THE NEW BOOK OF

Business
Quotations

Compiled by Martin H. Manser

Associate editor: Nicola L. Bull

Martin H. Manser

Martin Manser has been a professional reference book editor since 1980. He has compiled or edited more than 150 reference books, particularly English-language dictionaries, thesauruses, and Bible reference titles. He is also a Language Trainer and Consultant with national companies and organisations.

Text © 2007 Lawpack Publishing

Lawpack Publishing Limited
76–89 Alscot Road
London SE1 3AW

www.lawpack.co.uk

ISBN: 978-1-905261-62-8

Contents

Introduction

A well-chosen quotation can add fresh vigour to a spoken or written presentation. This selection of business quotations has been compiled with the aim of being both informative and entertaining. It will prove useful to those trying to find a quotation – serious or witty, contemporary or older – that will express a point of view for a report, article or speech.

Quotations have been drawn from a wide variety of sources: not only businessmen, businesswomen and economists, but also politicians, historians, philosophers, poets, etc., where their writings touch on business and topics related to the business world.

More than two thousand quotations have been selected. They are listed according to themes, which are arranged alphabetically within nine major sections. The index includes the authors of quotations and themes in one single alphabetical listing.

In the course of time, quotations change, too, as can be seen from the biblical 'The meek shall inherit the earth', through to John Paul Getty's 'The meek shall inherit the earth, but not the mineral rights' and on to the contemporary 'The geek shall inherit the earth'.

I hope that this book will prove to be not only an instructive work of reference but also an entertaining – and at times amusing – guide through the world of business.

Martin H. Manser

Success & Wealth

What are the secrets of becoming rich? How can you become prosperous and successful? Can money really buy anything … and everything? The quotations in this opening section reveal not only the great variety of ways of achieving success but also the extraordinary power exerted by money, wealth and property. Alongside less familiar quotes such as 'The two most beautiful words in the English language are "Cheque Enclosed"' (Dorothy Parker) are the more well-known 'Time is money' (Benjamin Franklin), 'Man does not live by GNP alone' (Paul Samuelson), and 'The meek shall inherit the earth, but not the mineral rights' (attributed to J. Paul Getty).

Money

Nothing defines human beings better than their willingness to do irrational things in the pursuit of phenomenally unlikely payoffs.
SCOTT ADAMS (1957–), American cartoonist: *The Dilbert Principle*

Money is better than poverty, if only for financial reasons.
WOODY ALLEN (Allen Stewart Konigsberg) (1935–), American film comedian, screenwriter and director: *Without Feathers, 'The Early Essays'*

Money isn't everything; usually it isn't even enough.
ANON

What comes by nature costs no money.
ANON

Money, it turned out, was exactly like sex, you thought of nothing else if you didn't have it and thought of other things if you did.

JAMES (ARTHUR) BALDWIN (1924–88), American novelist and essayist: *Nobody Knows My Name*

If you would know what the Lord God thinks of money, you have only to look at those to whom he gives it.

MAURICE BARING (1874–1945), English novelist, essayist, poet and playwright: quoted in Dorothy Parker, *Writers at Work, First Series*

A man accustomed to think in millions – other people's millions.

(ENOCH) ARNOLD BENNETT (1867–1931), English novelist: *Journal, June 1929*

For the love of money is the root of all evil.

The Bible, Authorised (King James) Version, 1 Timothy 6:10

Money: A blessing that is of no advantage to us excepting when we part with it. An evidence of culture and a passport to polite society. Supportable property.

AMBROSE (GWINETT) BIERCE (1842–?1914), American journalist and humorist: *The Devil's Dictionary*

It has been said that the love of money is the root of all evil. The want of money is so quite as truly.

SAMUEL BUTLER (1835–1902), English author, painter and musician: *Erewhon*

I consider in general that an increase of actual money causes in a State a corresponding increase of consumption which gradually brings about increased prices.

RICHARD CANTILLON (?1680–1734), British economist: *Essai sur la nature du commerce en général*

And here I say to parents, especially wealthy parents, 'Don't give your son money. As far as you can afford it, give him horses.'
SIR WINSTON LEONARD SPENCER CHURCHILL (1874–1965), English statesman, writer and prime minister: *My Early Life, 4*

How pleasant it is to have money.
ARTHUR HUGH CLOUGH (1819–61), English poet: *Dipsychus, 1:4*

A fool and his money are soon parted. What I want to know is how they got together in the first place.
CYRIL FLETCHER (1913–2005), British comedian: *BBC radio programme, 8 May 1969*

Remember that time is money.
BENJAMIN FRANKLIN (1706–90), American statesman, scientist and author: *Advice to a Young Tradesman*

Money is a singular thing. It ranks with love as a man's greatest source of joy. And with death as its greatest source of anxiety. Money differs from an automobile, a mistress or cancer in being equally important to those who have it and those who do not.
JOHN KENNETH GALBRAITH (1908–2006), Canadian-born American economist, diplomat and writer: *The Age of Uncertainty*

I find all this money a considerable burden.
J(EAN) PAUL GETTY (1892–1976), American financier

If you can actually count your money, then you are not a really rich man.
J(EAN) PAUL GETTY: quoted in Bernard Levin, *The Pendulum Years, chapter 1*

Money is like love; it kills slowly and painfully the one who withholds it, and it enlivens the other who turns it upon his fellow man.

KAHLIL GIBRAN (1883–1931), Lebanese-born writer

Bad money drives out good money.

SIR THOMAS GRESHAM (?1519–79), English financier

Put not your trust in money, but put your money in trust.

OLIVER WENDELL HOLMES, SR (1809–94), American physician, professor and author: *The Autocrat of the Breakfast Table*

Is this the sort of advice you're looking for? – 'Make money. Make it, if you can, fair and square. If not, make it anyway.'

HORACE (Quintus Horatius Flaccus) (65–8 BC), Roman poet and satirist: *Epistles*

Get money first; virtue comes afterward.

HORACE, as above

A man is usually more careful of his money than he is of his principles.

EDGAR WATSON HOWE (1853–1937), American journalist, novelist and essayist: *Ventures in Common Sense*

When a man says money can do anything, that settles it: he hasn't any.

EDGAR WATSON HOWE: *Sinner Sermons*

The safest way to double your money is to fold it over once and put it in your pocket.

FRANK MCKINNEY ('KIN') HUBBARD (1868–1930), American humorist

We all know how the size of sums of money appears to vary in a remarkable way according as they are being paid in or paid out.
JULIAN (SORELL) HUXLEY (1887–1975), English biologist: *Essays of a Biologist, 5*

Money, and not morality, is the principle of commercial nations.
THOMAS JEFFERSON (1743–1826), American statesman and president: *Letter to John Langdon, 1810*

There are few ways in which a man can be more innocently employed than in getting money.
SAMUEL JOHNSON (1709–84), English lexicographer, essayist and poet: quoted in James Boswell, *The Life of Samuel Johnson*

It needs to be said that the poor are poor because they don't have enough money.
SIR KEITH JOSEPH (1918–94), British politician: quoted in Adam Shaw, *Political Rhubarb*

For I don't care too much for money,
For money can't buy me love.
JOHN LENNON (1940–80), English rock musician and songwriter and PAUL MCCARTNEY (1942–), English rock musician and songwriter: *Can't Buy Me Love, song*

I am not rich. I am a poor man with money, which is not the same thing.
GABRIEL GARCÍA MÁRQUEZ (1928–), Colombian writer

Money:
A good thing to have. It frees you from doing things you dislike. Since I dislike doing nearly everything, money is handy.
GROUCHO MARX (1895–1977), American film comedian: quoted in Herbert V. Prochnow and Herbert V. Prochnow Jr, *Quotations for All Occasions*

What's a thousand dollars? Mere chicken feed. A poultry matter.
GROUCHO MARX: *The Cocoanuts, film, 1929*

Money is like a sixth sense without which you cannot make a complete use of the other five.
W(ILLIAM) SOMERSET MAUGHAM (1874–1965), English writer: *Of Human Bondage, chapter 51*

Money you haven't earned is not good for you.
ROBERT MAXWELL (1923–91), Czechoslovakian-born media owner

The chief value of money lies in the fact that one lives in a world in which it is overestimated.
HENRY LOUIS MENCKEN (1880–1956), American philologist, editor and satirist

Money can't buy friends but you can get a better class of enemy.
SPIKE MILLIGAN (1918–2002), Irish comedian: *Puckoon*

Money brings honour, friends, conquest, and realms.
JOHN MILTON (1608–74), English poet: *Paradise Regained, II*

After a certain point money is meaningless. It ceases to be the goal. The game is what counts.
ARISTOTLE ONASSIS (1900–75), Greek millionaire: *Esquire, 1969*

Within certain limits it is actually true that the less money you have, the less you worry.
GEORGE ORWELL (Eric Arthur Blair) (1903–50), English novelist and essayist: *Down and Out in Paris and London, chapter 3*

The two most beautiful words in the English language are 'Cheque Enclosed'.
DOROTHY (ROTHSCHILD) PARKER (1893–1967), American writer (Attributed)

You must spend money, if you wish to make money.
TITUS MACCIUS PLAUTUS (?254–?184 BC), Roman comic dramatist: *Asinaria*

A fool and his money are soon parted.
PROVERB

A man without money is like a wolf without teeth.
PROVERB

If you have no money, be polite.
PROVERB

Money is the best messenger.
PROVERB

Money isn't everything.
PROVERB

Money makes the man.
PROVERB

Money talks.
PROVERB

'Tis money that begets money.
PROVERB

Getting money is like digging with a needle; spending it is like water soaking into sand.
JAPANESE PROVERB

Money has no legs, but it runs.
JAPANESE PROVERB

Luxury either comes of riches or makes them necessary; it corrupts at once rich and poor, the rich by possession and the poor by covetousness.

JEAN-JACQUES ROUSSEAU (1712–78), Swiss-born French philosopher and writer: *The Social Contract*

My boy … always try to rub up against money, for if you rub up against money long enough, some of it may rub off on you.

(ALFRED) DAMON RUNYON (1884–1946), American writer and journalist: *Furthermore, 'A Very Honourable Guy'*

Corin:
He that wants money, means, and content, is without three good friends.

WILLIAM SHAKESPEARE (1564–1616), English dramatist and poet: *As You Like It, Act 3*

Money is indeed the most important thing in the world; and all sound and successful personal and national morality should have this fact for its basis.

GEORGE BERNARD SHAW (1856–1950), Irish dramatist and critic: *The Irrational Knot*

Money is the most important thing in the world. It represents health, strength, honour, generosity and beauty as conspicuously and undeniably as the want of it represents illness, weakness, disgrace, meanness and ugliness.

GEORGE BERNARD SHAW: *Major Barbara*

When declining to sell Samuel Goldwyn screen rights to his plays: The trouble, Mr Goldwyn, is that you are only interested in art and I am only interested in money.

GEORGE BERNARD SHAW

Look after the pounds and do not worry about the pence.

JIM SLATER (1929–), British finance guru and businessman: quoted in John Pollock, *Dear John*

Nothing in the world is worse than money. Money lays waste cities; it sets men to roaming from home; it seduces and corrupts honest men and turns virtue to baseness; it teaches villainy and impiety.

SOPHOCLES (?496–406 BC), Greek dramatist: *Antigone*

No man will take counsel, but every man will take money: therefore money is better than counsel.

JONATHAN SWIFT (1667–1745), Anglo-Irish satirist and churchman: *Thoughts on Various Subjects*

No one would remember the Good Samaritan if he'd only had good intentions. He had money as well.

MARGARET (HILDA) THATCHER (1925–), English politician and prime minister: *Observer, 'Sayings of 1980', 28 December 1980*

Make all you can, save all you can, give all you can.

JOHN WESLEY (1703–91), English preacher who founded Methodism

I don't want money. It is only people who pay their bills who want that, and I never pay mine.

OSCAR WILDE (1856–1900), Irish poet, dramatist and wit: *The Picture of Dorian Gray*

Property

Upon the sacredness of property civilisation itself depends – the right of the labourer to his hundred dollars in the savings bank, and equally the legal right of the millionaire to his millions.

ANDREW CARNEGIE (1835–1919), Scottish-born industrialist and philanthropist

Thieves respect property. They merely wish the property to become their property that they may more perfectly respect it.

G(ILBERT) K(EITH) CHESTERTON (1874–1936), English essayist, novelist, poet and critic: *The Man Who Was Thursday*

It will, generally, be found, that all great political questions end in the tenure of Land. What is the nature of that tenure is the first question a Statesman should ask himself, when forming an opinion on public events.

BENJAMIN DISRAELI, 1st Earl of Beaconsfield (1804–81), English statesman, prime minister and novelist: *Fragment of Reminiscence, 1860*

Property has its duties as well as its rights.

THOMAS DRUMMOND (1797–1840), Scottish engineer and statesman: *Letter to the Earl of Donoughmore, 22 May 1838*

If a man own land, the land owns him. Now let him leave home, if he dare.

RALPH WALDO EMERSON (1803–82), American poet, essayist and philosopher: *The Conduct of Life, 'Wealth'*

When it comes to divide an estate, the politest men quarrel.

RALPH WALDO EMERSON, Journals

The earth is the first condition of our existence. To make it an object of trade was the last step towards making human beings an object of trade. To buy and sell land is an immorality surpassed only by the immorality of selling oneself into slavery.

FRIEDRICH ENGELS (1820–95), German socialist leader and political philosopher: *Outlines of a Critique of Political Economy*

By socialism we mean above all an Islamic socialism. We are a Muslim nation. We shall therefore respect, as bidden in the

Qur'an, the principle of private property, even of hereditary property.

MOAMAR AL GADDAFI (1942–), Libyan army officer and statesman: *First Proclamation of the Revolutionary Command Council, 1 September 1969*

Private ownership of land is the nether millstone. Material progress is the upper millstone. Between them, with increasing pressure, the working classes are being ground.

HENRY GEORGE (1839–97), American economist: *Progress and Poverty*

The meek shall inherit the earth, but not the mineral rights.

J(EAN) PAUL GETTY (1892–1976), American financier (Attributed)

Property is necessary, but it is not necessary that it should remain forever in the same hands.

REMY DE GOURMONT (1858–1915), French literary critic and novelist

We stand for the maintenance of private property.

ADOLF HITLER (1889–1945), Austrian-born German Nazi dictator

Private property in land is an obstacle to the investment of capital on land … The possibilities of free investment of capital in land, free competition in agriculture, are much greater under the system of free renting than under the system of private property in land … landlordism without the landlord.

NIKOLAI LENIN (Vladimir Ilyich Ulyanov) (1870–1924), Russian statesman and Marxist theoretician: *Selected Works*

We abuse land because we regard it as a commodity belonging to us. When we see land as a community to which we belong, we may begin to use it with love and respect.

ALDO LEOPOLD (1886–1948), American forester and conservationist: quoted in Stewart L. Udall, *The Quiet Crisis*

A son can bear with equanimity the loss of his father, but the loss of his inheritance may drive him to despair.

NICCOLÒ MACHIAVELLI (1469–1527), Italian statesman and political philosopher: *The Prince*

Landlords, like all other men, love to reap where they never sowed.

KARL MARX (1818–83), German founder of modern communism: *Early Writings*

The theory of Communism may be summed up in one sentence: Abolish all private property.

KARL MARX and FRIEDRICH ENGELS (1820–95), German socialist leader: *The Communist Manifesto*

That which is built upon the land goes with the land.

MAXIM

No man made the land. It is the original inheritance of the whole species. Its appropriation is wholly a question of general expediency. When private property in land is not expedient, it is unjust. It is no hardship to any one to be excluded from what others have produced: they were not bound to produce it for his use, and he loses nothing by not sharing in what otherwise would not have existed at all. But it is some hardship to be born into the world and to find all nature's gifts previously engrossed, and no place left for the new-comer.

JOHN STUART MILL (1806–73), English philosopher and economist: *Principles of Political Economy, book 2*

The land of every country belongs to the people of that country. The individuals called landowners have no right in morality and justice to anything but the rent, or compensation for its saleable value.

JOHN STUART MILL, as above, *book 1*

Riches do not consist in the possession of treasures, but in the use made of them.

NAPOLEON I (Napoleon Bonaparte) (1769–1821), French emperor and general: *Maxims*

Property is theft.

PIERRE JOSEPH PROUDHON (1802–65), French political theorist: *Qu'est-ce que la propriété?, chapter I*

He that has lands, has quarrels.

PROVERB

We ask not what he is but what he has.

PROVERB

Whoever owns the river bank owns the fish.

RUSSIAN PROVERB

You cannot divorce property from power. You can only make them change hands.

JOHN RANDOLPH, Randolph of Roanoke (1773–1833), American politician: *Speech to the Senate, 1826*

Everything that is most beautiful in Britain has always been in private hands.

MALCOLM RIFKIND (1946–), British politician

It should be remembered that the foundation of the social contract is property; and its first condition, that every one should be maintained in the peaceful possession of what belongs to him.

JEAN-JACQUES ROUSSEAU (1712–78), Swiss-born French philosopher and writer: *A Discourse on Political Economy*

It is preoccupation with possession, more than anything else, that prevents men from living freely and nobly.

BERTRAND (ARTHUR WILLIAM) RUSSELL, 3rd Earl Russell (1872–1970), English philosopher and mathematician

One who knows how to show and to accept kindness
Will be a friend better than any possession.

SOPHOCLES (?496–406 BC), Greek dramatist: *Philoctetes*

Next to the right of liberty, the right of property is the most important individual right guaranteed by the Constitution and the one which, united with that of personal liberty, has contributed more to the growth of civilization than any other institution established by the human race ... Socialism proposes no adequate substitute for the motive of enlightened selfishness that today is at the basis of all human labour and effort, enterprise and new activity.

WILLIAM HOWARD TAFT (1857–1930), American statesman and president: *Popular Government, chapter 3*

If it takes you more than fifteen minutes to pack, you have too much stuff.

MOTHER TERESA (1910–97), Albanian nun, Nobel Peace Price winner 1979: quoted in D. Pytches, *Family Matters*

The earth is the general and equal possession of all humanity and therefore cannot be the property of individuals.

LEO TOLSTOY (1828–1910), Russian author

The want of a thing is perplexing enough, but the possession of it is intolerable.

SIR JOHN VANBRUGH (1664–1726), English dramatist and Baroque architect: *The Confederacy*

The spirit of property doubles a man's strength.

VOLTAIRE (François Marie Arouet) (1694–1778), French writer, philosopher and historian: *Philosophical Dictionary*

It is immoral to use private property in order to alleviate the horrible evils that result from the institution of private property. It is both immoral and unfair.

OSCAR WILDE (1856–1900), Irish poet, dramatist and wit: *Fortnightly Review, February 1891*

If property had simply pleasures, we could stand it, but its duties make it unbearable. In the interest of the rich we must get rid of it.

OSCAR WILDE, *The Soul of Man Under Socialism*

Prosperity

It is easy when we are in prosperity to give advice to the afflicted.

AESCHYLUS (525–426 BC), Greek playwright

In a day of prosperity, adversity is forgotten and in a day of adversity, prosperity is not remembered.

The Apocrypha, Ecclesiasticus 11:25

Prosperity is not without many fears and distastes, and adversity is not without comforts and hopes.

FRANCIS BACON, 1st Baron Verulam, Viscount St Albans (1561–1626), English writer, philosopher and statesman

There are those who believe that, if you will only legislate to make the well-to-do prosperous, their prosperity will leak through to those below. The Democratic idea, however, has been that if you legislate to make the masses prosperous, their prosperity will find its way up through every class which rests upon them.

WILLIAM JENNINGS BRYAN (1860–1925), American political leader and orator: *Speech at the Democratic National Convention, Chicago, 8 July 1896*

Adversity is sometimes hard upon a man; but for one man who can stand prosperity, there are a hundred that will stand adversity.

THOMAS CARLYLE (1795–1881), Scottish essayist and historian: *Heroes and Hero Worship*

The rich are the scum of the earth in every country.

G(ILBERT) K(EITH) CHESTERTON (1874–1936), English essayist, novelist, poet and critic: *The Flying Inn*

When prosperity comes, do not use all of it.

CONFUCIUS (Kong Zi) (551–479 BC), Chinese philosopher

The misfortune of the wise is better than the prosperity of the fool.

EPICURUS (341–270 BC), Greek philosopher: quoted in Diogenes Laertius, *Lives and Opinions of Eminent Philosophers*

Some men never find prosperity,
For all their voyaging,
While others find it with no voyaging.

EURIPIDES (?480–406 BC), Greek tragic dramatist: *Iphigenia in Tauris*

The human race has had long experience and a fine tradition in surviving adversity. But we now face a task for which we have little experience, the task of surviving prosperity.

ALAN GREGG (1890–1957), American physician and foundation official: *The New York Times, 4 November 1956*

We've got the most prosperous culture in human history and we've also got the biggest spiritual hole in human history.
MARK VICTOR HANSEN, American motivational speaker

Prosperity is a great teacher; adversity is a greater.
WILLIAM HAZLITT (1778–1830), English essayist: *Sketches and Essays, 'On the Conversation of Lords'*

Armaments, universal debt and planned obsolescence – those are the three pillars of Western prosperity.
ALDOUS (LEONARD) HUXLEY (1894–1963), English novelist and essayist: *Island*

If you don't want prosperity to falter, then Buy, Buy, Buy – on credit, of course. In other words, the surest way of bringing on a rainy day is to prepare for it.
JOSEPH WOOD KRUTCH (1893–1970), American critic, essayist and teacher: *Human Nature and the Human Condition*

He who wishes to be rich in a day will be hanged in a year.
LEONARDO DA VINCI (1452–1519), Italian artist, architect and engineer: *Notebooks*

Most of our people have never had it so good.
SIR (MAURICE) HAROLD MACMILLAN, 1st Earl of Stockton (1894–1986), English statesman and prime minister: *Speech, Bedford football ground, 20 July 1957*

In prosperity be cautious; in adversity, patient.
PROVERB

The prosperity of this world is like writing on water.
HINDU PROVERB

Prosperity makes friends, adversity tries them.
PUBLILIUS SYRUS (1st c. BC), Latin writer of mimes: *Moral Sayings*

Nothing contributes so much to the prosperity and happiness of a country as high profits.

DAVID RICARDO (1772–1823), English economist: *On Protection to Agriculture*

There's no reason to be the richest man in the cemetery. You can't do any business from there.

HARLAND DAVID (COLONEL) SANDERS (1890–1980), American businessman

If a nation could not prosper without the enjoyment of perfect liberty and perfect justice, there is not in the world a nation which could ever have prospered.

ADAM SMITH (1723–90), Scottish economist and philosopher: *Wealth of Nations, volume 2, book 4*

Few of us can stand prosperity. Another man's, I mean.

MARK TWAIN (Samuel Langhorne Clemens) (1835–1910), American novelist and humorist: *Pudd'nhead Wilson's New Calendar*

Prosperity is the best protector of principle.

MARK TWAIN, as above

Prosperity is necessarily the first theme of a political campaign.

(THOMAS) WOODROW WILSON (1836–1924), American statesman and president: *Address, 4 September 1912*

Success

Don't count your chickens before they are hatched.

AESOP (620–564 BC), Greek fabulist: *Fables, 'The Milkmaid and Her Pail'*

Begin to weave and God will provide the thread

ANON

Behind every successful man there stands an amazed woman.
ANON

It takes the hammer of persistence to drive the nail of success.
ANON

Pull off a coup and you're a national hero, fail and you're an evil criminal; in business it's the same difference between bankruptcy and making a fortune.
JEFFREY ARCHER (1940–), British politician and author: *A Quiver Full of Arrows*

One's religion is whatever he is most interested in, and yours is Success.
SIR JAMES MATTHEW BARRIE (1860–1937), Scottish novelist and dramatist: *The Twelve-Pound Look*

The toughest thing about success is that you've got to keep on being a success.
IRVING BERLIN (Israel Baline) (1888–1989), Russian-born American composer: *Theatre Arts, February 1958*

To be successful you have to be lucky, or a little mad, or very talented, or to find yourself in a rapid-growth field.
EDWARD DE BONO (1933–), Maltese-born British physician and writer: *Tactics: the art and science of success*

Success is counted sweetest
By those who ne'er succeed.
EMILY DICKINSON (1830–86), American poet: *Poems*

The secret of success is constancy to purpose.
BENJAMIN DISRAELI, 1st Earl of Beaconsfield (1804–81), English statesman, prime minister and novelist: *Speech, House of Commons, 24 June 1870*

She knows there's no success like failure
And that failure's no success at all.
BOB DYLAN (Robert Allen Zimmerman) (1941–), American folk singer and
songwriter: *Love Minus Zero/No Limit, song*

Success, as I see it, is a result, not a goal.
GUSTAVE FLAUBERT (1821–80), French novelist: *Letter to Maxime du Camp,*
26 June 1852

Nothing is more humiliating than to see idiots succeed in
enterprises we have failed in.
GUSTAVE FLAUBERT: *L'Éducation sentimentale*

You cannot win if you do not play.
STEVE FORBERT (1954–), songwriter: *song lyric*

Early to bed and early to rise, makes a man healthy, wealthy, and
wise.
BENJAMIN FRANKLIN (1706–90), American statesman, scientist and author:
Poor Richard's Almanac

Success has ruin'd many a man.
BENJAMIN FRANKLIN, as above

The truly successful businessman is essentially a dissenter, a rebel
who is seldom if ever satisfied with the status quo.
J(EAN) PAUL GETTY (1892–1976), American financier: *How to Be Rich*

He was a self-made man who owed his lack of success to nobody.
JOSEPH HELLER (1923–99), American novelist: *Catch-22*

Success and failure are both difficult to endure. Along with
success come drugs, divorce, fornication, bullying, travel,

meditation, medication, depression, neurosis and suicide. With failure comes failure.

JOSEPH HELLER

If at first you don't succeed,
Try, try again.

WILLIAM EDWARD HICKSON (1803–70), educational writer: *Try and Try Again*

Succeed we must, at all cost – even if it means being a dead millionaire at fifty.

LOUIS KRONENBERGER (1904–80), American critic, writer and editor: *The Cart and the Horse*

If at first you do succeed, try something harder.

ANN LANDERS (1918–2002), American advice columnist

To succeed in the world, we do everything we can to appear successful.

FRANÇOIS LA ROCHEFOUCAULD, Duc de la Rochefoucauld (1613–80), French writer: *Reflections*

Success is that old ABC – ability, breaks and courage.

CHARLES LUCKMAN (1909–99), American architect: *New York Mirror, 1955*

It is important for everyone to believe, whether they succeed or not, that success is linked with some kind of logic and beholden to some notion of legitimacy ... To put it another way, it is psychologically intolerable, having risen to the heights, to be badgered by doubt that you do not really deserve it.

ALISTAIR MANT: *The Rise and Fall of the British Manager*

To succeed in the world we must look foolish but be wise.

MONTESQUIEU (Charles de Secondat), Baron de la Brède et de Montesquieu (1689–1755), French philosopher, man of letters and lawyer: *Pensées*

People will listen a great deal more patiently when you explain
your mistakes than when you explain your success.
WILBUR D. NESBIT (1871–1927), American writer

No praying, it spoils business.
THOMAS OTWAY (1652–85), English dramatist: *Venice Preserv'd*

Gamesmanship or The Art of Winning Games Without Actually
Cheating.
STEPHEN POTTER (1900–69), English writer and radio producer: *Title of book*

If you wish to be a success in the world, acquire a knowledge of
Latin, a horse and money.
PROVERB

Nothing succeeds like success.
PROVERB

Success has many friends.
PROVERB

Of course there is no formula for success.
ARTUR RUBINSTEIN (1886–1982), Polish-born American concert pianist

Unless a man has been taught what to do with success after
getting it, the achievement of it must inevitably leave him a prey
to boredom.
BERTRAND (ARTHUR WILLIAM) RUSSELL, 3rd Earl Russell (1872–1970),
English philosopher and mathematician: *The Conquest of Happiness*

The only place where success comes before work is in a
dictionary.
VIDAL SASSOON (1928–), British hair stylist

Malvolio:

Some are born great, some achieve greatness, and some have greatness thrust upon 'em.

WILLIAM SHAKESPEARE (1564–1616), English dramatist and poet: *Twelfth Night, Act 2*

Man can climb to the highest summits, but he cannot dwell there long.

GEORGE BERNARD SHAW (1856–1950), Irish dramatist and critic: *Candida, Act 3*

There is no success without hardship.

SOPHOCLES (?496–406 BC), Greek dramatist: *Electra*

It's having the right stuff in the right place at the right time – and neither too much nor too little of it.

SIR ALAN SUGAR (1947–), British entrepreneur

Early to rise and early to bed makes a male healthy and wealthy and dead.

JAMES (GROVER) THURBER (1894–1961), American humorist and cartoonist: *Fables for Our Times, 'The Shrike and the Chipmunks'*

If you shoot for the stars and hit the moon, it's OK. But you've got to shoot for something. A lot of people don't even shoot.

ROBERT TOWNSEND (1957–), American company director

All you need in this life is ignorance and confidence, and then success is sure.

MARK TWAIN (Samuel Langhorne Clemens) (1835–1910), American novelist and humorist: *Letter to Mrs Foote, 2 December 1887*

Wealth

It is better to be miserable and rich than it is to be miserable and poor.
ANON

Wealth is not only what we have, but what we are.
ANON

Where some people are very wealthy and others have nothing, the result will be either extreme democracy or absolute oligarchy, or desperation will come from either of those excesses.
ARISTOTLE (384–322 BC), Greek philosopher and scientist: *Politics*

A man who has a million dollars is as well off as if he were rich.
JOHN JACOB ASTOR (1763–1848), American millionaire (Attributed)

Riches are for spending.
FRANCIS BACON, 1st Baron Verulam, Viscount St Albans (1561–1626), English writer, philosopher and statesman: *Essays, 'Of Expense'*

The control of the production of wealth is the control of human life itself.
(JOSEPH) HILAIRE (PIERRE) BELLOC (1870–1953), Anglo-French author

Life begets life. Energy becomes energy. It is by spending oneself that one becomes rich.
SARAH BERNHARDT (1844–1923), French stage actress

It is easier for a camel to go through the eye of a needle, than for a rich man to enter the kingdom of God.
The Bible, Authorised (King James) Version, Matthew 19:24

The poor is hated even of his neighbour: but the rich hath many friends.
The Bible, Authorised (King James) Version, Proverbs 14:20

It is true that wealth won't make a man virtuous, but I notice there isn't anybody who wants to be poor just for the purpose of being good.

JOSH BILLINGS (Henry Wheeler Shaw) (1818–85), American humorist

As wealth is power, so all power will infallibly draw wealth to itself by some means or other.

EDMUND BURKE (1729–97), British statesman, orator and writer: *Speech, House of Commons, 11 February 1780*

If you aren't rich, you should always look useful.

LOUIS-FERDINAND CELINE (Louis-Ferdinand Destouches) (1894–1961), French novelist: *Journey to the End of the Night*

The first wealth is health.

RALPH WALDO EMERSON (1805–82), American poet, essayist and philosopher: *The Conduct of Life*

Wealth stays with us a little moment if at all; Only our characters are steadfast, not our gold.

EURIPIDES (?480–406 BC), Greek tragic dramatist: *Electra*

There seem to be but three ways for a nation to acquire wealth. The first is by war, as the Romans did, in plundering their conquered neighbors. This is robbery. The second by commerce, which is generally cheating. The third by agriculture, the only honest way, wherein man receives a real increase of the seed thrown into the ground, in a kind of continual miracle, wrought by the hand of God in his favor, as a reward for his innocent life and his virtuous industry.

BENJAMIN FRANKLIN (1706–90), American statesman, scientist and author: *Positions to Be Examined Concerning National Wealth*

Riches have made more covetous men than covetousness hath made rich men.

THOMAS FULLER (1654–1734), English physician, writer and compiler: *Gnomologia*

Wealth has never been a sufficient source of honour in itself. It must be advertised, and the normal medium is obtrusively expensive goods.

JOHN KENNETH GALBRAITH (1908–2006), Canadian-born American economist, diplomat and writer: *The Affluent Society, chapter 7*

Wealth is not without its advantages, and the case to the contrary, although it has often been made, has never proved widely persuasive.

JOHN KENNETH GALBRAITH, as above, *chapter 1*

F. Scott Fitzgerald:
You know, Ernest, the rich are different from us.

Ernest Hemingway:
Yes I know. They have more money than we do.

ERNEST HEMINGWAY (1899–1961), American novelist and short-story writer: *The Crack-Up, 'Notebook E'*

The increase of riches and commerce in any one nation, instead of hurting, commonly promotes the riches and commerce of all its neighbours.

DAVID HUME (1711–76), Scottish philosopher and historian: *Essays, 'Of the Jealousy of Trade'*

It is better to live rich than to die rich.

SAMUEL JOHNSON (1709–84), English lexicographer, essayist and poet: quoted in James Boswell, *The Life of Samuel Johnson*

It is Enterprise which builds and improves the world's possessions ... if Enterprise is afoot, wealth accumulates whatever may be happening to Thrift; and if Enterprise is asleep, Wealth decays, whatever Thrift may be doing.

JOHN MAYNARD KEYNES (1883–1946), English economist: *Treatise on Money*

No just man ever became rich suddenly.

MENANDER (?342–?292 BC), Greek comic dramatist: *Adsentator*

The distribution of wealth ... depends on the laws and customs of society. The rules by which it is determined are what the opinions and feelings of the ruling portion of the community make them, and are very different in different ages and countries; and might be still more different, if mankind so chose.

JOHN STUART MILL (1806–73), English philosopher and economist: *Principles of Political Economy, book 2*

Men do not desire to be rich, but to be richer than other men.

JOHN STUART MILL: *Oxford and Cambridge Review, Posthumous Essay on Social Freedom, January 1907*

Give us the luxuries of life, and we will dispense with its necessities.

JOHN LOTHROP MOTLEY (1814–77), American historian and diplomat: *comment, O. W. Holmes, The Autocrat of the Breakfast Table, chapter 6*

God shows his contempt for wealth by the kind of person he selects to receive it.

AUSTIN O'MALLEY (1858–1932), American writer

Rich men long to be richer.

PROVERB

A man seldom gets rich without ill-got gain; as a horse does not fatten without feeding in the night.

CHINESE PROVERB

Nobody ever feels rich.

ESTHER RANTZEN (1940–), TV journalist: *Observer, 'Sayings of the Year',*
2 January 1983

When you're rich, it's not what money you might make but what
you might lose that matters.

EDMOND SAFRA (1932–99), Lebanese-born banker: *Financial Times,*
'Business Quotes of the Year', 24 December 1988

Man does not live by GNP alone.

PAUL ANTHONY SAMUELSON (1915–), American economist: *Economics*

Who so craves wealth is like a man who drinks seawater: the
more he drinks the more he increases his thirst. And he ceases
not to drink until he perishes.

MUSLIM SAYING

Many a man has found the acquisition of wealth only a change,
not an end of miseries.

MARCUS or LUCIUS ANNAEUS SENECA (The Elder) (?55 BC–?39 AD),
Roman writer on oratory and history: *Letters to Lucilius*

Petruchio:
Our purses shall be proud, our garments poor;
For 'tis the mind that makes the body rich;
And as the sun breaks through the darkest clouds,
So honour peereth in the meanest habit.

WILLIAM SHAKESPEARE (1564–1616), English dramatist and poet: *The*
Taming of the Shrew, Act 4

I am a Millionaire. That is my religion.

GEORGE BERNARD SHAW (1858–1950), Irish dramatist and critic: *Major*
Barbara, Act 1

The wretchedness of being rich is that you live with rich people.

LOGAN PEARSALL SMITH (1865–1946), American-born Englishman of letters: *Afterthoughts*

Nobody who has wealth to distribute ever omits himself.

LEON TROTSKY (Lev Davidovich Bronstein) (1879–1940), Russian revolutionary and Communist theorist: *Observer, 'Sayings of the Week', 23 March 1937*

When I was young I thought money was the most important thing in life; now that I am old I know that it is.

OSCAR WILDE (1856–1900), Irish poet, dramatist and wit

Business Activities

What are the functions of business? What is industry actually doing? 'Business? It's quite simple. It's other people's money', according to the French writer Alexandre Dumas; 'Business has only two functions – marketing and innovation', according to the management expert Peter Drucker. The quotations in this section move from decision-making and meetings ('A conference is a gathering of important people who singly can do nothing, but together can decide that nothing can be done' – Fred Allen) to the sheer hard graft of work. We also look at the industrial process from ideas and planning ('You can't really separate the inventor and the businessman' – Sir Clive Sinclair) through to production … and problems. Computers have become an indispensable part of business life: 'A computer makes it possible to do, in half an hour, tasks which were completely unnecessary to do before' as is email: 'The email of the species is more deadly than the mail.' We dare not ignore green issues: 'We are living beyond our means. As a people we have developed a life-style that is draining the earth of its priceless and irreplaceable resources without regard for the future of our children and people all around the world' (Margaret Mead).

Accountants

An accountant is a man hired to explain that you didn't make the money you did.

ANON

In your report here, it says that you are an extremely dull person. Our experts describe you as an appallingly dull fellow, unimaginative, timid, spineless, easily dominated, no sense of humour, tedious company and irrepressibly drab and awful. And whereas in most professions these would be considered drawbacks, in accountancy they are a positive boon.

JOHN CLEESE, GRAHAM CHAPMAN, TERRY JONES, MICHAEL PALIN and ERIC IDLE: *And Now for Something Completely Different, screenplay*

All the flower children were as alike as a congress of accountants and about as interesting.

JOHN MORTIMER (1923–), English barrister, writer and dramatist

Accountants are perpetually fighting their shiny pants, green eyeshades, number-cruncher image.

ALBERT NEWGARDEN: *Wall Street Journal, 26 April 1984*

Of course, it's a bit of a jump, isn't it? I mean, er ... chartered accountancy to lion taming in one go ... You don't think it might be better if you worked your way towards lion taming, say via banking?

MONTY PYTHON, British TV comedy

Administration

Those who can, do. Those who can't, teach. Those who can't teach, teach teachers to teach. Those who can't teach teachers to teach, administrate.

ANON

It is common for professional economists, when they first come in contact with administrators, to feel that the administrator is grossly ignorant of elementary economics. Sometimes this is justified; but it is equally true that the professional economist may be grossly ignorant of administration.

SIR ALEC CAIRNCROSS (1911–98), Scottish economist: *Essays in Economic Management*

An administration, like a machine, does not create. It carries on.
ANTOINE DE SAINT-EXUPÉRY (1900–44), French novelist and aviator: *Flight to Arras*

Bad administration, to be sure, can destroy good policy; but good administration can never save bad policy.
ADLAI (EWING) STEVENSON (1900–68), American statesman: *Speech, Los Angeles, 11 September 1952*

Advertising

Advertising agency: eighty-five per cent confusion and fifteen per cent commission.
FRED ALLEN (John F. Sullivan) (1894–1956), American comedian

Advertising is the fine art of making you think you have longed for something all your life that you never heard of before.
ANON

The man who stops advertising to save money is like the man who stops the clock to save time.
ANON

When business is good it pays to advertise; when business is bad you've got to advertise.
ANON

When the client moans and sighs
Make his logo twice the size.
If he still should prove refractory,
Show a picture of his factory.
Only in the gravest cases
Should you show the clients' faces.
ANON

Advertising is the very essence of democracy.
BRUCE BARTON (1886–1967), American advertising man: *Reader's Digest, 1955*

The advertisements in a newspaper are more full of knowledge in respect to what is going on in a state or community than the editorial columns are.
HENRY WARD BEECHER (1813–87), American clergyman, editor and writer: *Proverbs from Plymouth Pulpit*

The very first law in advertising is to avoid the concrete promise and cultivate the delightfully vague.
BILL COSBY (1937–), American comedy actor

I have always believed that writing advertisements is the second most profitable form of writing. The first, of course, is ransom notes …
PHILIP DUSENBERRY, American advertising executive

The philosophy behind much advertising is based on the old observation that every man is really two men – the man he is and the man he wants to be.
WILLIAM FEATHER (1889–1981), American businessman: *The Business of Life*

Few people at the beginning of the nineteenth century needed an adman to tell them what they wanted.
JOHN KENNETH GALBRAITH (1908–2006), Canadian-born American economist, diplomat and writer

It is not necessary to advertise food to hungry people, fuel to cold people, or houses to the homeless.
JOHN KENNETH GALBRAITH: *American Capitalism, chapter 8*

Give them quality. That's the best kind of advertising.
MILTON SNAVELY HERSHEY (1857–1945), American industrialist

Doing business without advertising is like winking at a girl in the dark: you know what you are doing, but nobody else does.

EDGAR WATSON HOWE (1853–1937), American journalist, novelist and essayist

Advertisements contain the only truths to be relied on in a newspaper.

THOMAS JEFFERSON (1743–1826), American statesman and president: *Letter to Nathaniel Macon, 1819*

Advertisements are now so numerous that they are very negligently perused, and it is therefore become necessary to gain attention by magnificence of promises, and by eloquences sometimes sublime and sometimes pathetic.

SAMUEL JOHNSON (1709–84), English lexicographer, essayist and poet: *The Idler*

Promise, large promise, is the soul of an advertisement.

SAMUEL JOHNSON, as above

Advertising may be described as the science of arresting human intelligence long enough to get money from it.

STEPHEN BUTLER LEACOCK (1869–1944), Canadian economist and humorist: *The Garden of Folly*

Half the money I spend on advertising is wasted, and the trouble is I don't know which half.

WILLIAM LEVER, 1st Viscount Leverhulme (1851–1925), English industrialist and philanthropist: quoted in D. Ogilvy, *Confessions of an Advertising Man*

You can fool all the people all of the time if the advertising is right and the budget is big enough.

JOSEPH E. LEVINE (1905–87), American film producer: *Joseph E. Levine Presents*

When producers want to know what the public wants, they graph it in curves. When they want to tell the public what to get, they say it in curves.

(HERBERT) MARSHALL MCLUHAN (1911–80), Canadian educator, author and media expert: *The Mechanical Bride*

Ads push the principle of noise all the way to the plateau of persuasion. They are quite in accord with the procedures of brain-washing.

(HERBERT) MARSHALL MCLUHAN: *Understanding Media*

Advertising is the greatest art form of the twentieth century.

(HERBERT) MARSHALL MCLUHAN: *Advertising Age*

Most of the people who are writing advertising today have never had to sell anything to anybody. They've never seen a consumer.

DAVID OGILVY (1911–99), British advertising executive

The Hidden Persuaders

VANCE (OAKLEY) PACKARD (1914–96), American writer and social critic: *Title of book*

Any publicity is good publicity.

PROVERB

Let us be a nation of shopkeepers as much as we please, but there is no necessity that we should become a nation of advertisers.

Punch, 1848

One Ad is worth more to a paper than forty Editorials.

WILL(IAM PENN ADAIR) ROGERS (1879–1935), American actor and humorist: *The Illiterate Digest*

I've written books on advertising … cheque books.

SIR ALAN SUGAR (1947–), British Entrepreneur

Advice

There is nothing which we receive with so much reluctance as advice.

JOSEPH ADDISON (1672–1719), English essayist and dramatist: *The Spectator, 1711*

Never trust the advice of a man in difficulties.

AESOP (c. 620–564 BC), Greek fabulist: *Fables, 'The Fox and the Goat'*

In the multitude of counsellors there is safety.

The Bible, Authorised (King James) Version, Proverbs 11:14

Consult:
To seek another's approval of a course already decided on.

AMBROSE (GWINETT) BIERCE (1842–?1914), American journalist and humorist: *The Devil's Dictionary*

Advice is seldom welcome; and those who want it the most always like it the least.

LORD CHESTERFIELD, Philip Dormer Stanhope, 4th Earl of (1694–1773), English statesman and writer: *Letter to his son, 29 January 1748*

Good advice is always certain to be ignored, but that's no reason not to give it.

AGATHA CHRISTIE (1890–1976), English crime fiction writer

When we feel a strong desire to thrust our advice upon others, it is usually because we suspect their weakness; but we ought rather to suspect our own.

CHARLES CALEB COLTON (?1780–1832), English clergyman and writer: *Lacon*

A word to the wise ain't necessary, it's the stupid ones who need the advice.

BILL COSBY (1937–), American comedy actor

Whatever your advice, make it brief.

HORACE (Quintus Horatius Flaccus) (65–8 BC), Roman poet and satirist: *De arte poetica*

Never explain – your friends do not need it and your enemies will not believe you anyway.

ELBERT (GREEN) HUBBARD (1856–1915), American businessman, writer and printer

Advice is what we ask for when we already know the answer but wish we didn't.

ERICA JONG (1942–), American author and educator

You will always find some Eskimos ready to instruct the Congolese on how to cope with heat waves.

STANISLAW (JERZY) LEC (1909–66), Polish poet and aphorist: *Unkempt Thoughts*

Advice after injury is like medicine after death.

PROVERB

Ask advice only of your equals.

PROVERB

Many receive advice, few profit by it.

PUBLILIUS SYRUS (1st c. BC), Latin writer of mimes: *Moral Sayings*

We should be careful and discriminating in all the advice we give. We should be especially careful in giving advice that we would not think of following ourselves. Most of all, we ought to avoid giving counsel which we don't follow when it damages those who take us at our word.

ADLAI (EWING) STEVENSON (1900–68), American statesman

No man will take counsel, but every man will take money: therefore money is better than counsel.

JONATHAN SWIFT (1667–1745), Anglo-Irish satirist and churchman: *Thoughts on Various Subjects*

I always pass on good advice. It is the only thing to do with it. It is never any use to oneself.

OSCAR WILDE (1856–1900), Irish poet, dramatist and wit: *An Ideal Husband*

Arguments

A single fact can spoil a good argument.

ANON

When quarrels and complaints arise, it is when people who are equal have not got equal shares, or vice versa.

ARISTOTLE (384–322 BC), Greek philosopher and scientist: *Nicomachean Ethics, book 5*

When an argument is over, how many weighty reasons does a man recollect which his heat and violence made him utterly forget?

EUSTACE BUDGELL (1686–1737), English essayist and man of letters: *The Spectator, 1711*

The only way to get the best of an argument is to avoid it.

DALE CARNEGIE (1888–1955), American writer

In every age and clime we see,
Two of a trade can ne'er agree.

JOHN GAY (1685–1732), English poet and dramatist: *Fables*

Don't take the wrong side of an argument just because your opponent has taken the right side.

BALTASAR GRACIÁN (1601–58), Spanish writer

The best way I know of to win an argument is to start by being in the right.

LORD HAILSHAM (Quintin McGarel Hogg) (1907–2001), British lawyer and government official: *The New York Times, 16 October 1960*

Sir, I have found you an argument; but I am not obliged to find you an understanding.

SAMUEL JOHNSON (1709–84), English lexicographer, essayist and poet: quoted in James Boswell, *The Life of Samuel Johnson*

We are never going to win the argument unless we put our head over the parapet.

SIR DIGBY JONES (1955–), trade and investment minister, Director, CBI

Discussion is an exchange of knowledge; argument is an exchange of ignorance.

ROBERT QUILLEN (1887–1948), American humorist

Least said soonest mended.

PROVERB

The test of a man or woman's breeding is how they behave in a quarrel.

GEORGE BERNARD SHAW (1856–1950), Irish dramatist and critic: *The Philanderer*

I am not arguing with you –
I am telling you.

JAMES ABBOTT MCNEILL WHISTLER (1834–1903), American painter: *Gentle Art of Making Enemies*

Arguments are to be avoided; they are always vulgar and often convincing.

OSCAR WILDE (1856–1900), Irish poet, dramatist and wit: *The Importance of Being Earnest*

Business

John Knightley:
Business, you know, may bring money, but friendship hardly ever does.

JANE AUSTEN (1775–1817), English novelist: *Emma, chapter 34*

The 'theory of business' leads a life of obstruction because theorists do not see the business, and the men of business will not reason out the theories.

WALTER BAGEHOT (1826–77), English economist and journalist: *Economic Studies*

There's a sucker born every minute.

PHINEAS T. BARNUM (1810–91), American showman (Attributed)

I wasn't a businessman, but a business magnate.

SILVIO BERLUSCONI (1936–), Italian politician and entrepreneur

A business must have a conscience as well as a counting house.

SIR MONTAGUE BURTON (1885–1952), British tailor

Few people do business well who do nothing else.

LORD CHESTERFIELD, Philip Dormer Stanhope, 4th Earl of (1694–1773), English statesman and writer: *Letter to his son, 7 August 1749*

The maxim of the British people is 'Business as usual'.

SIR WINSTON LEONARD SPENCER CHURCHILL (1874–1965), English statesman, writer and prime minister: *Speech, Guildhall, 9 November 1914*

The fact that a business is large, efficient and profitable does not mean it takes advantage of the public.

CHARLES CLORE (1904–79), British businessman

The business of America is business.

(JOHN) CALVIN COOLIDGE (1872–1933), US president: *Address before the Society of American Newspaper Editors, Washington, 17 January 1925*

Business has only two functions – marketing and innovation.

PETER F. DRUCKER (1909–2005), American management expert

Business? It's quite simple. It's other people's money.

ALEXANDRE DUMAS, known as Dumas Fils (1824–95), French novelist and dramatist: *La question d'argent*

Business is the salt of life.

THOMAS FULLER (1654–1734), English physician, writer and compiler: *Gnomologia*

Everything which is properly business we must keep carefully separate from life. Business requires earnestness and method; life must have a freer handling.

JOHANN WOLFGANG VON GOETHE (1749–1832), German poet, scientist and writer: *Elective Affinities*

Business is often about killing your favourite children to allow others to succeed.

SIR JOHN HARVEY-JONES (1924–), former chairman of ICI: *Troubleshooter*

Great businesses turn on a little pin.

GEORGE HERBERT (1593–1633), English metaphysical poet: *Outlandish Proverbs*

Business is a competition, and any high-level, sophisticated competition is almost exclusively a head game. The Inner Game of Business, as this could be called, is understanding the Business Paradox: the better you think you are doing, the greater should be your cause for concern; the more self-satisfied you are with your accomplishments, your past achievements, your 'right moves', the less you should be.

MARK H. MCCORMACK (1930–), Founder, International Management Group: *What They Don't Teach You at Harvard Business School*

The secret of business is knowing something that nobody else knows.

ARISTOTLE ONASSIS (1906–75), Greek businessman: quoted in Helen Exley, *The Best of Business Quotations*

I believe strongly in the social function of business … It is industry which creates our social patterns, it determines the whole form of our society, whether it is education or the design of cities. And I am concerned with the splits that I see in industry as they run right out into the fabric of our society.

SIR PETER PARKER (1924–2002), former chairman of British Rail: quoted in Cary L. Cooper and Peter Hingley, *The Change Makers*

Let business wait till tomorrow.

PROVERB

Live together like brothers and do business like strangers.

ARABIC PROVERB

[Of the music business] If you want to call it a business … it's more like a knife fight.

KEITH RICHARDS (1943–), English guitarist: *Uncut magazine*

We demand that big business give people a square deal; in return we must insist that when anyone engaged in big business honestly endeavours to do right, he shall himself be given a square deal.

THEODORE ROOSEVELT (1858–1919), American statesman and president

My own business always bores me to death; I prefer other people's.

OSCAR WILDE (1856–1900), Irish poet, dramatist and wit: *Lady Windermere's Fan*

I thought what was good for the country was good for General Motors and vice versa.

CHARLES ERWIN WILSON (1890–1961), American engineer and industrialist: *Statement to US Congressional Committee, 23 January 1953*

Big business is not dangerous because it is big, but because its business is an unwholesome inflation created by privileges and exemptions which it ought not to enjoy.

(THOMAS) WOODROW WILSON (1856–1924), American statesman and president: *Acceptance speech, Democratic National Convention, 7 July 1912*

Business underlies everything in our national life, including our spiritual life. Witness the fact that in the Lord's Prayer the first petition is for daily bread. No one can worship God or love his neighbor on an empty stomach.

(THOMAS) WOODROW WILSON: *Speech, New York, 1912*

Business is like riding a bicycle. Either you keep moving or you fall down.

JOHN DAVID WRIGHT (1905–), American businessman: *Money Talks*

Committees & Meetings

A conference is a gathering of important people who singly can do nothing, but together can decide that nothing can be done.

FRED ALLEN (John F. Sullivan) (1894–1956), American comedian

A camel looks like a horse that was planned by a committee.

ANON

Committee:
A group of men who keep minutes and waste hours.
ANON

If you had to identify, in one word, the reason why the human race has not achieved, and never will achieve, its full potential, that word would be 'meetings'.
DAVE BARRY (1947–), American humorist

Our meetings are held to discuss many problems which would never arise if we held fewer meetings.
ASHLEIGH BRILLIANT (1933–), English-born American cartoonist

A committee is a cul-de-sac down which ideas are lured and then quietly strangled.
SIR BARNETT COCKS (1907–89), clerk to House of Commons

Meetings … are rather like cocktail parties. You don't want to go, but you're cross not to be asked.
JILLY COOPER (1937–), British writer: *How to Survive from Nine to Five*

To get something done a committee should consist of no more than three men, two of whom are absent.
ROBERT COPELAND: quoted in *Penguin Dictionary of Modern Humorous Quotations*

Meetings are a symptom of bad organisation. The fewer meetings the better.
PETER F. DRUCKER (1909–2005), Austrian-born American management expert

Meetings are indispensable when you don't want to do anything.
JOHN KENNETH GALBRAITH (1908–2006), Canadian-born American economist, diplomat and writer: *Ambassador's Journal, 1969*

What is a committee? A group of the unwilling, picked from the unfit, to do the unnecessary.

RICHARD (LONG) HARKNESS (1907–), American radio and television commentator and journalist: *New York Herald Tribune, 1960*

A committee is a thing which takes a week to do what one good man can do in an hour.

ELBERT (GREEN) HUBBARD (1856–1915), American businessman, writer and printer

Civil servant:
What I mean is that I'm fully seized of your aims and, of course, I will do my utmost to see that they're put into practice. To that end, I recommend that we set up an inter-departmental committee with fairly broad terms of reference so that at the end of the day we'll be in a position to think through the various implications and arrive at a decision based on long-term considerations rather than rush prematurely into precipitate and possibly ill-conceived action which might well have unforeseen repercussions.

Minister:
You mean, no?

ANTHONY JAY and JONATHAN LYNN, scriptwriters: *Yes, Minister, BBC television, 1981*

Any committee is only as good as the most knowledgeable, determined and vigorous person on it. There must be somebody who provides the flame.

CLAUDIA (LADY BIRD) JOHNSON (1912–2007), widow of former American President Lyndon B. Johnson

Can anything be more Un-American than the Un-American committee?

BURT LANCASTER (1913–94), American film actor

A committee is an animal with four back legs.

JOHN LE CARRE (David John Cornwall) (1931–), English novelist: *Tinker Tailor Soldier Spy, Part 3*

A committee is organic rather than mechanical in its nature: it is not a structure but a plant. It takes root and grows, it flowers, wilts, and dies, scattering the seed from which other committees will bloom in their turn.

C(YRIL) NORTHCOTE PARKINSON (1909–93), English historian and journalist

The Law of Triviality ... means that the time spent on any item on the agenda will be in inverse proportion to the sum involved.

C(YRIL) NORTHCOTE PARKINSON: *Parkinson's Law*

We to a committee of the Council to discourse concerning pressing of men; but Lord how they meet; never sit down – one comes, now another goes, then comes another – one complaining that nothing is done, another swearing that he hath been there these two hours and nobody came. At last it came to this: 'my Lord Annesly,' says he, 'I think we must be forced to get the King to come to every committee, for I do not see that we do anything, at any time but when he is here.'

SAMUEL PEPYS (1633–1703), English diarist and naval administrator: *Diary, 27 February 1665*

If you see a snake, just kill it – don't appoint a committee on snakes.

ROSS PEROT (1930–), American businessman

The length of a meeting rises with the square of the number of people present.

EILEEN SHANAHAN, American newspaperwoman: quoted in Harold Faber, *The New York Times Magazine, 17 March 1968*

Compromise

All life is essentially the contributions that come from compromise.

SPIRO T. AGNEW (1918–96), American vice-president

Politics is compromise.

PADDY ASHDOWN (1941–), British politician

Compromise:
Such an adjustment of conflicting interests as gives each adversary the satisfaction of thinking he has got what he ought not to have, and is deprived of nothing except what was justly his due.

AMBROSE (GWINETT) BIERCE (1862–?1914), American journalist and humorist: *The Devil's Dictionary*

Compromise never pays. One must be intransigent. If you do something out of conviction, and you are wrong, you are wrong in an interesting way. But if you are wrong because you have compromised, all you have is a sense of failure and discouragement.

PIERRE BOULEZ (1925–), French composer: *Esquire, 1969*

All government – indeed, every human benefit and enjoyment, every virtue and every prudent act – is founded on compromise and barter.

EDMUND BURKE (1729–97), British statesman, orator and writer: *Speech, 'On Conciliation with the American Colonies', 22 March 1775*

What are facts but compromises? A fact merely marks the point where we have agreed to let investigation cease.

BLISS CARMAN (1861–1929), Canadian poet

Compromise used to mean that half a loaf was better than no bread. Among modern statesmen it really seems to mean that half a loaf is better than a whole loaf.

G(ILBERT) K(EITH) CHESTERTON (1874–1936), English essayist, novelist, poet and critic: *What's Wrong with the World*

They say it is better to be poor and happy than rich and miserable, but how about a compromise like moderately rich and just moody?

DIANA, PRINCESS OF WALES (1961–97), first wife of Charles, Prince of Wales

Compromise is but the sacrifice of one right or good in the hope of retaining another – too often ending in the loss of both.

TRYON EDWARDS (1805–94), American theologian

Most people hew the battlements of life from compromise, erecting their impregnable keeps from judicious submissions, fabricating their philosophical drawbridges from emotional retractions and scalding marauders in the boiling oil of sour grapes.

ZELDA FITZGERALD (1900–48), American writer and wife of F. Scott Fitzgerald: *Save Me the Waltz*

Don't compromise yourself. You are all you've got.

JANIS JOPLIN (1943–70), American singer

To be or not to be is not a question of compromise. Either you be or you don't be.

GOLDA MEIR (1898–1978), Russian-born Israeli stateswoman and prime minister

You still have to compromise and play some sort of game to stay in the game.

VAN MORRISON (1945–), Irish singer and songwriter

Be understanding of one another. Be willing to compromise.
YOKO ONO (LENNON) (1933–), Japanese-born artist and musician

If we don't stop somewhere, if we don't accept an unhappy
compromise, unhappy for both sides, if we don't learn how to
unhappily coexist and contain our burned sense of injustice – if
we don't learn how to do that, we end up in a doomed state.
AMOS OZ (1939–), Israeli writer

In a relationship, when does the art of compromise become
compromising?
SARAH JESSICA PARKER (1965–), American actress

Better bend than break.
SCOTTISH PROVERB

If you just set out to be liked, you would be prepared to
compromise on anything at any time, and you would achieve
nothing.
MARGARET (HILDA) THATCHER (1925–), English politician and prime
minister

From compromise and things half done,
Keep me with stern and stubborn pride;
And when at last the fight is won,
God, keep me still unsatisfied.
LOUIS UNTERMEYER (1885–1977), American author

You know what the Englishman's idea of compromise is? He says,
Some people say there is a God. Some people say there is no
God. The truth probably lies somewhere between these two
statements.
W(ILLIAM) B(UTLER) YEATS (1865–1939), Irish poet and dramatist

Computers & Automation

A computer makes it possible to do, in half an hour, tasks which were completely unnecessary to do before.

ANON

A thunderstorm is God's way of saying you spend too much time in front of the computer.

ANON

Don't worry about our future if we automate. Worry about our future if we don't automate.

ANON

GIGO:
Garbage in, garbage out.

ANON

Mac users swear by their computers. PC users swear at their computers.

ANON

To err is human, but to really foul things up requires a computer.

ANON

One cannot walk through a mass-production factory and not feel that one is in Hell.

W(YSTAN) H(UGH) AUDEN (1907–73), English poet, dramatist, critic and librettist

The most likely way for the world to be destroyed, most experts agree, is by accident. That's where we come in; we're computer professionals. We cause accidents.

NATHANIEL BORENSTEIN (1957–), American computer specialist

Computers are like Old Testament gods; lots of rules and no mercy.

JOSEPH CAMPBELL (1904–87), American writer

Automation is not gadgeteering, it is not even engineering; it is a concept of the structure and order of economic life, the design of its basic patterns integrated into a harmonious, balanced, organic whole.

PETER F. DRUCKER (1909–2005), American management expert: *America's Next Twenty Years*

The danger of the past was that men became slaves. The danger of the future is that men may become robots.

ERICH FROMM (1900–80), German-born American psychoanalyst and philosopher: *The Sane Society*

If you asked customers who they would rather have deciding what innovations go into their computer – the government or software companies – the answer would be clear. They'd want the decision left to the marketplace, with competition driving improvements.

BILL GATES (1955–), American businessman and philanthropist

People do play computer games at work, but they also doodle with pencils. Do you take away their pencils? … That's not the way a modern workforce is managed. You've got to trust people.

BILL GATES (1955–), American businessman and philanthropist: *The New York Times, 4 November 1996*

One machine can do the work of fifty ordinary men. No machine can do the work of one extraordinary man.

ELBERT (GREEN) HUBBARD (1856–1915), American businessman, writer and printer: *Roycroft Dictionary and Book of Epigrams*

Man is still the most extraordinary computer of all.

JOHN FITZGERALD KENNEDY (1917–63), American statesman and president: *Address, 21 May 1963*

We believe that if men have the talent to invent new machines that put men out of work, they have the talent to put those men back to work.

JOHN FITZGERALD KENNEDY: *Address, Wheeling, West Virginia, 27 September 1962*

It is critical vision alone which can mitigate the unimpeded operation of the automatic.

(HERBERT) MARSHALL MCLUHAN (1911–80), Canadian educator, author and media expert: *The Mechanical Bride*

The world is dying of machinery; that is the great disease, that is the plague that will sweep away and destroy civilization; man will have to rise against it sooner or later.

GEORGE MOORE (1852–1933), Irish novelist, poet and critic: *Confessions of a Young Man*

Computers are useless. They can only give you answers.

PABLO PICASSO (1881–1973), Spanish artist

Computers make it easier to do a lot of things, but most of the things they make it easier to do don't need to be done.

ANDY ROONEY (1919–), American humorist and writer

A computer will do what you tell it to do, but that may be much different from what you had in mind.

JOSEPH WEIZENBAUM (1923–), German-born professor of computer science

The evil that machinery is doing is not merely in the consequences of its work but in the fact that it makes men themselves machines also.

OSCAR WILDE (1856–1900), Irish poet, dramatist and wit: *(Omaha) Weekly Herald, 22 March 1882*

Deals & Contracts

If you deal in camels, make the doors high.

AFGHAN PROVERB

In honourable dealing you should consider what you intended, not what you said or thought.

MARCUS TULLIUS CICERO (106–43 BC), Roman statesman and orator

'My idea of an agreeable person,' said Hugo Bohun, 'is a person who agrees with me.'

BENJAMIN DISRAELI, 1st Earl of Beaconsfield (1804–81), English statesman, prime minister and novelist: *Lothair, chapter 35*

Your life works to the degree you keep your agreements.

WERNER ERHARD (1935–), American trainer

It is my fate and perhaps my temperament to sign agreements with fools.

E(DWARD) M(ORGAN) FORSTER (1879–1970), English novelist

You must never try to make all the money that's in a deal. Let the other fellow make some money too, because if you have a reputation for making all the money there is in a deal, you won't make many deals.

J(EAN) PAUL GETTY (1892–1976), American financier: quoted in Somerset de Chair, *Getty on Getty*

A verbal contract isn't worth the paper it's written on.

SAMUEL GOLDWYN (1882–1974), American film producer (Attributed)

Deals are my art form. Other people paint beautifully on canvas or write wonderful poetry. I like making deals, preferably big deals. That's how I get my kicks.

EDWARD KOCH (1924–), American politician and writer

Only free men can negotiate; prisoners cannot enter into contracts. Your freedom and mine cannot be separated.
NELSON MANDELA (1918–), South African statesman and president

Some people mistake weakness for tact. If they are silent when they ought to speak and so feign an agreement they do not feel, they call it being tactful. Cowardice would be a much better name.
SIR FRANK MEDLICOTT (1903–72), English solicitor: *Reader's Digest, July 1958*

You make very nice rules, you make agreements, you shake hands, but you know generally the exchange of information is only on specific cases when things have already happened.
ROMANO PRODI (1939–), Italian politician

Contract:
an agreement that is binding only on the weaker party.
FREDERICK SAWYER (1822–91), American senator

Every law is a contract between the king and the people and therefore to be kept.
JOHN SELDEN (1584–1634), English historian and antiquary: *Table Talk*

My style of dealmaking is quite simple and straightforward. I just keep pushing and pushing to get what I'm after.
DONALD TRUMP (1946–), American entrepreneur: *The Art of the Deal*

If Max [Beaverbrook] gets to Heaven he won't last long. He will be chucked out for trying to pull off a merger between Heaven and Hell … after having secured a controlling interest in key subsidiary companies in both places, of course.
H(ERBERT) G(EORGE) WELLS (1866–1946), English novelist, journalist and social philosopher: quoted in A. J. P. Taylor, *Beaverbrook*

There is nothing more likely to start disagreement among people or countries than an agreement.

E(LWYN) B(ROOKS) WHITE (1899–1985), American humorist and essayist: *One Man's Meat*

Ah! don't say you agree with me. When people agree with me I always feel that I must be wrong.

OSCAR WILDE (1856–1900), Irish poet, dramatist and wit: *The Critic as Artist, Part 2*

If two men on the same job agree all the time, then one is useless. If they disagree all the time, then both are useless.

DARRYL F(RANCIS) ZANUCK (1902–79), film executive: *Observer, 23 October 1949*

One of my favourite philosophical tenets is that people will agree with you only if they already agree with you. You do not change people's minds.

FRANK ZAPPA (1940–93), American rock musician and producer

Decision-Making & Indecision

In my house I'm the boss, my wife is just the decision-maker.

WOODY ALLEN (1935–), American film director and actor

We know what happens to people who stay in the middle of the road. They get run over.

ANEURIN BEVAN (1897–1960), British statesman: *Observer, 'Sayings of the Week', 9 December 1953*

What is a rebel? A man who says no.

ALBERT CAMUS (1913–60), French philosopher and writer: *The Rebel*

Resolve to perform what you ought. Perform without fail what you resolve.

BENJAMIN FRANKLIN (1706–90), American statesman, scientist and author: *Autobiography*

Each indecision brings its own delays and days are lost lamenting over lost days … What you can do or think you can do, begin it. For boldness has magic, power and genius in it.

JOHANN WOLFGANG VON GOETHE (1749–1832), German poet, scientist and writer

I'll give you a definite maybe.

SAMUEL GOLDWYN (1882–1974), American film producer (Attributed)

The minority is always right.

HENRIK IBSEN (1828–1906), Norwegian dramatist and poet: *An Enemy of the People, Act 4*

Take your life in your own hands and what happens? A terrible thing: no one to blame.

ERICA JONG (1942–), American author and educator

I actually did vote for the $87 billion, before I voted against it.

JOHN KERRY (1943–), American senator

The politician who never made a mistake never made a decision.

JOHN MAJOR (1943–), British prime minister

Like all weak men he laid an exaggerated stress on not changing one's mind.

W(ILLIAM) SOMERSET MAUGHAM (1874–1965), English writer: *Of Human Bondage, chapter 37*

Nothing is more difficult, and therefore more precious, than to be able to decide.

NAPOLEON I (Napoleon Bonaparte) (1769–1821), French emperor and general: *Maxims*

The man who is denied the opportunity of taking decisions of importance begins to regard as important the decisions he is allowed to take. He becomes fussy about filing, keen on seeing that pencils are sharpened, eager to ensure that the windows are open (or shut) and apt to use two or three different-coloured inks.

C(YRIL) NORTHCOTE PARKINSON (1909–93), English historian and journalist: *Parkinson's Law*

Between two stools one sits on the ground.

PROVERB

Choose always the way that seems the best, however rough it may be. Custom will soon render it easy and agreeable.

PYTHAGORAS (c. 575–500 BC), Greek philosopher

A decision is the action an executive must take when he has information so incomplete that the answer does not suggest itself.

ARTHUR WILLIAM RADFORD (1896–1973), American admiral and business consultant: *Time, 25 February 1957*

There are only two options regarding commitment. You're either in or out. There's no such thing as a life in-between.

PAT RILEY (1945–), American basketball coach and motivational speaker

Don't vacillate. A poor plan persevered in is better than a good one shifted while being performed.

ERWIN H. SCHELL (1889–1965): *The Technique of Executive Control*

The indispensable first step to getting the things you want out of life is this: decide what you want.

BEN STEIN (1944–), American lawyer, actor and comedian

Procrastination is the thief of time.

EDWARD YOUNG (1683–1765), English poet and dramatist: *Night Thoughts*

Eating & Drinking

There is no such thing as a free lunch.

ANON

You better cut the pizza in four pieces because I'm not hungry enough to eat six.

LAWRENCE PETER (YOGI) BERRA (1925–), American baseball player and manager

Tell me what you eat, and I will tell you what you are.

ANTHELME BRILLAT-SAVARIN (1755–1826), French politician and gourmet: *Physiologic du goût*

Coffee in England always tastes like a chemistry experiment.

AGATHA CHRISTIE (1890–1976), English crime fiction writer: quoted in *Wrinklies' Wit & Wisdom Forever*

Quick at meals, quick at work, is a saying as old as the hills.

WLLLIAM COBBETT (1762–1835), English farmer, social reformer and writer: *Advice to Young Men*

Never drink black coffee at lunch; it will keep you awake in the afternoon.

JILLY COOPER (1937–), British writer: *How to Survive from Nine to Five*

Lunch is for wimps.

MICHAEL DOUGLAS (1944–), American actor: as Gordon Gekko in *Wall Street*

I just can't eat without my sunglasses.

CALISTA FLOCKHART (1964–), American actress

More die in the United States of too much food than of too little.

JOHN KENNETH GALBRAITH (1908–2006), Canadian-born American economist, diplomat and writer: *The Affluent Society*

Conversation is the enemy of good wine and food.

SIR ALFRED (JOSEPH) HITCHCOCK (1889–1980), English film director

The morning cup of coffee has an exhilaration about it which the cheering influence of the afternoon or evening cup of tea cannot be expected to reproduce.

OLIVER WENDELL HOLMES, SR (1809–94), American physician, professor and author: *Over the Teacups*

Melancholy, indeed, should be diverted by every means but drinking.

SAMUEL JOHNSON (1709–84), English lexicographer, essayist and poet: quoted in James Boswell, *The Life of Samuel Johnson*

At a dinner party one should eat wisely but not too well, and talk well, but not too wisely.

W(ILLIAM) SOMERSET MAUGHAM (1874–1965), English writer: *A Writer's Notebook*

I've made it a rule never to drink by daylight and never to refuse a drink after dark.

HENRY LOUIS MENCKEN (1880–1956), American philologist, editor and satirist: *New York Post, 18 September 1945*

On the Continent people have good food; in England people have good table manners.

GEORGE MIKES (1912–87), Hungarian-English writer: *How to Be an Alien*

One should eat to live, not live to eat.

MOLIÈRE (Jean Baptiste Poquelin) (1622–73), French dramatist: *L'Avare, Act 3*

Mr Portpipe:
There are two reasons for drinking; one is, when you are thirsty, to cure it; the other, when you are not thirsty, to prevent it ... Prevention is better than cure.

THOMAS LOVE PEACOCK (1785–1866), English novelist: *Melincourt, chapter 16*

Strange to see how a good dinner and feasting reconciles everybody.

SAMUEL PEPYS (1633–1703), English diarist and naval administrator: *Diary, 9 November 1665*

[To a blind woman with a guide dog] Do you know they have eating dogs for the anorexic now?

PRINCE PHILIP, Duke of Edinburgh (1921–): *June 2002*

Appetite comes with eating.

FRANÇOIS RABELAIS (?1494–1553), French writer: *Gargantua 1:5*

You can't think rationally on an empty stomach, and a whole lot of people can't do it on a full one either.

LORD REITH, John (Charles Walsham), 1st Baron (1889–1971), British broadcasting executive (Attributed)

Miss a meal if you have to, but don't miss a book.

JIM ROHN, American motivational speaker

A dinner lubricates business.

WILLIAM SCOTT, 1st Baron Stowell (1745–1836), English judge: Boswell, *Life of Johnson*

If you are going to let the fear of poverty govern your life, your reward will be that you will eat, but you will not live.

GEORGE BERNARD SHAW (1856–1950), Irish dramatist and critic

Bad men live that they may eat and drink, whereas good men eat and drink that they may live.

SOCRATES (?470–399 BC), Athenian philosopher: *How a Young Man Ought to Hear Poems (Plutarch)*

But I'm not so think as you drunk I am.

SIR JOHN COLLINGS SQUIRE (1884–1958), English writer: *Ballade of Soporific Absorption*

Education & Training

Just because you're trained for something doesn't mean you're prepared for it.

ANON

Education is an ornament in prosperity and a refuge in adversity.

ARISTOTLE (384–322 BC), Greek philosopher and scientist: quoted in *Lives and Opinions of Eminent Philosophers*

I had a good education but it never went to my head, somehow. It should be a journey ending up with you at a different place. It didn't take with me. My degree was a kind of inoculation. I got just enough education to make me immune from it for the rest of my life.

ALAN BENNETT (1934–), English dramatist and actor: *Getting On, Act 1*

Education makes a people easy to lead, but difficult to drive; easy to govern, but impossible to enslave.

HENRY PETER BROUGHAM (1778–1868), Scottish statesman

The dons are too busy educating the young men to be able to teach them anything.

SAMUEL BUTLER (1835–1902), English author, painter and musician: *Notebooks*

Life at a university, with its intellectual and inconclusive discussions at a postgraduate level is on the whole a bad training for the real world. Only men of very strong character surmount this handicap.

PAUL CHAMBERS (1904–81), British chairman of ICI: *Observer, 1964*

Education is a sieve as well as a lift.

SID CHAPLIN: *The Day of the Sardine, chapter 1*

Headmasters have powers at their disposal with which Prime Ministers have never yet been invested.

SIR WINSTON LEONARD SPENCER CHURCHILL (1874–1965), English statesman, writer and prime minister: *My Early Life, chapter 2*

Examinations are formidable even to the best prepared, for the greatest fool may ask more than the wisest man can answer.

CHARLES CALEB COLTON (?1780–1832), English clergyman and writer: *Lacon, II*

Learning without thought is labour lost; thought without learning is perilous.

CONFUCIUS (Kong Zi) (551–479 BC), Chinese philosopher: *Analects*

I've over-educated myself in all the things I shouldn't have known at all.

SIR NOËL (PIERCE) COWARD (1899–1973), English actor and dramatist: *Wild Oats*

The one real object of education is to leave a man in the condition of continually asking questions.

BISHOP MANDEL CREIGHTON (1843–1901), English prelate and historian: quoted in C. A. Alington, *Things Ancient and Modern*

Higher education and business are basically interdependent. The one needs money to produce educated people. The other needs educated people to produce money.

MILTON EISENHOWER (1899–1985): *The Times Higher Education Supplement, 22 January 1982*

I pay the schoolmaster, but 'tis the schoolboys that educate my son.

RALPH WALDO EMERSON (1803–82), American poet, essayist and philosopher: *Journals, 1849*

It is not that the Englishman can't feel – it is that he is afraid to feel. He has been taught at his public school that feeling is bad form. He must not express great joy or sorrow, or even open his mouth too wide when he talks – his pipe might fall out if he did.

E(DWARD) M(ORGAN) FORSTER (1879–1970), English novelist: *Abinger Harvest, 'Notes on the English Character'*

Spoon feeding in the long run teaches us nothing but the shape of the spoon.

E(DWARD) M(ORGAN) FORSTER: *Observer, 'Sayings of the Week', 7 October 1951*

It horrifies me that ethics is only an optional extra at Harvard Business School.

SIR JOHN HARVEY-JONES (1924–), former chairman of ICI: quoted in Helen Exley, *The Best of Business Quotations*

The world's great men have not commonly been great scholars, nor great scholars great men.

OLIVER WENDELL HOLMES, SR (1809–94), American physician, professor and author: *The Autocrat of the Breakfast Table, chapter 6*

Perhaps the most valuable result of all education is the ability to make yourself do the thing you have to do, when it ought to be done, whether you like it or not; it is the first lesson that ought to be learned; and however early a man's training begins, it is probably the last lesson that he learns thoroughly.

THOMAS HENRY HUXLEY (1825–95), English biologist, teacher and writer: *Technical Education*

State a moral case to a ploughman and a professor. The former will decide it as well, and often better than the latter, because he has not been led astray by artificial rules.

THOMAS JEFFERSON (1743–1826), American statesman and president: *Letter to Peter Can, 10 August 1787*

The goal of education is the advancement of knowledge and the dissemination of truth.

JOHN FITZGERALD KENNEDY (1917–63), American statesman and president: *Address, Harvard University, Cambridge, Massachusetts, 1956*

Universities are the cathedrals of the modern age. They shouldn't have to justify their existence by utilitarian criteria.

DAVID LODGE (1935–), British author

A man who knows a subject thoroughly, a man so soaked in it that he eats it, sleeps it and dreams it – this man can always teach it with success, no matter how little he knows of technical pedagogy.

HENRY LOUIS MENCKEN (1880–1956), American philologist, editor and satirist: *Prejudices: Third Series*

All education is, in a sense, vocational, vocational for living.

SIR JOHN NEWSOM (1910–71), Chairman of Central Advisory Council for Education (England): *Observer, 'The Education Women Need', 6 September 1964*

A little learning is a dangerous thing.

ALEXANDER POPE (1688–1744), English poet and satirist: *An Essay on Criticism*

Experience is the best teacher.
PROVERB

Give a man a fish and you feed him for one day. Teach a man to fish and you feed him for a lifetime.
CHINESE PROVERB

The schools of the country are its future in miniature.
CHINESE PROVERB

Education is the leading human souls to what is best … the training which makes men happiest in themselves also makes them most serviceable to others.
JOHN RUSKIN (1819–1900), English art critic and social reformer: *The Stones of Venice*

He who can, does. He who cannot, teaches.
GEORGE BERNARD SHAW (1856–1950), Irish dramatist and critic: *Man and Superman, Maxims for Revolutionists*

Education has for its object the formation of character.
HERBERT SPENCER (1820–1903), English philosopher: *Social Statics*

There is nothing training cannot do. Nothing is above its reach. It can turn bad morals to good; it can destroy bad principles and recreate good ones; it can lift men to angelship.
MARK TWAIN (Samuel Langhorne Clemens) (1835–1910), American novelist and humorist

Education is an admirable thing, but it is well to remember from time to time that nothing that is worth knowing can be taught.
OSCAR WILDE (1856–1900), Irish poet, dramatist and wit: *Intentions, 'The Critic As Artist'*

Email, Fax & Telephone

Email – when it absolutely positively has to get lost at the speed of light.

ANON

Fax is stranger than fiction.

ANON

For people who like peace and quiet: a phoneless cord.

ANON, quoted in *Quotations with an Attitude*

Home is where you hang your @.

ANON

Speak softly and carry a mobile phone.

ANON

The email of the species is more deadly than the mail.

ANON

Letters of thanks, letters from banks,
Letters of joy from girl and boy.

W(YSTAN) H(UGH) AUDEN (1907–73), English poet, dramatist, critic and librettist: *Night Mail*

Telephone:
An invention of the devil which abrogates some of the advantages of making a disagreeable person keep his distance.

AMBROSE (GWINETT) BIERCE (1842–?1914), American journalist and humorist: *The Devil's Dictionary*

The great secret in life ... not to open your letters for a fortnight.

At the expiration of that period you will find that nearly all of them have answered themselves.

ARTHUR BINSTEAD (1861–1914), journalist and author: *Pitcher's Proverbs*

The hills are alive with the sound of mobiles.

Headline: *Daily Telegraph*, 2 November 2000: quoted in D. Pytches, *Family Matters*

I can't think of life without the BlackBerry.

NICHOLAS EVANS, British executive

I'm afraid I was very much the traditionalist. I went down on one knee and dictated a proposal which my secretary faxed over straight away.

STEPHEN FRY (1957–), English comedian and actor

No. I don't know his telephone number. But it was up in the high numbers.

JOHN MAYNARD KEYNES (1883–1946), English economist (Attributed)

President Bush said for security reasons, he's sworn off all email communication. He will not be using email at the White House at all. Is that a good idea? I mean, it's not like that speaking thing was working out so good.

JAY LENO (1950–), American comedian

Electronic communication is an instantaneous and illusory contact that creates a sense of intimacy without the emotional investment that leads to close friendships.

CLIFFORD STOLL, American astronomer and author: *Silicon Snake Oil*

Facts

Where facts are few, experts are many.
ANON

On Harold Wilson:
All facts – no bloody ideas.
ANEURIN BEVAN (1897–1960), British statesman

The trouble with facts is that there are so many of them.
SAMUEL MCCHORD CROTHERS (1857–1927), *The Gentle Reader*

Gradgrind:
Now, what I want is Facts … Facts alone are wanted in life.
CHARLES (JOHN HUFFAM) DICKENS (1812–70), English novelist: *Hard Times*

It is a capital mistake to theorise before one has data. Insensibly one begins to twist facts to suit theories, instead of theories to suit facts.
SIR ARTHUR CONAN DOYLE (1859–1930), English writer: *The Adventures of Sherlock Holmes, 'Scandal in Bohemia'*

I think there is one smashing rule – never face the facts.
RUTH GORDON (1896–1985), American actress: *New York Post, 1971*

A wise man recognizes the convenience of a general statement, but he bows to the authority of a particular fact.
OLIVER WENDELL HOLMES, SR (1809–94), American physician, professor and author: *The Poet at the Breakfast Table*

All fact-collectors, who have no aim beyond their facts, are one-story men. Two-story men compare, reason, generalize, using the labors of the fact-collectors as well as their own. Three-story men

idealize, imagine, predict; their best illumination comes from
above, through the skylight.
OLIVER WENDELL HOLMES, SR, as above

Facts do not cease to exist because they are ignored.
ALDOUS (LEONARD) HUXLEY (1894–1963), English novelist and essayist:
Proper Studies

Facts by themselves are silent.
ALFRED MARSHALL (1842–1924), English classical economist: *The Present
Position of Economics*

Why, a four-year-old child could understand this report. Run out
and find me a four-year-old child. I can't make head or tail out of it.
GROUCHO MARX (1895–1977), American film comedian: *Duck Soup, film*

There are no facts, only interpretations.
FRIEDRICH WILHELM NIETZSCHE (1844–1900), German philosopher, poet
and critic

The facts are to blame, my friend. We are all imprisoned by facts:
I was born, I exist.
LUIGI PIRANDELLO (1867–1936), Italian playwright and novelist: *The Rules of
the Game*

When you have duly arrayed your 'facts' in logical order, lo, it is
like an oil-lamp that you have made, filled and trimmed, but
which sheds no light unless first you light it.
ANTOINE DE SAINT-EXUPÉRY (1900–44), French novelist and aviator:
The Wisdom of the Sands

Comment is free but facts are sacred.
C(HARLES) P(RESTWICK) SCOTT (1846–1932), newspaper editor:
Manchester Guardian, 6 May 1926

Get your facts first, and then you can distort them as much as you please.

MARK TWAIN (Samuel Langhorne Clemens) (1835–1910), American novelist and humorist

Gifts

A hug is the perfect gift; one size fits all, and nobody minds if you exchange it.

ANON

What you get free costs too much.

JEAN ANOUILH (1910–87), French dramatist: *The Lark*

Bath salts and inexpensive scent
And hideous tie so kindly meant.

SIR JOHN BETJEMAN (1906–84), English poet: *Christmas*

I sense a new spirit in Britain: that the people of Britain want this massive demonstration of generosity [following the 2004 tsunami] to be given enduring purpose.

GORDON BROWN (1951–), British prime minister

The only gift is a portion of thyself.

RALPH WALDO EMERSON (1803–82), American poet, essayist and philosopher: *Essays: Second Series, 'Gifts'*

It is not good to refuse a gift.

HOMER (c. 800 BC), Greek poet: *Odyssey*

The charity that is a trifle to us can be precious to others.

HOMER, as above

You never want to give a man a present when he's feeling good. You want to do it when he's down.

LYNDON B(AINES) JOHNSON (1908–73), American statesman and president (Attributed)

The selection of presents for children is never easy, because in order to extract real pleasure from the purchase, it is necessary to find something that excites the donor as much as it is likely to excite the recipient.

SIR COMPTON MACKENZIE (1883–1972), British author: *Poor Relations*

He who cannot give anything away cannot feel anything either.

FRIEDRICH WILHELM NIETZSCHE (1844–1900), German philosopher, poet and critic: *The Will to Power*

Say it with flowers.

PATRICK O'KEEFE (1874–1934), American advertising agent: *Slogan for Society of American Florists*

Fear the Greeks bearing gifts.

PROVERB

Small gifts make friends, great ones make enemies.

PROVERB

Give whatever you are doing and whoever you are with the gift of your attention.

JIM ROHN, American motivational speaker

The spirit in which a thing is given determines that in which the debt is acknowledged; it's the intention, not the face-value of the gift, that's weighed.

MARCUS or Lucius ANNAEUS SENECA (The Elder) (?55 BC–?AD 39), Roman writer on oratory and history: *Letters to Lucilius*

A friend is a gift you give yourself.
ROBERT LOUIS BALFOUR STEVENSON (1850–94), Scottish writer

Let us not be satisfied with just giving money. Money is not enough, money can be got, but they need your hearts to love them. So, spread your love everywhere you go.
MOTHER TERESA (1910–97), Albanian nun, Nobel Peace Price winner 1979

Globalisation

It has been said that arguing against globalisation is like arguing against the laws of gravity.
KOFI ANNAN (1938–), Ghanaian diplomat, secretary-general of the United Nations, Nobel Peace Prize winner 2001

I'm against this huge globalisation on the basis of economic advantage.
SIR DAVID ATTENBOROUGH (1926–), English broadcaster and naturalist

Globalisation, which benefits only multinational companies and takes away all sense of local or national pride and identity, is the biggest threat facing all the member states of the EU.
STEVE BLAKE

Globalisation has altered the dynamics in the White House, as well as between the White House and the Treasury.
GEORGE W. BUSH (1946–), American president

Globalisation, as defined by rich people like us, is a very nice thing … you are talking about the internet, you are talking about cell phones, you are talking about computers. This doesn't affect two-thirds of the people of the world.
JIMMY CARTER (1924–), American president, Nobel Peace Prize winner 2002

Not much is to be gained simply by religious groups and religious leaders repeating slogans about the costs and evils of globalisation.

ROWAN WILLIAMS (1950–), Welsh-born theologian and Archbishop of Canterbury

Green Issues

Global warming is not a political issue. It's a moral issue, an ethical issue, a survival issue.

AL GORE (1948–), American politician, businessman and environmentalist; American vice-president

We are living beyond our means. As a people we have developed a life-style that is draining the earth of its priceless and irreplaceable resources without regard for the future of our children and people all around the world.

MARGARET MEAD (1901–78), American anthropologist: *Redbook*

I think the environment should be put in the category of our national security. Defence of our resources is just as important as defence abroad. Otherwise what is there to defend?

ROBERT REDFORD (1937–), American actor

Action on climate change will also create significant business opportunities, as new markets are created in low-carbon energy technologies and other low-carbon goods and services.

Stern Review: The Economics of Climate Change

Using the results from formal economic models, the Review estimates that if we don't act, the overall costs and risks of climate change will be equivalent to losing at least 5% of global GDP each year, now and forever.

Stern Review: The Economics of Climate Change

We're in a giant car heading towards a brick wall and everyone's arguing over where they're going to sit.

DAVID SUZUKI (1936–), Canadian environmentalist

Over the long haul of life on this planet, it is the ecologists, and not the bookkeepers of business, who are the ultimate accountants.

STEWART L. UDALL (1920–), American politician

To the average British farmer, organic farming is about as relevant as caviar and a flight on Concorde.

OLIVER WALSTON (1941–), British farmer and journalist

Hospitality

Hospitality is making your guests feel at home, even though you wish they were.

ANON

When hospitality becomes an art it loses its very soul.

SIR MAX BEERBOHM (1872–1956), English writer and caricaturist

Hospitality:
The virtue which induces us to feed and lodge certain persons who are not in need of food and lodging.

AMBROSE (GWINETT) BIERCE (1842–?1914), American journalist and humorist: *The Devil's Dictionary*

When I sell liquor, it's called bootlegging; when my patrons serve it on Lake Shore Drive, it's called hospitality.

AL CAPONE (1899–1947), American gangster

My master is of churlish disposition
And little recks to find the way to heaven

By doing deeds of hospitality.

WILLIAM SHAKESPEARE (1564–1616), English dramatist and poet: *As You Like It*

Hotels

I have always had a hidden wish, a frustrated desire, to run a hotel.

EDWARD (RICHARD GEORGE) HEATH (1916–2005), British statesman and prime minister: *Observer, 'Sayings of the Year', 18 December 1966*

Switzerland is a small, steep country, much more up and down than sideways, and is all stuck over with large brown hotels built on the cuckoo style of architecture.

ERNEST HEMINGWAY (1899–1961), American novelist and short-story writer

The great advantage of a hotel is that it's a refuge from home life.

GEORGE BERNARD SHAW (1856–1950), Irish dramatist and critic: *You Never Can Tell*

It used to be a good hotel, but that proves nothing – I used to be a good boy.

MARK TWAIN (Samuel Langhorne Clemens) (1835–1910), American novelist and humorist: *Letter from New York to the Alta Californian (San Francisco), 19 April 1867*

I prefer temperance hotels – although they sell worse kinds of liquor than any other kind of hotels.

ARTEMUS WARD (Charles Farrar Browne) (1834–67), American humorist, editor and lecturer: *Artemus Ward's Lecture*

Ideas & Innovations

Don't worry about people stealing your ideas. If your ideas are any good, you'll have to ram them down people's throats.

HOWARD AIKEN (1900–73), American computer pioneer

As the births of living creatures at first are ill-shapen, so are all innovations, which are the births of time.

FRANCIS BACON, 1st Baron Verulam, Viscount St Albans (1561–1626), English writer, philosopher and statesman: *Essays*

There is no new thing under the sun.

The Bible, Authorised (King James) Version, Ecclesiastes 1:9

I never actually set out to see how I could make the most cash. I've always merely tried to make the figures fit the ideas I've had rather than the other way around. I guess that's doing it backwards.

RICHARD BRANSON (1950–), Head of Virgin Group: quoted in Jeffrey Robinson, *The Risk Takers, chapter 4*

Let's remind ourselves that last year's fresh idea is today's cliché.

AUSTEN BRIGGS (1931–), American commercial artist

A new idea is delicate. It can be killed by a sneer or a yawn; it can be stabbed to death by a quip and worried to death by a frown on the right man's brow.

CHARLES (HENDRICKSON) BROWER (1901–84), American advertising executive: *Advertising Age, 10 August 1959*

I want to thank the astronauts who are with us, the courageous spacial entrepreneurs who set such a wonderful example for the young of our country.

GEORGE W. BUSH (1946–), American president

We must beware of needless innovation, especially when guided by logic.

SIR WINSTON LEONARD SPENCER CHURCHILL (1874–1965), English statesman, writer and prime minister

Without tradition, art is a flock of sheep without a shepherd.
Without innovation, it is a corpse.
SIR WINSTON LEONARD SPENCER CHURCHILL

Creative people must entertain lots of silly ideas in order to
receive the occasional strokes of genius.
MARSHALL COOK, American professor of journalism and communications

Where ideas lead, progress is rapid.
EDWARD DE BONO (1933–), British physician and writer

Inventors and men of genius have almost always been regarded as
fools at the beginning (and very often at the end) of their careers.
FYODOR MIKHAILOVICH DOSTOEVSKY (1821–81), Russian novelist: *The Idiot*

Innovation is the new conservatism.
PETER F. DRUCKER (1909–2005), American management expert: quoted in
Jeremy Tunstall, *The Advertising Man*

Invention breeds invention.
RALPH WALDO EMERSON (1803–82), American poet, essayist and
philosopher: *Society and Solitude*

No grand idea was ever born in a conference, but a lot of foolish
ideas have died there.
FRANCIS SCOTT (KEY) FITZGERALD (1896–1940), American novelist: *The
Crack-Up*

It is easy to overlook the absence of appreciable advance in an
industry. Inventions that are not made, like babies that are not
born, are rarely missed.
JOHN KENNETH GALBRAITH (1908–2006), Canadian-born American
economist, diplomat and writer: *The Affluent Society, chapter 9*

One doesn't discover new lands without consenting to lose sight of the shore for a very long time.

ANDRÉ GIDE (1869–1951), French novelist, dramatist, critic, diarist and translator: *The Counterfeiters*

Art has to move you and design does not, unless it's a good design for a bus.

DAVID HOCKNEY (1937–), British painter

As soon as an idea is accepted it is time to reject it.

HOLBROOK JACKSON (1874–1948), English literary scholar and editor

Writing is not hard. Just get paper and pencil, sit down and write it as it occurs to you. The writing is easy – it's the occurring that's hard.

STEPHEN BUTLER LEACOCK (1869–1944), Canadian economist and humorist

If you are possessed by an idea, you find it expressed everywhere, you even smell it.

THOMAS MANN (1875–1955), German novelist and essayist: *Death in Venice*

An idea isn't responsible for the people who believe in it.

DON(ALD ROBERT PERRY) MARQUIS (1878–1937), American humorist: *New York Sun, 'Sun Dial'*

The full importance of an epoch-making idea is often not perceived in the generation in which it is made … The mechanical inventions of every age are apt to be underrated relatively to those of earlier times. For a new discovery is seldom fully effective for practical purposes till many minor improvements and subsidiary discoveries have gathered themselves around it.

ALFRED MARSHALL (1842–1924), English classical economist: *Principles of Economics, book 4*

But modernise is such a tedious phrase because everyone now claims to be a moderniser and it's obvious really.

FRANCIS MAUDE (1953–), British politician

By his very success in inventing labor-saving devices, modern man has manufactured an abyss of boredom that only the privileged classes in earlier civilizations have ever fathomed.

LEWIS MUMFORD (1895–1990), American sociologist, historian and critic: *The Conduct of Life*

As soon as we are shown the existence of something old in a new thing, we are pacified.

FRIEDRICH WILHELM NIETZSCHE (1844–1900), German philosopher, poet and critic: *The Will to Power*

Thinking is the endeavor to capture reality by means of ideas.

JOSÉ ORTEGA Y GASSET (1883–1955), Spanish philosopher and statesman: *The Dehumanization of Art*

One thing about pioneers that you don't hear mentioned is that they are invariably, by their nature, mess makers. They go forging ahead, seeing only their noble, distant goal, and never notice any of the crud and debris they leave behind.

ROBERT M. PIRSIG (1928–), American author: *Zen and the Art of Motorcycle Maintenance*

Necessity is the mother of invention.

PROVERB

The great difficulty in education is to get experience out of ideas.

GEORGE SANTAYANA (1863–1952), American philosopher and poet: *The Life of Reason: Reason in Common Sense*

You can't really separate the inventor and the businessman. The idea of the lone inventor sitting in an attic somewhere is pretty impractical. By its very nature, invention itself is improbable. If you rush around with all your ideas in a brown paper bag, knocking on doors of big companies, those big companies are going to say, no. The way society arranges things makes it very difficult for all inventors. So the way you get around that problem, the way you turn your invention into something, is by being a sort of businessman. You go out there and you start a company and you get your own invention off the ground.

SIR CLIVE (MARLES) SINCLAIR (1940–), English computer entrepreneur: quoted in Jeffrey Robinson, *The Risk Takers*

An entrepreneur, if there is such a thing, is a born schemer and thinker-up of things.

SIR ALAN SUGAR (1947–), British entrepreneur

Name the greatest of all the inventors. Accident.

MARK TWAIN (Samuel Langhorne Clemens) (1835–1910), American novelist and humorist: *Notebook*

The radical invents the views.
When he has worn them out the conservative adopts them.

MARK TWAIN, as above

Wit is the sudden marriage of ideas which before their union were not perceived to have any relation.

MARK TWAIN, as above

Everyone likes innovation until it affects himself, and then it's bad.

WALTER WRISTON, Chairman, First National City Bank, New York: *Observer*, 'Sayings of the Year', 29 December 1974

Insurance

There are worse things in life than death. Have you ever spent an evening with an insurance salesman?

WOODY ALLEN (1935–), American film director and actor

I don't want to tell you how much insurance I carry with the Prudential, but all I can say is: when I go, they go.

JACK BENNY (1894–1974), American comedian (Attributed)

Insurance:
An ingenious modern game of chance in which the player is permitted to enjoy the comfortable conviction that he is beating the man who keeps the table.

AMBROSE (GWINETT) BIERCE (1842–?1914), American journalist and humorist: *The Devil's Dictionary*

When the praying does no good, insurance does help.

BERTOLT BRECHT (1898–1956), German dramatist: *The Mother*

The Act of God designation on all insurance policies … means roughly that you cannot be insured for the accidents that are most likely to happen to you. If your ox kicks a hole in your neighbour's Maserati, however, indemnity is instantaneous.

ALAN COREN (1938–), British humorist: *The Lady from Stalingrad Mansions*

Physically you are a human being, but mentally you are incomplete. Given that we have this physical human form, we must safeguard our mental capacity for judgement. For that, we cannot take out insurance; the insurance company is within: self-discipline, self-awareness, and a clear realisation of the disadvantages of anger and the positive effects of kindness.

TENZIN GYATSO (1935–), Dalai Lama, Nobel Peace Prize winner 1989

I detest life-insurance agents; they always argue that I shall some day die, which is not so.

STEPHEN BUTLER LEACOCK (1869–1944), Canadian economist and humorist: *Literary Lapses, 'Insurance Up to Date'*

Intellectual Property

The internet is nothing but a crudely patched-together digital misappropriation of long-established intellectual property of the city of New York.
ANON

Intellectual property has the shelf life of a banana.
BILL GATES (1955–), American businessman and philanthropist

Internet

A chat has nine lives.
ANON

A journey of a thousand sites begins with a single click.
ANON

A user and his leisure time are soon parted.
ANON

C:\ is the root of all directories.
ANON

Don't byte off more than you can view.
ANON

Don't put all your hypes in one home page.
ANON

Give a person a fish and you feed them for a day; teach them to use the net, and they won't bother you for weeks.
ANON

Great groups from little icons grow.
ANON

In Gates we trust (and our tender is legal).
ANON

Know what to expect before you connect.
ANON

Modulation in all things.
ANON

Pentium wise; pen and paper foolish.
ANON

The geek shall inherit the earth.
ANON

The modem is the message.
ANON

There's no place like http://www.home.com.
ANON

Too many clicks spoil the browse.
ANON

Virtual reality is its own reward.
ANON

What boots up must come down.
ANON

Windows will never cease.

ANON

You can't teach an old mouse new clicks.

ANON

I regularly read internet user groups filled with messages from people trying to solve software incompatibility problems that, in terms of complexity, make the US Tax Code look like Dr Seuss.

DAVE BARRY (1947–), American humorist

What, exactly, is the internet? Basically it is a global network exchanging digitised data in such a way that any computer, anywhere, that is equipped with a device called a 'modem', can make a noise like a duck choking on a kazoo.

DAVE BARRY

The internet might define the way we live in the next century, or it could be the CB radio of the 1990s.

GRAHAM BOWLEY, journalist

Will the highways on the internet become more few?

GEORGE W. BUSH (1946–), American president

The new information technology, internet and email, have practically eliminated the physical costs of communications.

PETER F. DRUCKER (1909–2005), Austrian-born American management expert

The internet is the first thing that humanity has built that humanity doesn't understand, the largest experiment in anarchy that we have ever had.

ERIC SCHMIDT (1955–), American computer company chairman

Anyone can post messages to the net. Practically everyone does. The resulting cacophony drowns out serious discussion.

CLIFFORD STOLL, American astronomer and author: *Silicon Snake Oil*

The internet is a telephone system that's gotten uppity.

CLIFFORD STOLL, American astronomer and author

Machinery

Faith in machinery is our besetting danger; often in machinery most absurdly disproportioned to the end which this machinery, if it is to do any good at all, is to serve; but always in machinery, as if it had a value in and for itself.

MATTHEW ARNOLD (1822–88), English poet, essayist and literary critic: *Culture and Anarchy*

If it works, it's out of date.

STAFFORD BEER (1926–2002), British writer and scientist: *Brain of the Firm*

Man will never be enslaved by machinery if the man tending the machine be paid enough.

KAREL CAPEK (1890–1938), Czechoslovakian writer

Man is a tool-using animal.

THOMAS CARLYLE (1795–1881), Scottish essayist and historian: *Sartor Resartus*

One machine can do the work of fifty ordinary men. No machine can do the work of one extraordinary man.

ELBERT (GREEN) HUBBARD (1856–1915), American businessman, writer and printer

It is only when they go wrong that machines remind you how powerful they are.

CLIVE JAMES (1939–), Australian critic: *Observer, 1976*

We believe that if men have the talent to invent new machines that put men out of work, they have the talent to put those men back to work.

JOHN FITZGERALD KENNEDY (1917–63), American statesman and president: *Address, Wheeling, West Virginia, 27 September 1962*

Without doubt, machinery has greatly increased the number of well-to-do idlers.

KARL MARX (1818–83), German founder of modern communism: *Capital, volume 1*

Since the introduction of inanimate mechanism into British manufactories, man, with few exceptions, has been treated as a secondary and inferior machine; and far more attention has been given to perfect the raw materials of wood and metals than those of body and mind. Give but due reflection to the subject, and you will find that man, even as an instrument for the creation of wealth, may be still greatly improved.

ROBERT OWEN (1771–1858), Welsh industrialist and social reformer: *A New View of Society or Essays on the Principle of the Formation of the Human Character and the Application of the Principle of Practice*

The great mechanical impulses of the age, of which most of us are so proud, are a mere passing fever, half-speculative, half-childish.

JOHN RUSKIN (1819–1900), English art critic and social reformer: *Modern Painters*

I think I should not go far wrong if I asserted that the amount of genuine leisure available in a society is generally in inverse proportion to the amount of labour-saving machinery it employs.

ERNST FRIEDRICH SCHUMACHER (1911–77), German-born economist and conservationist

There is nothing in machinery, there is nothing in embankments and railways and iron bridges and engineering devices to oblige

them to be ugly. Ugliness is the measure of imperfection.
H(ERBERT) G(EORGE) WELLS (1866–1946), English novelist, journalist and social philosopher

Negotiation & Persuasion

The single most powerful tool for winning a negotiation is the ability to get up and walk away from the table without a deal.
ANON

Negotiation in the classic diplomatic sense assumes parties more anxious to agree than to disagree.
DEAN ACHESON (1893–1971), American politician

How to Win Friends and Influence People.
DALE CARNEGIE (1888–1955), American writer: *Title of book*

Most people have ears, but few have judgment; tickle those ears, and, depend upon it, you will catch their judgments, such as they are.
LORD CHESTERFIELD, Philip Dormer Stanhope, 4th Earl of (1694–1773), English statesman and writer: *Letter to his son, 9 December 1749*

Money is the best bait to fish for man with.
THOMAS FULLER (1654–1734), English physician, writer and compiler: *Gnomologia*

When a man tells me he's going to put all his cards on the table, I always look up his sleeve.
LORD (ISAAC) LESLIE HORE-BELISHA (1893–1957), British politician

Whenever you're sitting across from some important person, always picture him sitting there in a suit of long red underwear. That's the way I always operated in business.
JOSEPH PATRICK KENNEDY (1888–1969), American businessman and diplomat

By winning words to conquer willing hearts,
And make persuasion do the work of fear.

JOHN MILTON (1608–74), English poet: *Paradise Regained*

We are more easily persuaded, in general, by the reasons we
ourselves discover than by those which are given to us by others.

BLAISE PASCAL (1623–62), French philosopher, mathematician and physicist:
Pensées

There are two fools in every market: one asks too little, one asks
too much.

PROVERB

There is a danger in being persuaded before one understands.

(THOMAS) WOODROW WILSON (1856–1924), American statesman and
president: *Maxims of Piety and of Christianity*

Offices

No man on his death bed ever looked up into the eyes of his family
and friends and said, 'I wish I'd spent more time at the office.'

ANON

A tremendous number of people in America work very hard at
something that bores them. Even a rich man thinks he has to go
down to the office everyday. Not because he likes it but because
he can't think of anything else to do.

W(YSTAN) H(UGH) AUDEN (1907–73), English poet, dramatist, critic and
librettist

Gutenberg made everybody a reader. Xerox makes everybody a
publisher.

(HERBERT) MARSHALL MCLUHAN (1911–80), Canadian educator, author
and media expert: *Guardian Weekly, 12 June 1977*

He and I had an office so tiny that an inch smaller and it would have been adultery.

DOROTHY (ROTHSCHILD) PARKER (1893–1967), American writer

Papyromania:
Compulsive accumulation of papers.

Papyrophobia:
Abnormal desire for 'a clean desk'.

DR LAURENCE J. PETER (1919–90), Canadian educator and RAYMOND HULL (1919–), *The Peter Principle, glossary*

A man who has no office to go to – I don't care who he is – is a trial of which you can have no conception.

GEORGE BERNARD SHAW (1856–1950), Irish dramatist and critic: *The Irrational Knot*

I yield to no one in my admiration for the office as a social centre, but it's no place actually to get any work done.

KATHARINE WHITEHORN (1928–), British journalist: *Sunday Best, Introduction*

Filing is concerned with the past; anything you actually need to see again has to do with the future.

KATHARINE WHITEHORN, as above: '*Sorting Out*'

Philanthropy

Giving away money effectively is almost as hard as earning it in the first place.

BILL GATES (1955–), American businessman and philanthropist

Philanthropy is entertainment with a purpose. For the consumer, giving online is all about emotion – they expect to feel as good or better than when they go to eBay or Amazon. That means the non-profit's site needs to offer engaging stories, compelling artwork, and powerful viral marketing tools.

HARRY GRUBER, American entrepreneur

I think the great livers, the people who are fully self-actualizing and alive, are the great givers.

MARK VICTOR HANSEN, American motivational speaker

I never have any regrets about having spent a lot of money trying to make things better.

GEORGE SOROS (1930–), Hungarian-born businessman and philanthropist

Problems

There's no problem so big or complicated that it can't be run away from.

ANON

If you can't tell me what you'd like to be happening ... you don't have a problem yet. You're just complaining. A problem exists only if there is a difference between what is actually happening and what you desire to be happening.

KENNETH BLANCHARD, American management consultant and SPENCER JOHNSON, American doctor, psychologist and author: *The One Minute Manager*

When I look back on all these worries I remember the story of the old man who said on his deathbed that he had had a lot of trouble in his life, most of which had never happened.

SIR WINSTON LEONARD SPENCER CHURCHILL (1874–1965), English statesman, writer and prime minister: *Their Finest Hour*

You're either part of the solution or part of the problem.

ELDRIDGE CLEAVER (1935–), American writer and radical: *Slogan, 1968*

The government solution to a problem is usually as bad as the problem.

MILTON FRIEDMAN (1912–2006), American economist (Attributed)

It is not always by plugging away at a difficulty and sticking at it that one overcomes it; but, rather, often by working on the one next to it. Certain people and certain things require to be approached on an angle.

ANDRÉ GIDE (1869–1951), French novelist, dramatist, critic, diarist and translator: *Journals, 26 October 1924*

There are two problems in my life. The political ones are insoluble and the economic ones are incomprehensible.

SIR ALEC DOUGLAS-HOME, Lord Home of Hirsel (1903–95), British statesman and prime minister: *Speech, January 1964*

Never let a problem to be solved become more important than a person to be loved.

BARBARA JOHNSON, American writer

Nothing will ever be attempted, if all possible objections must be first overcome.

SAMUEL JOHNSON (1709–84), English lexicographer, essayist and poet: *Rasselas*

Problems are only opportunities in work clothes.

HENRY J. KAISER (1882–1967), American industrialist

There cannot be a crisis next week. My schedule is already full.

HENRY KISSINGER (1923–), German-born American academic and diplomat: *The New York Times Magazine, 1969*

Obstacles cannot crush me. Every obstacle yields to stern resolve. He who is fixed to a star does not change his mind.

LEONARDO DA VINCI (1452–1519), Italian artist and inventor

To solve the problems of today, we must focus on tomorrow.
ERIK NUPPONEN

No problem is so formidable that you can't walk away from it.
CHARLES (MONROE) SCHULZ (1922–2000), American cartoonist

Learn from the mistakes of others – you can't live long enough to make them all yourself.
MARTIN VANBEE

Production

Man produces in order to consume.
FREDERIC BASTIAT (1801–50): *Sophistries économiques, chapter I*

A market is never saturated with a good product, but it is very quickly saturated with a bad one.
HENRY FORD (1863–1947), American car manufacturer

Production only fills a void that it has itself created.
JOHN KENNETH GALBRAITH (1908–2006), Canadian-born American economist, diplomat and writer: *The Affluent Society, chapter 11*

An object of art creates a public capable of finding pleasure in its beauty. Production, therefore, not only produces an object for the subject, but also a subject for the object.
KARL MARX (1818–83), German founder of modern communism: *A Critique of Political Economy*

Capitalist production, therefore, develops technology, and the combining together of various processes into a social whole, only by sapping the original sources of all wealth – the soil and the labourer.
KARL MARX (1818–83), German founder of communism

Production goes up and up because high pressure advertising and salesmanship constantly create new needs that must be satisfied: this is Admass – a consumer's race with donkeys chasing an electric carrot.

J(OHN) B(OYNTON) PRIESTLEY (1894–1984), English author: *Thoughts in the Wilderness*

It is production which opens a demand for production … a product is no sooner created, than it, from that instant, affords a market for other products to the full extent of its own value … the only way of getting rid of money is in the purchase of some product or other.

JEAN-BAPTISTE SAY (1767–1832), French economist: *A Treatise on Political Economy, volume I*

Had we gone the way of France and got 60 per cent of our electricity from nuclear power, we should not have environmental problems.

MARGARET (HILDA) THATCHER (1925–), English politician and prime minister

Industry does nothing but produce scarce things.

(MARIE-ESPRIT) LEON WALRAS (1834–1910), French economist and reformer: *Elements of Pure Economics, Part 1*

Progress

Change does not necessarily assure progress, but progress implacably requires change.

ANON

In the youth of a state arms do flourish; in the middle age of a state, learning; and then both of them together for a time; in the declining age of a state, mechanical arts and merchandise.

FRANCIS BACON, 1st Baron Verulam, Viscount St Albans (1561–1626), English writer, philosopher and statesman: *Essays, 'Of Vicissitude of Things'*

All progress is based upon a universal innate desire of every organism to live beyond its income.

SAMUEL BUTLER (1835–1902), English author, painter and musician: *Notebooks*

All conservatism is based upon the idea that if you leave things alone you leave them as they are. But you do not. If you leave a thing alone you leave it to a torrent of change.

G(ILBERT) K(EITH) CHESTERTON (1874–1936), English essayist, novelist, poet and critic: *Orthodoxy, chapter 7*

As enunciated today, 'progress' is simply a comparative of which we have not settled the superlative.

G(ILBERT) K(EITH) CHESTERTON: *Heretics, chapter 2*

Economic advance is not the same thing as human progress.

SIR JOHN CLAPHAM (1873–1946), British economic historian: *A Concise Economic History of Britain*

Change comes about because of two factors broadly, I think. One is the interaction of other nations on us, who are exploiting our lack of competitiveness … And then you've got people like me who bring about change with a view to trying to recoup the situation and to make us more competitive; and it is thought that the only way you do that is now by rushing out and employing a lot of people. You do it, in fact, by scaling down organizations to be lean, hungry and competitive, and to take on the Japanese and the Americans and the Germans.

SIR MICHAEL EDWARDES (1930–), British industrialist: quoted in Cary L. Cooper and Peter Hingley, *The Change Makers*

The strongest principle of growth lies in human choice.

GEORGE ELIOT (Mary Ann Evans) (1819–90), English novelist: *Daniel Deronda, book 6*

There is always a certain meanness in the argument of conservatism, joined with a certain superiority in its fact.

RALPH WALDO EMERSON (1803–82), American poet, essayist and philosopher: *The Conservative*

All is change; all yields its place and goes.

EURIPIDES (?480–406 BC), Greek tragic dramatist: *Heracles*

So the grand oaks grow that once were acorns; so the grand deeds, too, that once were only dreams.

MARIANNE FARNINGHAM (1834–1909), English hymn-writer

The modern conservative is engaged in one of man's oldest exercises in moral philosophy, that is the search for a superior moral justification for selfishness.

JOHN KENNETH GALBRAITH (1908–2006), Canadian-born American economist, diplomat and writer

All that is human must retrograde if it do not advance.

EDWARD GIBBON (1737–94), English historian: *Decline and Fall of the Roman Empire*

There is no way to make people like change. You can only make them feel less threatened by it.

FREDERICK HAYES, American bureaucrat: *Fortune, 1969*

Progress comes from the intelligent use of experience.

ELBERT (GREEN) HUBBARD (1856–1915), American businessman, writer and printer

The reason men oppose progress is not that they hate progress, but that they love inertia.

ELBERT (GREEN) HUBBARD: *The Note Book*

Progress is the life-style of man. The general life of the human race is called Progress, and so is its collective march. Progress advances, it makes the great human and earthly journey towards what is heavenly and divine.
VICTOR HUGO (1802–85), French writer

Is it progress if a cannibal uses knife and fork?
STANISLAW (JERZY) LEC (1909–66), Polish poet and aphorist

What is conservatism? Is it not adherence to the old and tried, against the new and untried?
ABRAHAM LINCOLN (1809–65), American statesman and president: *Speech, New York, 27 February 1860*

If we have had a formula for growth it has been: start with the best; learn from the best, expand slowly and solidify our position; then horizontally diversify our expertise.
MARK H. MCCORMACK (1930–), Founder, International Management Group: *What They Don't Teach You at Harvard Business School*

Progress – progress is the dirtiest word in the language – who ever told us – And made us believe it – that to take a step forward was necessarily, was always a good idea?
EDNA ST VINCENT MILLAY (1892–1950), American poet: *Make Bright the Arrows*

[On launch of Sky TV] It's not until we get people being equally entrepreneurial and really driving at it that Britain is going to get going again.
RUPERT MURDOCH (1931–), Australian-born media executive

No progress is going back.
PROVERB

If you are planning for one year plant rice. If you are planning for ten years plant trees. If you are planning for 100 years plant people.
INDIAN PROVERB

Small is Beautiful: Economics as if People Mattered.
ERNST FRIEDRICH SCHUMACHER (1911–77), German-born economist and conservationist: *Title of book*

Economic progress, in capitalist society, means turmoil.
JOSEPH ALOIS SCHUMPETER (1883–1950), Austrian-born American economist: *Capitalism, Socialism and Democracy*

All progress means war with Society.
GEORGE BERNARD SHAW (1856–1950), Irish dramatist and critic: *Getting Married*

The reasonable man adapts himself to the world: the unreasonable one persists in trying to adapt the world to himself. Therefore all progress depends on the unreasonable man.
GEORGE BERNARD SHAW: *Man and Superman, Maxims for Revolutionists*

Economic growth is not only unnecessary, but ruinous.
ALEXANDER ISAYEVICH SOLZHENITSYN (1918–), Russian novelist

Things do not change; we change.
HENRY DAVID THOREAU (1817–62), American essayist and poet: *Walden, 'Economy'*

Progress was all right. Only it went on too long.
JAMES (GROVER) THURBER (1894–1961), American humorist and cartoonist (Attributed)

I like thinking big. I always have. To me, it's very simple; if you're going to be thinking anyway, you might as well think big.
DONALD TRUMP (1946–), American entrepreneur: *The Art of the Deal*

Civilisation advances by extending the number of important operations which we can perform without thinking about them.

ALFRED NORTH WHITEHEAD (1861–1947), English mathematician and philosopher

Conservatism is the policy of 'make no change and consult your grandmother when in doubt'.

(THOMAS) WOODROW WILSON (1856–1924), American statesman and president

Public Speaking

Since I am used to speaking in public, I know that it is useless.

FRANKLIN PIERCE ADAMS (1881–1960), American journalist and humorist

An after-dinner speech should be like a lady's dress: long enough to cover the subject and short enough to be interesting.

ANON

KISS: Keep it short, stupid.

ANON

I do not object to people looking at their watches when I am speaking – but I strongly object when they start shaking them to make certain they are still going.

LORD BIRKETT: quoted in A. Andrews, *Quotations for Speakers and Writers*

Blessed is the man who, having nothing to say, abstains from giving in words evidence of the fact.

GEORGE ELIOT (Mary Ann Evans) (1819–80), English novelist: *Impressions of Theophrastus Such*: quoted in *A Collection of Quotable Quotes*

First learn the meaning of what you say, and then speak.

EPICTETUS (?AD 50–?120), Greek philosopher: *Discourses*

I guess I should warn you, if I turn out to be particularly clear, you've probably misunderstood what I said.

ALAN GREENSPAN (1926–), American businessman: *Financial Times*, *'Business Quotes of the Year'*, 24 December 1988

There may be other reasons for a man's not speaking in publick than want of resolution: he may have nothing to say.

SAMUEL JOHNSON (1709–84), English lexicographer, essayist and poet: quoted in James Boswell, *The Life of Samuel Johnson*

English is the perfect language for preachers because it allows you to talk until you think of what to say.

GARRISON KEILLOR (1942–), American author and humorist

Public speaking is the art of diluting a two-minute idea with a two-hour vocabulary.

JOHN FITZGERALD KENNEDY (1917–63), American president

Beware of the conversationalist who adds 'In other words'. He is merely starting afresh.

ROBERT MORLEY (1908–92), British actor and wit: *Observer, 1964*

According to most studies, people's number one fear is public speaking. Number two is death. Death is number two. Does that sound right? This means to the average person, if you go to a funeral, you're better off in the casket than doing the eulogy.

JERRY SEINFELD (1954–), American comic actor

Polonius:
Brevity is the soul of wit.

WILLIAM SHAKESPEARE (1564–1616), English dramatist and poet: *Hamlet, Act 2*

Men of few words are the best men.

WILLIAM SHAKESPEARE, *King Henry the Fifth, Act 3*

I am the most spontaneous speaker in the world because every word, every gesture and every retort has been carefully rehearsed.
GEORGE BERNARD SHAW (1856–1950), Irish dramatist and critic

It is terrible to speak well and be wrong.
SOPHOCLES (?496–406 BC), Greek dramatist: *Electra*

It usually takes me more than three weeks to prepare a good impromptu speech.
MARK TWAIN (Samuel Langhorne Clemens) (1835–1910), American novelist and humorist

Sport & Business

Money plays an important role in football but it is not the dominating factor.
ROMAN ABRAMOVICH (1966–), Russian-born oil billionaire and football club owner

In an increasingly dynamic sports and entertainment marketplace, new technology and entertainment vehicles have impacted the way sports leagues function and how we deliver the NHL experience to our business partners and fans.
GARY BETTMAN (1952–), American lawyer

I still love the sport of boxing but I don't care for the business part of it.
CHRIS BYRD (1970–), American boxer

[On David Beckham] He has transcended the classic footballing context. He is an integral part of show business.
MARCEL DESAILLY (1968–), Ghanaian-born French footballer

[On improvements to Silverstone] What have they done?

Nothing. They've spent £14m on a car park.
SIR BERNIE ECCLESTONE (1930–), British Formula One manager

When you look at other sports, like golf, the players earn a lot more money without running around. I wish I had that little cart to take me to the corner kicks.
THIERRY HENRY (1977–), French-born footballer

[To Rio Ferdinand] Just because you are paid £120,000 a week and play well for 20 minutes against Tottenham, you think you are a superstar.
ROY KEANE (1971–), Irish footballer and manager

Fifty years on from now, Britain will still be the country of long shadows on cricket grounds, warm beer, invincible green suburbs, dog lovers and pools fillers.
JOHN MAJOR (1943–), British prime minister

[On Roman Abramovich, owner of Chelsea FC] He's going to try to make it to as many games as he can, which is easy when you have your own plane.
JOHN MANN, Roman Abramovich's media relations officer

Business is a combination of war and sport.
ANDRÉ MAUROIS (1885–1967), French author

[On footballers] In the real world they would be hard pushed to get a job that paid them £20,000 a year, never mind a week.
SIR BOBBY ROBSON (1933–), English football manager

The money coming into the game [football] is incredible. But it is just the prune-juice effect – it comes in and goes out straight away. Agents run the game.
SIR ALAN SUGAR (1947–), British entrepreneur

Technology

Any sufficiently advanced technology is indistinguishable from magic.

ARTHUR C. CLARKE (1917–), British science-fiction author: *Profiles of the Future*

Technology frightens me to death. It's designed by engineers to impress other engineers, and they always come with instruction books that are written by engineers for other engineers – which is why almost no technology ever works.

JOHN CLEESE (1939–), English comedian and actor: quoted in *Wrinklies' Wit & Wisdom Forever*

It is appallingly obvious our technology has exceeded our humanity.

ALBERT EINSTEIN (1879–1955), German-Swiss-American physicist

Technology … the knack of so arranging the world that we don't have to experience it.

MAX FRISCH (1911–91), Swiss dramatist and novelist: *Homo Faber*

Humanity is acquiring all the right technology for all the wrong reasons.

R(ICHARD) BUCKMINSTER FULLER (1895–1983), American author and inventor: quoted in *Quotations with an Attitude*

The most important and urgent problems of the technology of today are no longer the satisfactions of primary needs or of archetypal wishes, but the reparation of the evils and damages by technology of yesterday.

DENNIS GABOR (1900–79), Hungarian physicist and inventor

If GM [General Motors] had kept up with technology like the computer industry has, we would all be driving $25 cars that got 1000 MPG.

BILL GATES (1955–), American businessman and philanthropist

For tribal man space was the uncontrollable mystery. For technological man it is time that occupies the same role.

(HERBERT) MARSHALL MCLUHAN (1911–80), Canadian educator, author and media expert: *The Mechanical Bride, 'Magic that Changes Mood'*

I've thrown three mobile phones into the Thames in the past because I couldn't work them. I've never been on the internet in my life. My wife Barbara gave me a computer but I haven't a clue how to work it.

RICHARD (RIK) MAYALL (1958–), English comedian and actor: quoted in *Wrinklies' Wit & Wisdom Forever*

Anyone who has spent time sitting in front of a computer screen, as we are doing, must frequently have thought that the new technology is a drag on productivity.

HERBERT STEIN (1916–99), American economist

Technology feeds on itself. Technology makes more technology possible

ALVIN TOFFLER (1928–), American writer: *Future Shock*

Thought

Analysis kills spontaneity. The grain once ground into flour springs and germinates no more.

HENRI FREDERIC AMIEL (1821–81), Swiss philosopher and poet: *Journal, 7 November 1878*

A conclusion is simply the place where someone got tired of thinking.

ANON

Logic:
The art of thinking and reasoning in strict accordance with the limitations and incapacities of the human misunderstanding.

AMBROSE (GWINETT) BIERCE (1842–?1914), American journalist and humorist: *The Devil's Dictionary*

Reflection:
An action of the mind whereby we obtain a clearer view of our relation to the things of yesterday and are able to avoid the perils that we shall not again encounter.

AMBROSE (GWINETT) BIERCE, as above

If a man sits down to think, he is immediately asked if he has the headache.

RALPH WALDO EMERSON (1803–82), American poet, essayist and philosopher: *Journals*

What is the hardest task in the world? To think.

RALPH WALDO EMERSON: *Intellect*

Second thoughts are ever wiser.

EURIPIDES (?480–406 BC), Greek tragic dramatist: *Hippolytus*

Thinking is more interesting than knowing, but less interesting than looking.

JOHANN WOLFGANG VON GOETHE (1749–1832), German poet, scientist and writer

When half the people believe one thing, and the other half

another, it is usually safe to accept either opinion.

EDGAR WATSON HOWE (1853–1937), American journalist, novelist and essayist: *Ventures in Common Sense*

Most of one's life … is one prolonged effort to prevent oneself thinking.

ALDOUS (LEONARD) HUXLEY (1894–1963), English novelist and essayist: *Mortal Coils*, 'Green Tunnels'

Thinking is one thing no one has ever been able to tax.

CHARLES FRANKLIN KETTERING (1876–1958), American inventor and philosopher

As the development of the mind proceeds, symbols, instead of being employed to convey images, are substituted for them. Civilized men think as they trade, not in kind but by means of a circulating medium.

THOMAS BABINGTON MACAULAY (1800–59), English historian, essayist and statesman: *Edinburgh Review, January 1828*, 'John Dryden'

Profundity of thought belongs to youth, clarity of thought to old age.

FRIEDRICH WILHELM NIETZSCHE (1844–1900), German philosopher, poet and critic: *Miscellaneous Maxims and Opinions*

We do not live to think, but, on the contrary, we think in order that we may succeed in surviving.

JOSÉ ORTEGA Y GASSET (1883–1955), Spanish philosopher and statesman: *Partisan Review, December 1949*

There are two distinct classes of what are called thoughts: those that we produce in ourselves by reflection and the act of thinking, and those that bolt into the mind of their own accord.

THOMAS PAINE (1737–1809), English philosopher and writer: *The Age of Reason*

After you've done a thing the same way for two years look it over carefully. After five years look at it with suspicion and after ten years throw it away and start all over again.

ALFRED EDWARD PERLMAN (1902–83), American railway executive: *The New York Times, 1958*

While we stop to think, we often miss our opportunity.

PUBLILIUS SYRUS (1st c. BC), Latin writer of mimes: *Sententiae*

The real problem is not whether machines think but whether men do.

B(URRHUS) F(REDERIC) SKINNER (1904–90), American behaviourist: *Contingencies of Reinforcement*

Thoughts may be bandits. Thoughts may be raiders. Thoughts may be invaders. Thoughts may be disturbers of the international peace.

(THOMAS) WOODROW WILSON (1856–1924), American statesman and president: *Speech, 16 May 1916*

Travel

Telegram of employee during traffic crisis:
Regret cannot come today; have not yet got home yesterday.

ANON

Travel teaches toleration.

BENJAMIN DISRAELI, 1st Earl of Beaconsfield (1804–81), English statesman, prime minister and novelist: *Contarini Fleming*

No man should travel until he has learned the language of the country he visits. Otherwise he voluntarily makes himself a great baby – so helpless and so ridiculous.

RALPH WALDO EMERSON (1803–82), American poet, essayist and philosopher: *Journals, 1833*

Of railway termini:
They are our gates to the glorious and the unknown. Through them we pass out into adventure and sunshine, and to them, alas! we return.

E(DWARD) M(ORGAN) FORSTER (1879–1970), English novelist: *Howard's End, chapter 2*

Travel is atavistic, the day will come when there will be no more traffic at all and only newlyweds will travel.

MAX FRISCH (1911–91), Swiss dramatist and novelist: quoted in D. J. Boorstin, *The Image*

A gentleman ought to travel abroad but dwell at home.

THOMAS FULLER (1654–1734), English physician, writer and compiler: *Gnomologia*

He that travels much knows much.

THOMAS FULLER, as above

One of the pleasantest things in the world is going a journey; but I like to go by myself.

WILLIAM HAZLITT (1778–1830), English essayist: *On Going a Journey*

Flying? I've been to almost as many places as my luggage!

BOB HOPE (1903–2003), English-born American comedian and comic actor

Travelling makes men wiser, but less happy. When men of sober age travel, they gather knowledge which they may apply usefully for their country; but they are subject ever after to recollections mixed with regret; their affections are weakened by being extended over more objects; and they learn new habits which cannot be gratified when they return home.

THOMAS JEFFERSON (1743–1826), American statesman and president: *Letter to Peter Carr*

In the space age, man will be able to go around the world in two hours – one hour for flying and the other to get to the airport.

NEIL H. MCELROY (1904–72), American business executive and public official: *Look, 18 February 1958*

The car has become the carapace, the protective and aggressive shell, of urban and suburban man.

(HERBERT) MARSHALL MCLUHAN (1911–80), Canadian educator, author and media expert: *Understanding Media*

A pleasant companion reduces the length of the journey.

PUBLILIUS SYRUS (1st c. BC), Latin writer of mimes: *Senteniae*

He who would travel happily must travel light.

ANTOINE DE SAINT-EXUPÉRY (1900–44), French novelist and aviator

The more I see of other countries the more I love my own.

MADAME DE STAEL, Baronne Anne Louise Germaine de Stael-Holstein (1766–1817), Swiss-born French writer: *Corinne*

For my part, I travel not to go anywhere, but to go. I travel for travel's sake. The great affair is to move.

ROBERT LOUIS BALFOUR STEVENSON (1850–94), Scottish writer: *Travels with a Donkey*

To travel hopefully is a better thing than to arrive, and the true success is to labour.

ROBERT LOUIS BALFOUR STEVENSON: *Virginibus puerisque, 'El Dorado'*

You and I come by road or rail, but economists travel on infrastructure.

MARGARET (HILDA) THATCHER (1925–), English politician and prime minister

Everything in life is somewhere else, and you get there in a car.
E(LWYN) B(ROOKS) WHITE (1899–1985), American humorist and essayist: *One Man's Meat*

I never travel without my diary. One should always have something sensational to read in the train.
OSCAR WILDE (1856–1900), Irish poet, dramatist and wit

Work

We continue to overlook the fact that work has become a leisure activity.
MARK ABRAMS: *Observer, 'Sayings of the Week', 3 June 1962*

Work was like cats were supposed to be: if you disliked and feared it and tried to keep out of its way, it knew at once and sought you out.
KINGSLEY AMIS (1922–95), English novelist and poet: *Take a Girl Like You*

Even the best plan degenerates into work.
ANON

The difficult we do immediately. The impossible takes a little longer.
ANON

The first 90% of the project takes the first 90% of the time. The last 10% of the project takes the last 90% of the time.
ANON

Work is the price you pay for money.
ANON

How can I take an interest in my work when I don't like it?
FRANCIS BACON (1909–92), Irish artist

He had insomnia so bad that he couldn't sleep when he was working.

ARTHUR BAER (1885–1969): quoted in Robert W. Kent, *Money Talks*

It is necessary to work, if not from inclination, at least from despair. Everything considered, work is less boring than amusing oneself.

CHARLES PIERRE BAUDELAIRE (1821–67), French poet: *Mon coeur mis à nu*

Anyone can do any amount of work, provided it isn't the work he is supposed to be doing at that moment.

ROBERT BENCHLEY (1889–1945), American humorist

Sooner or later in life everything turns into work, including work.

ALAN BENNETT (1934–), English actor and writer

Overwork:
A dangerous disorder affecting high public functionaries who want to go fishing.

AMBROSE (GWINETT) BIERCE (1842–?1914), American journalist and humorist: *The Devil's Dictionary*

What is the use of health, or of life, if not to do some work therewith?

THOMAS CARLYLE (1795–1881), Scottish essayist and historian: *Sartor Resartus*

Work is much more fun than fun.

SIR NOËL (PIERCE) COWARD (1899–1973), English actor and dramatist: *Observer*, 'Sayings of the Week', 21 June 1963

[On House of Commons reform] I'm sick and tired of strong women pretending that they can't cope with a 'masculine' working environment. If they can't deal with it, then they should go back home and do some knitting.

GWYNETH DUNWOODY (1930–), British politician

Genius is one percent inspiration and ninety-nine percent perspiration.

THOMAS ALVA EDISON (1847–1931), American inventor: *Life*

The idea that to make a man work you've got to hold gold in front of his eyes is a growth, not an axiom. We've done that for so long that we've forgotten there's any other way.

FRANCIS SCOTT (KEY) FITZGERALD (1896–1940), American novelist: *This Side of Paradise, book 2*

Diligence is the mother of good luck, and God gives all things to industry. Then plough deep while sluggards sleep, and you shall have corn to sell and to keep.

BENJAMIN FRANKLIN (1706–90), American statesman, scientist and author: *Poor Richard's Almanac*

One of the best ways of avoiding necessary and even urgent tasks is to seem to be busily employed on things that are already done.

JOHN KENNETH GALBRAITH (1908–2006), Canadian-born American economist, diplomat and writer: *The Affluent Society*

Perseverance is the hard work you do after you get tired of doing the hard work you already did.

NEWT GINGRICH (1943–), American politician

I like work; it fascinates me. I can sit and look at it for hours. I love to keep it by me: the idea of getting rid of it nearly breaks my heart.

JEROME K(LAPKA) JEROME (1859–1927), English humorous writer: *Three Men in a Boat, chapter 15*

It is impossible to enjoy idling thoroughly unless one has plenty of work to do.
JEROME K(LAPKA) JEROME: *Idle Thoughts of an Idle Fellow*

It's all in the day's work, as the huntsman said when the lion ate him.
CHARLES KINGSLEY (1819–75), English clergyman, novelist and poet

Too much work and too much energy kill a man just as effectively as too much assorted vice or too much drink.
(JOSEPH) RUDYARD KIPLING (1865–1936), English novelist, poet and short story writer: *Plain Tales from the Hills, 'Thrown Away'*

My father taught me to work; he did not teach me to love it.
ABRAHAM LINCOLN (1809–65), American statesman and president

Work … does not exist in a non-literate world … Where the whole man is involved there is no work. Work begins with the division of labour.
(HERBERT) MARSHALL MCLUHAN (1911–80), Canadian educator, author and media expert: *Understanding Media*

It seems to me that a great deal of nonsense is talked about the dignity of work. Work is a drug that dull people take to avoid the pangs of unmitigated boredom.
W(ILLIAM) SOMERSET MAUGHAM (1874–1965), English writer: *The Explorer, chapter 3*

The really exhausting and the really repulsive labours, instead of being better paid than others, are almost invariably paid the worst of all … The hardships and the earnings, instead of being directly proportional, as in any just arrangements of society they would be, are generally in an inverse ratio to one another.
JOHN STUART MILL (1806–73), English philosopher and economist: *Principles of Political Economy, book 2*

Work seven days a week and nothing can stop you.
SIR JOHN MOORES (1896–1993), British businessman

Work expands so as to fill the time available for its completion.
C(YRIL) NORTHCOTE PARKINSON (1909–93), English historian and
journalist: *Parkinson's Law*

Work is accomplished by those employees who have not yet
reached their level of incompetence.
DR LAURENCE J. PETER (1919–90), Canadian educator and RAYMOND
HULL (1919–): *The Peter Principle, chapter I*

Elbow-grease is the best polish.
PROVERB

Nothing is got without pain but dirt and long nails.
PROVERB

The test of a vocation is the love of the drudgery it involves.
LOGAN PEARSALL SMITH (1865–1946), American-born Englishman of
letters: *Afterthoughts*

Nothing so difficult but it may be won by industry.
TERENCE (Publius Terentius Afer) (?190–159 BC) Roman comic dramatist:
Heauton Timoroumenos

Of work:
It is about a search, too, for daily meaning as well as daily bread,
for recognition as well as cash, for astonishment rather than
torpor; in short, for a sort of life rather than a Monday through
Friday sort of dying.
STUDS TERKEL (1912–): *Working*

The buck stops here.

HARRY S. TRUMAN (1884–1972), American statesman and president: *Notice on the presidential desk*

Work spares us from three great evils: boredom, vice and need.

VOLTAIRE (François Marie Arouet) (1694–1778), French writer, philosopher and historian: *Candide*

When a man says he wants to work, what he means is that he wants wages.

BISHOP RICHARD WHATELY (1787–1863), English Archbishop of Dublin

Work is the refuge of people who have nothing better to do.

OSCAR WILDE (1856–1900), Irish poet, dramatist and wit

Work is the curse of the drinking classes.

OSCAR WILDE

Finance & Institutions

Finance is vital to the functioning of business. Opinions vary, however, on the morality of borrowing and profit-making, as the quotations in this section show. The quotations here also reveal a range of attitudes on the role of institutions such as banks, the law and government, from the humorous 'A bank is a place that will lend you money if you can prove that you don't need it' (Bob Hope), through the descriptive 'Owning capital is not a productive activity' (Joan Robinson), to the sobering 'Be content with your wages' (The Bible). 'Profits, like sausages ... are esteemed most by those who know least about what goes into them' (Alvin Toffler).

Banking

A banker is a man who lends you an umbrella when the weather is fair, and takes it away from you when it rains.
ANON

O Gold! I still prefer thee unto paper
Which makes bank credit like a bank of vapour.
LORD BYRON, George Gordon Byron, 6th Baron Byron of Rochdale (1788–1824), English poet: *Don Juan*

Political Ravishment, or, The Old Lady of Threadneedle Street.
JAMES GILRAY (1757–1815), British caricaturist: *Title of cartoon*

Put not your trust in money, but put your money in trust.
OLIVER WENDELL HOLMES, SR (1809–94), American physician, professor and author: *The Autocrat of the Breakfast Table*

A bank is a place that will lend you money if you can prove that you don't need it.

BOB HOPE (1903–2003), English-born American comedian and comic actor: quoted in Alan Harrington, *Life in the Crystal Palace*

Banking establishments are more dangerous than standing armies.

THOMAS JEFFERSON (1743–1826), American statesman and president: *Letter to Elbridge Gerry, 26 January 1799*

It is better that a man should tyrannize over his bank balance than over his fellow citizens.

JOHN MAYNARD KEYNES, 1st Baron (1883–1946), English economist: *General Theory of Employment*

Bankers Are Just Like Anybody Else, Except Richer.

OGDEN NASH (1902–71), American humorous poet: *I'm a Stranger Here Myself*

A banker is a person who is willing to make a loan if you present sufficient evidence to show you don't need it.

HERBERT V. PROCHNOW (1897–1998): quoted in Robert W. Kent, *Money Talks*

There have been three great inventions since the beginning of time: fire, the wheel, and central banking.

WILL(IAM PENN ADAIR) ROGERS (1879–1935), American actor and humorist: quoted in P. A. Samuelson, *Economics*

It is not by augmenting the capital of the country, but by rendering a greater part of that capital active and productive than would otherwise be so, that the most judicious operations of banking can increase the industry of the country.

ADAM SMITH (1723–90), Scottish economist and philosopher

Bonuses

Golden Handcuffs: The Lowly Life of a High Flyer.
POLLY COURTNEY, English author: *Book title*

Golden handshake:
What many executives receive despite poor performance.
Guardian Unlimited, 12 April 2007

I gotta tell ya, with our $2.4 billion in profits last year, they gave me a great big bonus. Really, it's almost obscene.
LEE IACOCCA (1924–), American industrialist

A top state school found it so difficult to recruit a new headteacher it was forced to offer a reported £40,000 'golden hello' to attract the right candidate.
TIM ROSS, journalist: *Independent, 24 March 2007*

The big winners … are first and foremost the 'fat-cat' company bosses who have managed to grab a bigger slice than almost anyone else of the economy's growing wealth, even though their companies' profits have only grown in line with the overall economy.
ASHLEY SEAGER, journalist: *Guardian, 22 April 2006*

Bureaucracy

Join in the new game that's sweeping the country. It's called 'Bureaucracy'. Everybody stands in a circle. The first person to do anything loses.
ANON

The perfect bureaucrat everywhere is the man who manages to

make no decisions and escape all responsibility.

(JUSTIN) BROOKS ATKINSON (1894–1984), American dramatic critic and essayist: *Once Around the Sun*

I think we have more machinery of government than is necessary, too many parasites living on the labor of the industrious.

THOMAS JEFFERSON (1743–1826), American statesman and president: *Letter to William Ludlow*

If the first person who answers the phone cannot answer your question it's a bureaucracy. If the first person can answer your question, it's a miracle.

GERALD F. LIEBERMAN (1923–86), American writer

The only governments, not representative, in which high political skill and ability have been other than exceptional, whether under monarchial or aristocratic forms, have been essentially bureaucracies. The work of government has been in the hands of governors by profession; which is the essence and meaning of bureaucracy.

JOHN STUART MILL (1806–73), English philosopher and economist: *Representative Government*

It's all papers and forms, the entire Civil Service is like a fortress made of papers, forms and red tape.

ALEXANDER NIKOLAYEVICH OSTROVSKY (1823–86), Russian playwright: *The Diary of a Scoundrel*

Bureaucracy defends the status quo long past the time when the quo has lost its status.

DR LAURENCE J. PETER (1919–90), Canadian educator

Bureaucracy is not an obstacle to democracy but an inevitable complement to it.

JOSEPH ALOIS SCHUMPETER (1883–1950), Austrian-born American economist: *Capitalism, Socialism and Democracy, chapter 18*

You will never understand bureaucracies until you understand that for bureaucrats procedure is everything and outcomes are nothing.

THOMAS SOWELL (1930–), American economist and writer

Capital

Just as a cautious businessman avoids investing all his capital in one concern, so wisdom would probably admonish us also not to anticipate all our happiness from one quarter alone.

SIGMUND FREUD (1856–1939), Austrian neurologist and psychiatrist

The great dialectic in our time is not, as anciently and by some still supposed, between capital and labor; it is between economic enterprise and the state.

JOHN KENNETH GALBRAITH (1908–2006), Canadian-born American economist, diplomat and writer

Capital is a result of labor, and is used by labor to assist it in further production. Labor is the active and initial force, and labor is therefore the employer of capital.

HENRY GEORGE (1839–97), American economist: *Progress and Poverty, book 3*

Each needs the other: capital cannot do without labour, nor labour without capital.

POPE LEO XIII (Gioacchino Pecci) (1810–1903): *Rerum novarum, 15 May 1891*

Labor is prior to, and independent of, capital. Capital is only the fruit of labor, and could never have existed if labor had not first existed. Labor is the superior of capital, and deserves much the higher consideration.

ABRAHAM LINCOLN (1809–65), American statesman and president: *Message to Congress, 3 December 1861*

Capital consists in a great part of knowledge and organisation: and of this some part is private property and other part is not.

ALFRED MARSHALL (1842–1924), English classical economist: *Principles of Economics, book 4*

Capital is dead labour that, vampire-like, lives only by sucking living labour, and lives the more, the more labour it sucks.

KARL MARX (1818–83), German founder of modern communism: *Capital*

In bourgeois society capital is independent and has individuality, while the living person is dependent and has no individuality.

KARL MARX and FRIEDRICH ENGELS (1820–95), German socialist leader: *The Communist Manifesto*

Industry is limited by capital.

JOHN STUART MILL (1806–73), English philosopher and economist: *Principles of Political Economy, book 1*

Capital is that part of the wealth of a country which is employed in production, and consists of food, clothing, tools, raw materials, machinery, etc., necessary to give effect to labour.

DAVID RICARDO (1772–1823), English economist: *Principles of Political Economy*

Owning capital is not a productive activity.

JOAN VIOLET ROBINSON (1903–83), English economist: *An Essay on Marxian Economics, chapter 3*

Parsimony, and not industry, is the immediate cause of the increase of capital. Industry, indeed, provides the subject which parsimony accumulates. But whatever industry might acquire, if parsimony did not save and store up, the capital would never be the greater.

ADAM SMITH (1723–90), Scottish economist and philosopher: *The Wealth of Nations*

Credit & Borrowing

Borrow money from a pessimist – they don't expect it back.

ANON

In God we trust. All others pay cash.

ANON

In our modern economy it seems unlikely that the middle-class morality about money will be able to survive. I, for example, was brought up never to buy anything until I had the cash to pay for it. If everyone did the same, i.e. bought nothing on credit, our economy would go smash.

W(YSTAN) H(UGH) AUDEN (1907–73), English poet, dramatist, critic and librettist: *A Certain World*

I don't borrow on credit cards because it is too expensive.

MATT BARRETT, Barclays Bank chief executive

The borrower is servant to the lender.

The Bible, Authorised (King James) Version, Proverbs 22:7

Live within your income, even if you have to borrow money to do so.

JOSH BILLINGS (Henry Wheeler Shaw) (1818–85)

Credit buying is much like being drunk. The buzz happens immediately, and it gives you a lift. The hangover comes the day after.

JOYCE BROTHERS (1928–), American psychologist and advice columnist

Neither borrow money of a friend; but of a mere stranger; where, paying for it, thou shalt hear of it no more: otherwise thou shalt eclipse thy credit, lose thy friend, and yet pay as dear as to another.

WILLIAM CECIL, 1st Baron Burghley (1520–98), English statesman: *Advice to his son*

Lend money to an enemy, and thou shalt gain him; to a friend, and thou shalt lose him.

BENJAMIN FRANKLIN (1706–90), American statesman, scientist and author: *Poor Richard's Almanac*

Better give a shilling than lend and lose half a crown.

THOMAS FULLER (1654–1734), English physician, writer and compiler: *Gnomologia*

Borrowed garments never fit well.

THOMAS FULLER, as above

Would you know what money is, go borrow some.

GEORGE HERBERT (1593–1633), English metaphysical poet: *Outlandish Proverbs*

The human species, according to the best theory I can form of it, is composed of two distinct races, the men who borrow, and the men who lend.

CHARLES (ELIA) LAMB (1775–1834), English essayist: *Essays of Elia, The Two Races of Men*

A pig bought on credit is forever grunting.

PROVERB

He that lends, gives.

PROVERB

A borrowed cloak does not keep one warm.

ARABIC PROVERB

A small loan makes a debtor; a great one, an enemy.
PUBLILIUS SYRUS (1st c. BC), Latin writer of mimes: *Moral Sayings*

First payments is what made us think we were prosperous, and the other nineteen is what showed us we were broke.
WILL(IAM PENN ADAIR) ROGERS (1879–1935), American actor and humorist: *The Autobiography of Will Rogers*

Words are weapons, and it is dangerous in speculation, as in politics, to borrow them from the arsenal of the enemy.
GEORGE SANTAYANA (1863–1952), American philosopher and poet

Polonius:
Neither a borrower nor a lender be;
For loan oft loses both itself and friend.
And borrowing dulls the edge of husbandry.
WILLIAM SHAKESPEARE (1564–1616), English dramatist and poet: *Hamlet, Act I*

Words pay no debts.
WILLIAM SHAKESPEARE: *Troilus and Cressida, Act 3*

Let us all be happy and live within our means, even if we have to borrow the money to do it with.
ARTEMUS WARD (Charles Farrar Browne) (1834–67), American humorist, editor and lecturer

Currency & Devaluation

The crown has the sole right to issue money.
Decision of the English Privy Council 1603

There is no subtler, no surer means of overturning the existing basis of society than to debauch the currency. The process engages all the hidden forces of economic law on the side of destruction, and does it in a manner which not one man in a million is able to diagnose.

JOHN MAYNARD KEYNES, 1st Baron (1883–1946), English economist: *The Economic Consequences of the Peace*

Currency trading is unnecessary, unproductive and totally immoral. It should be stopped.

MAHATHIR BIN MOHAMAD (1925–), Malaysian politician and prime minister

A currency, to be perfect, should be absolutely invariable in value.

DAVID RICARDO (1772–1823), English economist: *Works, volume 4*

Finance is the art of passing currency from hand to hand until it finally disappears.

ROBERT W. SARNOFF (1918–), American media executive

Devaluation, whether of sterling, or the dollar, or both, would be a lunatic, self-destroying operation.

SIR (JAMES) HAROLD WILSON, Lord Wilson of Rievaulx (1916–95), English statesman and prime minister: *Speech, 1963*

From now, the pound is worth 14 per cent or so less in terms of other currencies. It does not mean, of course, that the pound here in Britain, in your pocket or purse or in your bank, has been devalued.

SIR (JAMES) HAROLD WILSON: *Speech after devaluation of the pound, 20 November 1967*

European Union

Well, the simple answer to that is that the EU only has

competence where the EU has competence. If it's a law or a constitution provision that is just for the nation that doesn't change.

BERTIE AHERN (1951–), Irish politician

If there is one thing Britain should learn from the last 50 years, it is this: Europe can only get more important for us.

TONY (ANTHONY CHARLES LYNTON) BLAIR (1953–), British prime minister

We had a discussion of what we at this historic time could as European Union finance ministers do to improve that process in peace and development.

GORDON BROWN (1951–), British prime minister

Brussels is a madness. I will fight it from within.

SIR JAMES GOLDSMITH (1933–97), British businessman and politician

The problem with the EU is that at times its very nature exacerbates internal tensions. That is why the euro may eventually break up.

NORMAN LAMONT, Baron Lamont of Lerwick (1942–), British politician and former Chancellor of the Exchequer: *Financial Times, 22 June 2005*

I do not share the half-in, half-out attitude to the EU of some in Britain. Britain's place is in Europe.

PETER MANDELSON (1953–), British politician

Of course, the EU is not going to fall apart, but at best it will stagnate for the foreseeable future and we will be dealing with quite a lot of internal chaos.

PETER MANDELSON

Finance & the Economy

Rags make Paper
Paper makes Money
Money makes Banks
Banks make Loans
Loans make Beggars
Beggars make Rags

ANON

Finance:
The art or science of managing revenues and resources for the best advantage of the manager.

AMBROSE (GWINETT) BIERCE (1842–?1914), American journalist and humorist: *The Devil's Dictionary*

A mixed economy is essential to social democracy.

ANTHONY CROSLAND (1918–77), British politician: *The Daily Telegraph*, 25 *January 1979*

The private sector is the part of the economy the Government controls and the public sector is that part that nobody controls.

SIR JAMES GOLDSMITH (1933–97), British businessman: *Observer*, 'Sayings of the Year', 30 December 1979

Booms and slumps are simply the expression of the results of an oscillation of the terms of credit about their equilibrium position.

JOHN MAYNARD KEYNES (1883–1946), English economist: *A Treatise on Money, volume 1*

I only make movies to finance my fishing.

LEE MARVIN (1924–87), American actor

A financier is a pawnbroker with imagination.

SIR ARTHUR WING PINERO (1855–1934), English dramatist: *The Second Mrs Tanqueray*

Our analysis leads us to believe that recovery is sound only if it does come of itself. For any revival which is merely due to artificial stimulus leaves part of the work of depressions undone and adds, to an undigested remnant of maladjustment, new maladjustments of its own.

JOSEPH ALOIS SCHUMPETER (1883–1950), Austrian-born American economist: *Essays*

It's a recession when your neighbor loses his job; it's a depression when you lose yours.

HARRY S. TRUMAN (1884–1972), American president: quoted in *A Collection of Quotable Quotes*

When it comes to finances, remember that there is no withholding taxes on the wages of sin.

MAE WEST (1892–1980), American stage and film actress

All these financiers, all the little gnomes of Zurich and the other financial centres, about whom we keep on hearing.

SIR (JAMES) HAROLD WILSON, Lord Wilson of Rievaulx (1916–95), English statesman and prime minister: *Speech, House of Commons, 12 November 1956*

Gambling

If the first super-casino goes ahead in the UK, we will see the damaging consequences of such a development, predicted to include an increase in problem gambling in the local area and ruin for many local businesses.

STEVEN BATE, campaigner against super-casinos in the UK

Gambling with cards or dice or stocks is all one thing. It's getting money without giving an equivalent for it.

HENRY WARD BEECHER (1813–87), American clergyman, editor and writer

Whoever plays deep must necessarily lose his money or his character.

LORD CHESTERFIELD, Philip Dormer Stanhope, 4th Earl of (1694–1773), English statesman and writer: *Letters to his godson*

Gambling is a disease of barbarians superficially civilised.

WILLIAM RALPH INGE (1860–1954), English theologian

Las Vegas is not coming to Great Britain.

TESSA JOWELL (1947–), British politician: quoted in *Guardian, 30 January 2007*

The sure way of getting nothing for something.

WILSON MIZNER (1876–1933), American dramatist

Gambling is the child of avarice and the father of despair.

PROVERB

The best throw of the dice is to throw them away.

PROVERB

There is no moral difference between gambling at cards or in lotteries or on the race track and gambling in the stock-market. One method is just as pernicious to the body politic as the other kind, and in degree the evil worked is far greater.

THEODORE ROOSEVELT (1858–1919), American statesman and president: *Message to Congress, 31 January 1908*

A gambler with a system must be, to a greater or lesser extent, insane.

GEORGE AUGUSTUS SALA (1828–95), English writer and journalist

In gambling the many must lose in order that the few may win.

GEORGE BERNARD SHAW (1856–1950), Irish dramatist and critic: *Fabian Essays, 'The Economic Basis of Socialism'*

Adventure upon all the tickets in the lottery, and you lose for certain; and the greater the number of your tickets the nearer your approach to this certainty.

ADAM SMITH (1723–90), Scottish economist and philosopher: *The Wealth of Nations, volume 1*

Life is a gamble, at terrible odds – if it was a bet, you wouldn't take it.

TOM STOPPARD (1937–), Czechoslovakian-born British playwright: *Rosencrantz and Guildenstern Are Dead, 1967*

He that puts confidence in … dice, cards, balls, bowls, or any game lawful or unlawful doth adventure to be laughed at for a fool, or die a beggar unpitied.

JOHN TAYLOR (1580–1653), English writer: *A Kicksey Winsey*

Government & Institutions

The divine science of government is social happiness, and the blessings of society depend entirely on the constitutions of government.

JOHN ADAMS (1735–1826), American president: *Discourses on Davila*

A democracy is a government in the hands of men of low birth, no property, and vulgar employments.

ARISTOTLE (384–322 BC), Greek philosopher and scientist: *Politics*

Democracy means government by discussion but it is only effective if you can stop people talking.

CLEMENT RICHARD ATTLEE, 1st Earl Attlee (1883–1967), English statesman and prime minister: *Anatomy of Britain*

All Governments like to interfere; it elevates their position to make out that they can cure the evils of mankind.

WALTER BAGEHOT (1826–77), English economist and journalist: *Economic Studies*

This island is almost made of coal and surrounded by fish. Only an organising genius could produce a shortage of coal and fish in Great Britain at the same time.

ANEURIN BEVAN (1897–1960), British statesman: *Speech, 1945*

The State is, or can be, master of money; but in a free society it is master of very little else.

LORD BEVERIDGE, William Henry Beveridge, 1st Baron Beveridge (1879–1963), British economist: quoted in Jonathon Green, *A Dictionary of Contemporary Quotations*

The trouble in modern democracy is that men do not approach to leadership until they have lost the desire to lead anyone.

LORD BEVERIDGE: *Observer, 'Sayings of the Week', 15 April 1934*

All government, – indeed, every human benefit and enjoyment, every virtue and every prudent act, – is founded on compromise and barter.

EDMUND BURKE (1729–97), British statesman, orator and writer: *Speech, 'On Conciliation with the American Colonies', 22 March 1775*

And having looked to government for bread, on the very first scarcity they will turn and bite the hand that fed them.

EDMUND BURKE, *Thoughts and Details on Scarcity*

Government is a contrivance of human wisdom to provide for human wants. Men have a right that these wants should be provided for by this wisdom.

EDMUND BURKE, *Reflections on the Revolution in France*

All modern revolutions have ended in a reinforcement of the power of the State.

ALBERT CAMUS (1913–60), French philosopher and writer: *The Rebel*

Government is emphatically a machine: to the discontented a 'taxing machine', to the contented a 'machine for securing property'.

THOMAS CARLYLE (1795–1881), Scottish essayist and historian: *Signs of the Times*

It has been said that Democracy is the worst form of government except all those other forms that have been tried from time to time.

SIR WINSTON LEONARD SPENCER CHURCHILL (1874–1965), English statesman, writer and prime minister: *Speech, House of Commons, November 1947*

In a country well governed poverty is something to be ashamed of. In a country badly governed wealth is something to be ashamed of.

CONFUCIUS (Kong Zi) (551–479 BC), Chinese philosopher: *Analects*

Every time the government attempts to handle our affairs, it costs more and the results are worse than if we had handled them ourselves.

BENJAMIN CONSTANT (Henri Benjamin Constant de Rebecque) (1767–1830), French writer and politician: *Cours de politique constitutionnelle*

Most people favour an incomes policy – provided it doesn't apply to them.

FRANK COUSINS (1904–86), English trade union leader: *Observer, 'Sayings of the Decade', 28 December 1969*

A good government produces citizens distinguished for courage, love of justice, and every other good quality; a bad government makes them cowardly, rapacious, and the slaves of every foul desire.

DIONYSIUS OF HALICARNASSUS (?40–8 BC), Greek historian and rhetorician: *Antiquities of Rome*

Individuals may form communities, but it is institutions alone that can create a nation.

BENJAMIN DISRAELI, 1st Earl of Beaconsfield (1804–81), English statesman, prime minister and novelist: *Speech, Manchester, 1866*

The State is made for man, not man for the State.

ALBERT EINSTEIN (1879–1955), German-Swiss-American physicist: *The World as I See it*

We do not make a world of our own, but fall into institutions already made, and have to accommodate ourselves to them to be useful at all.

RALPH WALDO EMERSON (1803–82), American poet, essayist and philosopher: *Journals, 1832*

Governments never learn. Only people learn.

MILTON FRIEDMAN (1912–2006), American economist: *Observer, 'Sayings of the Year', 28 December 1980*

In a community where public services have failed to keep abreast of private consumption things are very different. Here in an atmosphere of private opulence and public squalor, the private goods have full sway.

JOHN KENNETH GALBRAITH (1908–2006), Canadian-born American economist, diplomat and writer: *The Affluent Society*

The government that is big enough to give you all you want is big enough to take it all away.

BARRY (MORRIS) GOLDWATER (1909–98), American politician: *Speech, 1964*

Government after all is a very simple thing.

WARREN G(AMALIEL) HARDING (1865–1923), American president

What I do object to is living in a country where governments make their decisions without any understanding whatsoever of their bloody effect on business.

SIR JOHN HARVEY-JONES (1924–), former chairman of ICI

No government can save the country unless the country is determined to save itself.

EDWARD (RICHARD GEORGE) HEATH (1916–2005), British statesman and prime minister: *Observer, 'Sayings of the Year', 29 December 1974*

We are gradually moving towards a situation where everybody is subsidising everybody else.

H. S. HOUTHAKKER: *The Economics of Federal Subsidy Programmes, May 1972*

Agriculture, manufactures, commerce, and navigation, the four pillars of our prosperity, are the most thriving when left most free to individual enterprise.

THOMAS JEFFERSON (1743–1826), American statesman and president: *Message to Congress, 1801*

I would not give half a guinea to live under one form of Government rather than another. It is of no moment to the happiness of an individual.

SAMUEL JOHNSON (1709–84), English lexicographer, essayist and poet: quoted in James Boswell, *The Life of Samuel Johnson*

I sometimes think that given half a chance politicians would like to give extra tax and social security concessions to marginal constituencies only.

WILLIAM KEEGAN: *Observer, 17 September 1978*

That this nation, under God, shall have a new birth of freedom; and that government of the people, by the people, and for the people, shall not perish from the earth.

ABRAHAM LINCOLN (1809–65), American statesman and president: *Address at Dedication of National Cemetery, Gettysburg, 19 November 1863*

It is perfectly true that that government is best which governs least. It is equally true that that government is best which provides most.

WALTER LIPPMANN (1889–1974), American teacher, editor and journalist: *A Preface to Politics, 'The Red Herring'*

Thrift should be the guiding principle in our government expenditure.

MAO TSE-TUNG (Mao Zedong) (1893–1976), Chinese Communist leader: *Quotations from Chairman Mao Tse-Tung*

The worst government is the most moral. One composed of cynics is often very tolerant and human. But when fanatics are on top there is no limit to oppression.

HENRY LOUIS MENCKEN (1888–1956), American philologist, editor and satirist: *Notebooks, 'Minority Report'*

The art of governing consists in not allowing men to grow old in their jobs.

NAPOLEON I (Napoleon Bonaparte) (1769–1821), French emperor and general: *Maxims*

Government, even in its best state, is but a necessary evil; in its worst state, an intolerable one.

THOMAS PAINE (1737–1809), English philosopher and writer: *Common Sense, chapter 1*

All money nowadays seems to be produced with a natural homing instinct for the Treasury.
PRINCE PHILIP, Duke of Edinburgh (1921–): *Observer, 'Sayings of the Week', 26 May 1963*

Public money is like holy water; everyone helps himself.
ITALIAN PROVERB

Strange women lying in ponds distributing swords is no basis for a system of government!
MONTY PYTHON: *Monty Python and the Holy Grail, 1975*

The business of government is to keep the government out of business – that is, unless business needs government aid.
WILL(IAM PENN ADAIR) ROGERS (1879–1935), American actor and humorist

What institution of government could tend so much to promote the happiness of mankind as the general prevalence of wisdom and virtue? All government is but an imperfect remedy for the deficiency of these.
ADAM SMITH (1723–90), Scottish economist and philosopher: *The Theory of Moral Sentiments*

Whenever you have an efficient government you have a dictatorship.
HARRY S. TRUMAN (1884–1972), American statesman and president: *Lecture, Columbia University, 1959*

The Treasury could not, with any marked success, run a fish and chip shop.
SIR (JAMES) HAROLD WILSON, Lord Wilson of Rievaulx (1916–95), English statesman and prime minister: *Observer, 'Sayings of the Year', 30 December 1984*

Interest

Interest works night and day, in fair weather and in foul. It gnaws at a man's substance with invisible teeth.

HENRY WARD BEECHER (1813–87), American clergyman, editor and writer: *Proverbs from Plymouth Pulpit*

The most powerful force in the universe is compound interest.

ALBERT EINSTEIN (1879–1955), German-Swiss-American physicist

The Theory of Interest, As Determined by IMPATIENCE to Spend Income and OPPORTUNITY to Invest it.

IRVING FISHER (1867–1947), American mathematician and economist: *The Theory of Interest*

Interest springs from the power of increase which the reproductive forces of nature give to capital. It is not an arbitrary, but a natural thing; it is not the result of a particular social organization, but of laws of the universe which underlie society. It is, therefore, just.

HENRY GEORGE (1839–97), American economist: *Progress and Poverty*

High interest arises from three circumstances: a great demand for borrowing, little riches to supply that demand, and great profits arising from commerce.

DAVID HUME (1711–76), Scottish philosopher and historian: *Essays, 'Of Interest'*

No law can reduce the common rate of interest below the lowest ordinary market rate at the time when that law is made.

ADAM SMITH (1723–90), Scottish economist and philosopher: *The Wealth of Nations*

There are three forms of usury: interest on money, rent of land

and houses, and profit in exchange. Whoever is in receipt of any of these is a usurer.

BENJAMIN R. TUCKER (1854–1939), American anarchist: *Instead of a Book*

Every half-year's interest costs half a year of life.

HORACE WALPOLE, 4th Earl of Orford (1717–97), English writer and historian: *Letter to the Countess of Upper Ossory, 10 November 1793*

Investment

The best investments are often those that looked dead wrong when they were made.

ANON

The purchase and quick resale of stocks is not any more gambling than the purchase and quick resale of lots, and the length of time a man may hold stocks or lots depends largely upon the temperament and ability of the man.

BISHOP JAMES CANNON, JR: *Unspotted from the World, 3 August 1929*

There is no finer investment for any community than putting milk into babies.

SIR WINSTON LEONARD SPENCER CHURCHILL (1874–1965), English statesman, writer and prime minister: *Radio Broadcast, 21 March 1943*

'Tis money that begets money.

THOMAS FULLER (1654–1734), English physician, writer and compiler: *Gnomologia*

Of all the mysteries of the stock exchange there is none so impenetrable as why there should be a buyer for everyone who seeks to sell.

JOHN KENNETH GALBRAITH (1908–2006), Canadian-born American economist, diplomat and writer: *The Great Crash, 1929, chapter 6*

The best investment on earth is earth.

LOUIS GLICKMAN (1933–): *New York Post, 3 September 1957*

Both public and private investment should be carried out only to the extent to which they are considered useful. If the effective demand thus generated fails to provide full employment, the gap should be filled by increasing consumption and not by piling up unwanted public or private capital equipment.

M. KALECKI (1899–1970), Polish economist: *The Economics of Full Employment, 'Three Ways to Full Employment'*

Speculators may do no harm as bubbles on a steady stream of enterprise. But the position is serious when enterprise becomes the bubble on a whirlpool of speculation. When the capital development of the country becomes a by-product of the activities of a casino, the job is likely to be ill-done.

JOHN MAYNARD KEYNES (1883–1946), English economist: *The General Theory of Employment, Interest and Money, book 4*

The fact that so many opportunities for the profitable investment of resources in the development of human potentialities are neglected, and so many wasteful investments of the same kind made, is perhaps one of the most serious criticisms of existing society.

FRANK H. KNIGHT (1885–1972), Professor of Economics: *Risk, Uncertainty and Profit*

Let every man divide his money into three parts, and invest a third in land, a third in business, and a third let him keep by him in reserve.

HEBREW PROVERB

You get out of an investment what you put into it, so the first decision you have to make is how much time you are prepared to devote to the initial task of acquiring a basic knowledge of investment.

JIM SLATER (1929–), British finance guru and businessman

It's not whether you're right or wrong that's important, but how much money you make when you're right and how much you lose when you're wrong.

GEORGE SOROS (1930–), Hungarian-born businessman and philanthropist

October. This is one of the peculiarly dangerous months to speculate in stocks in. The others are July, January, September, April, November, May, March, June, December, August, and February.

MARK TWAIN (Samuel Langhorne Clemens) (1835–1910), American novelist and humorist: *Pudd'nhead Wilson, chapter 13*

There are two times in a man's life when he should not speculate: when he can't afford it, and when he can.

MARK TWAIN: *Following the Equator*

Law

A lawyer has been defined as a man who helps you get what's coming to him.

ANON: quoted in Edward Phillips, *The World's Best Lawyer Jokes*

It has been said that Moses was a great lawgiver but the fact that he limited himself to only ten commandments and kept them short and easy to understand shows that he was no lawyer.

ANON: quoted in Edward Phillips, *The World's Best Lawyer Jokes*

Riches without law are more dangerous than is poverty without law.

HENRY WARD BEECHER (1813–87), American clergyman, editor and writer: *Proverb from Plymouth Pulpit*

We do not get good laws to restrain bad people. We get good people to restrain bad laws.

G(ILBERT) K(EITH) CHESTERTON (1874–1936), English essayist, novelist, poet and critic: *All Things Considered*

The Law of England is a very strange one; it cannot compel anyone to tell the truth … But what the Law can do is to give you seven years for not telling the truth.

CHARLES JOHN DARLING, 1st Baron (1849–1936), English judge: *D. Walker-Smith, Lord Darling*

'If the law supposes that,' said Mr Bumble … 'the law is a ass – a idiot.'

CHARLES (JOHN HUFFAM) DICKENS (1812–70), English novelist: *Oliver Twist, chapter 51*

People say law but they mean wealth.

RALPH WALDO EMERSON (1803–82), American poet, essayist and philosopher: *Journals, 1839*

As in law so in war, the longest purse finally wins.

MAHATMA GANDHI (Mohandas Karamchand Gandhi) (1869–1948), Hindu nationalist leader: *Paper read to the Bombay Provincial Co-operative Conference, 17 September 1917*

Lord Chancellor
The Law is the true embodiment
Of everything that's excellent.
It has no kind of fault or flaw,
And I, my lords, embody the Law.

SIR WILLIAM SCHWENK GILBERT (1836–1911), English parodist and librettist: *Iolanthe, Act 1*

Laws grind the poor, and rich men rule the law.

OLIVER GOLDSMITH (?1728–74), Irish dramatist, novelist and poet: *The Traveller*

Men are not hanged for stealing Horses, but that Horses may not be stolen.

HALIFAX, 1st Marquis of, Sir George Savile (1633–95), English statesman, writer and orator: *Political Thoughts and Reflections: Of Punishment*

The main foundations of every state, new states as well as ancient or composite ones, are good laws and good arms … you cannot have good laws without good arms, and where there are good arms, good laws inevitably follow.

NICCOLÒ MACHIAVELLI (1469–1527), Italian statesman and political philosopher: *The Prince, chapter 12*

Who saves his country violates no law.

NAPOLEON I (Napoleon Bonaparte) (1769–1821), French emperor and general: *Maxims*

Laws were made to be broken.

CHRISTOPHER NORTH (John Wilson) (1785–1854), Scottish poet, essayist and critic: *Noctes ambrosianae, 24 May 1830*

The first of all laws is to respect the laws: the severity of penalties is only a vain resource, invented by little minds in order to substitute terror for that respect which they have no means of obtaining.

JEAN-JACQUES ROUSSEAU (1712–78), Swiss-born French philosopher and writer: *A Discourse on Political Economy*

Ignorance of the law excuses no man; not that all men know the law, but because 'tis an excuse every man will plead, and no man can tell how to confute him.

JOHN SELDEN (1584–1654), English historian and antiquary: *Table Talk*

Let all the laws be clear, uniform and precise; to interpret laws is almost always to corrupt them.

VOLTAIRE (François Marie Arouet) (1694–1778), French writer, philosopher and historian: *Philosophical Dictionary*

Media

In day-to-day commerce, television is not so much interested in the business of communications as in the business of delivering audiences to advertisers. People are the merchandise, not the shows. The shows are merely the bait.

ANON

The media's power is frail. Without the people's support, it can be shut off with the ease of turning a light switch.

CORAZON C. AQUINO (1933–), President of the Philippines

What the mass media offer is not popular art, but entertainment which is intended to be consumed like food, forgotten, and replaced by a new dish.

W(YSTAN) H(UGH) AUDEN (1907–73), English poet, dramatist, critic and librettist: *The Dyer's Hand, 'The Poet and the City'*

The printing-press is either the greatest blessing or the greatest curse of modern times, one sometimes forgets which.

SIR JAMES MATTHEW BARRIE (1860–1937), Scottish novelist and dramatist: *Sentimental Tommy*

I read the newspaper avidly. It is my one form of continuous fiction.

ANEURIN BEVAN (1897–1960), British statesman (Attributed)

TV is an evil medium. It should never have been invented. But since we have to live with it, let's try to do something about it.

RICHARD (JENKINS) BURTON (1925–84), British stage and film actor: *Observer, 'Sayings of the Decade', 28 December 1969*

Journalism largely consists in saying 'Lord Jones Dead' to people who never knew Lord Jones was alive.

G(ILBERT) K(EITH) CHESTERTON (1874–1936), English essayist, novelist, poet and critic

Television is more interesting than people. If it were not, we should have people standing in the corners of our rooms.

ALAN COREN (1938–), British humorist: *The Times*

Television:
It is a medium of entertainment which permits millions of people to listen to the same joke at the same time, and yet remain lonesome.

T(HOMAS) S(TEARNS) ELIOT (1888–1965), American-born British poet, dramatist and critic: *New York Post, 22 September 1963*

A newspaper consists of just the same number of words, whether there be any news in it or not.

HENRY FIELDING (1707–54), English novelist and dramatist: *Tom Jones*

Why should people go out and pay money to see bad films when they can stay at home and see bad television for nothing?

SAMUEL GOLDWYN (1882–1974), American film producer: *Observer, 'Sayings of the Week', 9 September 1956*

All media exist to invest our lives with artificial perceptions and arbitrary values.

(HERBERT) MARSHALL MCLUHAN (1911–80), Canadian educator and philosopher

The medium is the message. This is merely to say that the personal and social consequences of any medium … result from the new scale that is introduced into our affairs by each extension of ourselves or by any new technology.

(HERBERT) MARSHALL MCLUHAN: *Understanding Media, chapter 1*

The new electronic interdependence recreates the world in the image of a global village.

(HERBERT) MARSHALL MCLUHAN: *The Medium Is the Message*

Journalism:
A profession whose business it is to explain to others what it personally does not understand.

LORD NORTHCLIFFE, Alfred Charles William Harmsworth, 1st Viscount (1865–1922), Irish-born British newspaper proprietor

All the news that's fit to print.

ADOLPH S(IMON) OCHS (1858–1935), American publisher and editor: *The New York Times, motto*

Early in life I had noticed that no event is ever correctly reported in a newspaper.

GEORGE ORWELL (Eric Arthur Blair) (1903–50), English novelist and essayist: *Collected Essays, Journalism and Letters*

For a politician to complain about the press is like a ship's captain complaining about the sea.

ENOCH POWELL (1912–98), British politician

Television? No good will come of this device. The word is half Greek and half Latin.

C(HARLES) P(RESTWICH) SCOTT (1846–1932), Editor, *Manchester Guardian* (Attributed)

An editor is one who separates the wheat from the chaff and prints the chaff.

ADLAI (EWING) STEVENSON (1900–68), American statesman: *The Stevenson Wit*

On the start of British commercial television:

A stake in commercial television is the equivalent of having a licence to print money.

LORD THOMSON, KENNETH ROY, 2nd Baron Thomson of Fleet (1923–2006), British newspaper proprietor (Attributed)

We write frankly and freely but then we 'modify' before we print.

MARK TWAIN (Samuel Langhorne Clemens) (1835–1910), American novelist and humorist: *Life on the Mississippi*

News is what a chap who doesn't care much about anything wants to read. And it's only news until he reads it. After that it's dead.

EVELYN (ARTHUR ST JOHN) WAUGH (1903–66), English novelist: *Scoop*

Newspapers have degenerated. They may now be absolutely relied upon.

OSCAR WILDE (1856–1900), Irish poet, dramatist and wit: *The Decay of Lying*

National Debt

Nothing is so well calculated to produce a death-like torpor in the country as an extended system of taxation and a great national debt; and, therefore, all Ministers who, like Mr Pitt, have no notion of governing but by means of the baser passions, have regarded a public debt as a public blessing.

WILLIAM COBBETT (1762–1835), English farmer, social reformer and writer: *Letter to W. Windham, 10 February 1804*

Public credit means the contracting of debts which a nation never can pay.

WILLIAM COBBETT: *Advice to Young Men*

Solvency is maintained by means of a national debt, on the principle, 'If you will not lend me the money, how can I pay you?'

RALPH WALDO EMERSON (1803–82), American poet, essayist and philosopher

A national debt, if it is not excessive, will be to us a national blessing.

ALEXANDER HAMILTON (?1757–1804), American Federalist politician: *Letter to Robert Morris, 30 April 1781*

Blessed are the young, for they shall inherit the national debt.

HERBERT (CLARK) HOOVER (1894–1964), American statesman and president

It is incumbent on every generation to pay its own debts as it goes – a principle which, if acted on, would save one-half the wars of the world.

THOMAS JEFFERSON (1743–1826), American statesman and president: *Letter to Destutt Tracy, 1820*

A nation is not in danger of financial disaster merely because it owes itself money.

ANDREW WILLIAM MELLON (1855–1937), American financier: *Aside, 1933*

No nation ought to be without a debt. A national debt is a national bond.

THOMAS PAINE (1737–1809), English philosopher and writer: *Common Sense, 'Of the Present Ability of America'*

It would be easier to pay off the national debt overnight than to neutralise the long-range effects of our national stupidity.

FRANK ZAPPA (1940–93), American rock musician and producer

Payment & Wages

Be content with your wages.

The Bible, Authorised (King James) Version, Luke 3:14

I don't pay good wages because I have a lot of money; I have a lot of money because I pay good wages.

ROBERT BOSCH (1861–1942), German industrialist

A fair day's wages for a fair day's work: it is as just a demand as governed men ever made of governing.

THOMAS CARLYLE (1795–1881), Scottish essayist and historian: *Past and Present*

We have profoundly forgotten everywhere that cash-payment is not the sole relation of human beings.

THOMAS CARLYLE

There is one rule for industrialists and that is: Make the best quality of goods possible at the lowest cost possible, paying the highest wages possible

HENRY FORD (1863–1947), American car manufacturer

It is but a truism that labor is most productive where its wages are largest. Poorly paid labor is inefficient labor, the world over.

HENRY GEORGE (1839–97), American economist: *Progress and Poverty*

We're overpaying him but he's worth it.

SAMUEL GOLDWYN (1882–1974), American film producer

The theory of the determination of wages in a free market is simply a special case of the general theory of value. Wages are the price of labour.

SIR JOHN RICHARD HICKS (1904–89), British economist: *The Theory of Wages, Part 1*

Folks who never do any more than they are paid for, never get paid more than they do.

ELBERT (GREEN) HUBBARD (1856–1915), American businessman, writer and printer

It is an economic axiom as old as the hills that goods and services can be paid for only with goods and services.

ALBERT J. NOCK (1873–1945): *Memoirs of a Superfluous Man*

Only in our dreams are we free. The rest of the time we need wages.
TERRY PRATCHETT (1948–), English science-fiction author

A good paymaster never wants workmen.
PROVERB

He who pays the piper may call the tune.
PROVERB

If you pay peanuts, you get monkeys.
PROVERB

Everything is worth what its purchaser will pay for it.
PUBLILIUS SYRUS (1st c. BC), Latin writer of mimes: *Moral Sayings*

Wages should be left to the fair and free competition of the market, and should never be controlled by the interference of the legislature.
DAVID RICARDO (1772–1823), English economist: *Principles of Political Economy*

No business which depends for existence on paying less than living wages to its workers has any right to continue in this country. By business I mean the whole of commerce as well as the whole of industry; by workers I mean all workers – the white-collar class as well as the man in overalls; and by living wages I mean more than a bare subsistence level – I mean the wages of decent living.
FRANKLIN DELANO ROOSEVELT (1882–1945), American statesman and president: *Address, 16 June 1933*

If you do things by the job, you are perpetually driven: the hours are scourges. If you work by the hour, you gently sail on the stream of Time, which is always bearing you on to the haven of Pay, whether you make any effort, or not.

CHARLES DUDLEY WARNER (1829–1900), American essayist, editor and novelist: *My Summer in a Garden*

For two days' labour, you ask two hundred guineas? No, I ask it for the knowledge of a lifetime.

JAMES ABBOTT MCNEILL WHISTLER (1834–1903), American painter: *D. C. Seitz, Whistler Stories*

One man's wage rise is another man's price increase.

SIR (JAMES) HAROLD WILSON, Lord Wilson of Rievaulx (1916–95), English statesman and prime minister: *Observer, 'Sayings of the Week', 11 January 1970*

Pensions & Saving

Goodbye Tension, Hello Pension.

ANON

Men are divided between those who are as thrifty as if they would live for ever, and those who are as extravagant as if they were going to die the next day.

ARISTOTLE (384–322 BC), Greek philosopher and scientist: quoted in *Diogenes Laertius, Lives and Opinions of Eminent Philosophers*

Economy:
Purchasing the barrel of whiskey that you do not need for the price of the cow that you cannot afford.

AMBROSE (GWINETT) BIERCE (1842–?1914), American journalist and humorist: *The Devil's Dictionary*

Mere parsimony is not economy … Expense, and great expense, may be an essential part of true economy. Economy is a distributive virtue, and consists not in saving but selection.

Parsimony requires no providence, no sagacity, no powers of combination, no comparison, no judgment.

EDMUND BURKE (1729–97), British statesman, orator and writer: *Letter to a Noble Lord*

You see, anybody can plan a new Jerusalem with proper pensions and insurance and the rest of it, but to carry it out at a time when your country has been bankrupted by war is a very different kettle of fish.

BARBARA CASTLE (1910–2002), British politician

Saving is a very fine thing. Especially when your parents have done it for you.

SIR WINSTON LEONARD SPENCER CHURCHILL (1874–1965), English statesman, writer and prime minister (Attributed)

It is better to have a hen tomorrow than an egg today.

THOMAS FULLER (1654–1734), English physician, writer and compiler: *Gnomologia*

Whenever you save five shillings, you put a man out of work for a day.

JOHN MAYNARD KEYNES (1883–1946), English economist: *Essays in Persuasion, 'Inflation and Deflation'*

When I was young, academics were proud people, they were well paid, they had jobs for life, pensions, they were respected then.

JAMES LOVELOCK (1919–), British scientist, author and environmentalist

A good saver is a good server.

PROVERB

Take care of the pence, and the pounds will take care of themselves.

PROVERB

It is not economical to go to bed early to save the candles if the results are twins.

CHINESE PROVERB

The time to save is now. When a dog gets a bone, he doesn't go out and make a down payment on a bigger bone. He buries the one he's got.

WILL(IAM PENN ADAIR) ROGERS (1879–1935), American actor and humorist

What is annually saved is as regularly consumed as what is annually spent, and nearly in the same time too; but it is consumed by a different set of people.

ADAM SMITH (1723–90), Scottish economist and philosopher: *The Wealth of Nations, volume 1*

I advise you to go on living solely to enrage those who are paying your annuities. It is the only pleasure I have left.

VOLTAIRE (François Marie Arouet) (1694–1778), French writer, philosopher and historian

To recommend thrift to the poor is both grotesque and insulting. It is like advising a man who is starving to eat less.

OSCAR WILDE (1856–1900), Irish poet, dramatist and wit: *The Soul of Man under Socialism*

Profit & Loss

Remind people that profit is the difference between revenue and expense. This makes you look smart.

SCOTT ADAMS (1957–), American cartoonist, creator of Dilbert

I think the railways can be made to pay. This is the first time I have said this so flat-footedly.

LORD BEECHING, Dr Richard Beeching (1913–84), chairman, British Railways Board: *Observer, 'Sayings of the Decade', 28 December 1969*

It is a socialist idea that making profits is a vice; I consider the
real vice is making losses.
SIR WINSTON LEONARD SPENCER CHURCHILL (1874–1965), English
statesman, writer and prime minister

Civilization and profits go hand in hand.
(JOHN) CALVIN COOLIDGE (1872–1933), American president

What is a man if he is not a thief who openly charges as much as
he can for the goods he sells?
MAHATMA GANDHI (Mohandas Karamchand Gandhi) (1869–1948), Hindu
nationalist leader: *Non-Violence in Peace and War*

The smell of profit is clean
And sweet, whatever the source.
JUVENAL (Decimus Junius Juvenalis) (?60–?140 AD), Roman satirist: *Satires*

Even genius is tied to profit.
PINDAR (?518–?438 BC), Greek lyric poet: *Odes*

There are occasions when it is undoubtedly better to incur loss
than to make gain.
TITUS MACCIUS PLAUTUS (?254–?184 BC), Roman comic dramatist: *The
Captives*

Profit is better than fame.
PROVERB

Where profit is, loss is hidden near by.
JAPANESE PROVERB

The loss which is unknown is no loss at all.
PUBLILIUS SYRUS (1st c. BC), Latin writer of mimes: *Moral Sayings*

When wages are low profits must be high.

DAVID RICARDO (1772–1823), English economist: *Works, volume 2, 'Notes on Malthus'*

Nothing contributes so much to the prosperity and happiness of a country as high profits.

DAVID RICARDO: *On Protection to Agriculture*

Profit is the ignition system of our economic engine.

CHARLES SAWYER (1868–1954), American photographer

The earnings of an entrepreneur sometimes represent nothing but the spoliation of the workmen. A profit is made not because the industry produces much more than it costs, but because it fails to give to the workman sufficient compensation for his toil. Such an industry is a social evil.

JEAN CHARLES LEONARD SIMONDE DE SISMONDI (1773–1842), Swiss historian and economist: *Nouveaux principes d'economie politique, volume 1*

Profits, like sausages … are esteemed most by those who know least about what goes into them.

ALVIN TOFFLER (1928–), American writer

The trouble with the profit system has always been that it was highly unprofitable to most people.

E(LWYN) B(ROOKS) WHITE (1899–1985), American humorist and essayist: *One Man's Meat*

Economics & Background Sciences

In this section we consider economics and other related social sciences, together with some of the distinctive political teachings and theories. The quotations indicate widely ranging – and at times conflicting – opinions on these significant subjects that determine different approaches to business and economics. We move from the more familiar 'Politics is the art of the possible' (R. A. Butler), 'The unpleasant and unacceptable face of capitalism' (Edward Heath), and 'The theory of Communism may be summed up in one sentence: Abolish all private property' (Marx and Engels) to the less well-known 'The Communist is a Socialist in a violent hurry' (G. W. Gough) and 'Other Things Being Equal … you can generally tell whether a man is an economist by the number of times he uses this particular phrase' (William Davis), and 'Ask five economists and you'll get five different explanations (six if one went to Harvard)' (Edgar R. Fiedler).

Capitalism

There is a good deal of solemn cant about the common interests of capital and labor. As matters stand, their only common interest is that of cutting each other's throat.

(JUSTIN) BROOKS ATKINSON (1894–1984), American dramatic critic and essayist: *Once Around the Sun*

Unemployment is capitalism's way of getting you to plant a garden.

ORSON SCOTT CARD (1951–), American author

The inherent vice of capitalism is the unequal sharing of blessings; the inherent virtue of socialism is the equal sharing of miseries.
SIR WINSTON LEONARD SPENCER CHURCHILL (1874–1965), English statesman, writer and prime minister

History suggests that capitalism is a necessary condition for political freedom.
MILTON FRIEDMAN (1912–2006), American economist

The unpleasant and unacceptable face of capitalism.
EDWARD (RICHARD GEORGE) HEATH (1916–2005), English statesman and prime minister: *Speech, House of Commons, 15 May 1973*

Labour, under capitalism, is doubly enslaved. It is directed towards ends which it has not chosen by means which are forced upon it.
JEAN LEON JAURES (1859–1914), French politician and writer: *Études socialistes*

When I was young I worked for a capitalist twelve hours a day and I was always tired. Now I work for myself twenty hours a day and I never get tired.
NIKITA (SERGEYEVICH) KHRUSHCHEV (1894–1971), Soviet statesman and premier

In the Soviet Union, capitalism triumphed over communism. In this country, capitalism triumphed over democracy.
FRAN LEBOWITZ (1950–), American author

Capitalists are no more capable of self-sacrifice than a man is capable of lifting himself by his own bootstraps.
NIKOLAI LENIN (Vladimir Ilyich Ulyanov) (1870–1924), Russian statesman and Marxist theoretician: *Letters from Afar*

Imperialism is the monopoly stage of capitalism.
NIKOLAI LENIN: *Imperialism, the Highest Stage of Capitalism*

Under capitalism we have a state in the proper sense of the word, that is, a special machine for the suppression of one class by another.
NIKOLAI LENIN: *The State and Revolution*

The basic law of capitalism is you or I, not both you and I.
KARL LIEBKNECHT (1871–1919), German socialist leader: *Speech before the Fourth Socialist Young People's Conference, Stuttgart 1907*

You show me a capitalist, I'll show you a bloodsucker.
MALCOLM X (Malcolm Little) (1925–65), American Black Muslim leader: *Malcolm X Speaks*

There is a serious tendency towards capitalism among the well-to-do peasants.
MAO TSE-TUNG (Mao Zedong) (1893–1976), Chinese Communist leader: *Quotations from Chairman Mao Tse-Tung*

Capitalist production begets, with the inexorability of a law of nature, its own negation.
KARL MARX (1818–83), German founder of modern communism: *Capital, chapter 15*

The conflict between capitalism and democracy is inherent and continuous; it is often hidden by misleading propaganda and by the outward forms of democracy, such as parliaments, and the sops that the owning classes throw to the other classes to keep them more or less contented.
JAWAHARLAL NEHRU (1889–1964), Indian prime minister: *Glimpses of World History*

Under capitalism man exploits man; under socialism the reverse is true.
POLISH PROVERB

Man is born perfect, it is the capitalist system which corrupts him.
ARTHUR SCARGILL (1938–), British trade unionist: *Debate, Wakefield, 20 November 1981*

Under fully developed Capitalism civilization is always on the verge of revolution. We live as in a villa on Vesuvius.

GEORGE BERNARD SHAW (1856–1950), Irish dramatist and critic: *The Intelligent Woman's Guide to Socialism, Capitalism, Sovietism and Fascism, chapter 66*

Capitalism was doomed ethically before it was doomed economically, a long time ago.

ALEXANDER ISAYEVICH SOLZHENITSYN (1918–), Russian novelist: *Cancer Ward, Part 2*

Industrial crisis, unemployment, waste, widespread poverty, these are the incurable diseases of capitalism.

JOSEPH STALIN (Iosif Vissarionovich Dzhugashvili) (1879–1953), Soviet premier: *Speech before the conference of managers of the Soviet industry, 4 February 1931*

Marxian economics is essentially the economics of capitalism, while 'capitalist' economics is in a very real sense the economics of socialism.

PAUL M. SWEEZY: *'Economics and the Crisis of Capitalism', Economic Forum, Spring 1935*

You can't be a feminist and a capitalist.

RUTH WALLSGROVE: *Spare Rib: Observer, 'Sayings of 1982', 2 January 1983*

Class & Rank

The rich man in his castle,
The poor man at his gate,
God made them, high or lowly,
And order'd their estate.

CECIL FRANCES ALEXANDER (1818–95), Irish hymn-writer: *All Things Bright and Beautiful*

Inferiors revolt in order that they may be equal and equals that they may be superior. Such is the state of mind which creates revolutions.

ARISTOTLE (384–322 BC), Greek philosopher and scientist: *Politics*

There are three classes of citizens. The first are the rich, who are indolent and yet always crave more. The second are the poor, who have nothing, are full of envy, hate the rich, and are easily led by demagogues. Between the two extremes lie those who make the state secure and uphold the laws.

EURIPIDES (?480–406 BC), Greek tragic dramatist: *The Suppliant Women*

All the world over, I will back the masses against the classes.

WILLIAM EWART GLADSTONE (1809–98), English statesman and prime minister: *Speech, Liverpool, 28 June 1886*

One man is born with a silver spoon in his mouth, and another with a wooden ladle.

OLIVER GOLDSMITH (?1728–74), Irish dramatist, novelist and poet: *The Citizen of the World*

We are, by our occupations, education and habits of life, divided almost into different species, which regard one another, for the most part, with scorn and malignity.

SAMUEL JOHNSON (1709–84), English lexicographer, essayist and poet: *The Rambler, 28 September 1751*

Our loyalties must transcend our race, our tribe, our class and our nation; and this means we must develop a world perspective.

MARTIN LUTHER KING, JR (1929–68), American Baptist minister and civil rights leader

Class is the sure-footedness that comes with having proved you can meet life.

ANN LANDERS (1918–2002), American advice columnist

There is merit without rank, but there is no rank without some merit.

FRANÇOIS LA ROCHEFOUCAULD, Duc de la Rochefoucauld (1613–80), French writer: *Maxims*

Those who hold and those who are without property have ever formed distinct interests in society. Those who are creditors, and those who are debtors, fall under a like discrimination. A landed interest, a manufacturing interest, a mercantile interest, a moneyed interest, with many lesser interests, grow up of necessity in civilized nations, and divide them into different classes, actuated by different sentiments and views.

JAMES MADISON (1751–1836), American statesman and president: *The Federalist*

In class society everyone lives as a member of a particular class, and every kind of thinking, without exception, is stamped with the brand of a class.

MAO TSE-TUNG (Mao Zedong) (1893–1976), Chinese Communist leader: *Quotations from Chairman Mao Tse-Tung*

The history of all hitherto existing society is the history of class struggles.

KARL MARX (1818–83), German founder of modern communism and FRIEDRICH ENGELS (1820–95), German socialist leader: *The Communist Manifesto*

Money can't buy friends but it can get you a better class of enemy.

SPIKE MILLIGAN (1918–2002), Irish comedian

The most grinding poverty is a trifling evil compared with the inequality of classes.

WILLIAM MORRIS (1834–96), English writer and social reformer: *Letter to Andreas Scheu, 5 September 1883*

A throne is only a bench covered with velvet.

NAPOLEON I (Napoleon Bonaparte) (1769–1821), French emperor and
general: *Maxims*

Money is related to class only in the minds of people who have
too much of the former, too little of the latter or none of either.

DOUG ROBARCHEK, American journalist

We must be thoroughly democratic and patronize everybody
without distinction of class.

GEORGE BERNARD SHAW (1856–1950), Irish dramatist and critic:
Heartbreak House, Act 4

Communism & Marxism

A communist is one who has nothing and wishes to share it with
the world.

ANON

Virtually the whole British establishment has been, at least until
recently, educated without any real knowledge of Marxism, and is
determined to see that these ideas do not reach the public …
Anyone today who speaks of class in the context of politics runs
the risk of excommunication and outlawry.

TONY (ANTHONY NEIL WEDGWOOD) BENN (1925–), English politician:
Marx Memorial Lecture, London 1982

There is not one single social or economic principle or concept
in the philosophy of the Russian Bolshevik which has not been
realized, carried into action, and enshrined in immutable laws a
million years ago by the white ant.

SIR WINSTON LEONARD SPENCER CHURCHILL (1874–1965), English
statesman, writer and prime minister: quoted in *Bill Adler, The Churchill Wit,
'Politics'*

Marxism has not only failed to promote human freedom, it has failed to produce food.

JOHN DOS PASSOS (1896–1970), American novelist

What is a Communist? One who hath yearnings
For equal division of unequal earnings.
Idler or bungler, or both, he is willing,
To fork out his copper and pocket your shilling.

EBENEZER ELLIOTT (1781–1849), English poet: *Epigram*

The Communist is a Socialist in a violent hurry.

G. W. GOUGH: *The Economic Consequences of Socialism*

Communism possesses a language which every people can understand – its elements are hunger, envy and death.

HEINRICH HEINE (1797–1856), German journalist and essayist

Far from being a classless society, Communism is governed by an elite as steadfast in its determination to maintain its prerogatives as any oligarchy known to history.

ROBERT FRANCIS KENNEDY (1925–68), American statesman: *The Pursuit of Justice*

Communists who believed we could completely alter the economic form of society in three years were visionaries. I say it will take at least a century.

NIKOLAI LENIN (Vladimir Ilyich Ulyanov) (1870–1924), Russian statesman and Marxist theoretician: *Observer, 'Sayings of the Week', 7 April 1921*

There may be thousands of principles of Marxism, but in the final analysis they can be summed up in one sentence: Rebellion is justified.

MAO TSE-TUNG (Mao Zedong) (1893–1976), Chinese Communist leader: *The Times, 31 October 1966*

We Communists are like seeds and the people are like the soil. Wherever we go, we must unite with the people, take root and blossom among them.

MAO TSE-TUNG: *Quotations from Chairman Mao Tse-Tung*

The theory of Communism may be summed up in one sentence: Abolish all private property.

KARL MARX (1818–83), German founder of modern communism and FRIEDRICH ENGELS (1820–95), German socialist leader: *The Communist Manifesto*

What is thine is mine, and all of mine is thine.

TITUS MACCIUS PLAUTUS (?254–?84 BC), Roman comic dramatist: *Trinummus*

Communism is inequality, but not as property is. Property is exploitation of the weak by the strong. Communism is exploitation of the strong by the weak.

PIERRE JOSEPH PROUDHON (1809–65), French political theorist: *What Is Property?*

Communism is like Prohibition, it's a good idea but it won't work.

WILL(IAM PENN ADAIR) ROGERS (1879–1935), American actor and humorist: *The Autobiography of Will Rogers*

Vincentio:

What's mine is yours and what is yours is mine.

WILLIAM SHAKESPEARE (1564–1616), English dramatist and poet: *Measure for Measure, Act 5*

Of the Communist party:

As soon as classes have been abolished, and the dictatorship of the proletariat has been done away with, the party will have fulfilled its mission and can be allowed to disappear.

JOSEPH STALIN (Iosif Vissarionovich Dzhugashvili) (1879–1953), Soviet premier: *Speech at Sverdloff University, April 1924*

Money is related to class only in the minds of people who have too much of the former, too little of the latter or none of either.

ADLAI (EWING) STEVENSON (1900–68), American statesman

In reply to a question on whether Communism had failed:
It depends on the way you measure the concept of good, bad, better, worse, because, if you choose the example of what we Polish have in our pockets and in our shops, then I answer that Communism has done very little for us. If you choose the example of what is in our souls, instead, I answer that Communism has done very much for us. In fact our souls contain exactly the contrary of what they wanted. They wanted us not to believe in God and our churches are full. They wanted us to be materialistic and incapable of sacrifices: we are anti-materialistic, capable of sacrifice. They wanted us to be afraid of the tanks, of the guns, and instead we don't fear them at all.

LECH WALESA (1943–), Polish trade-union leader: *The Sunday Times, 22 March 1981*

Marxism is the opium of the intellectuals.

EDMUND WILSON (1895–1972), American writer and literary critic

Economics & Economists

'Do you have anything on economics?' asked a colleague in his local bookshop. 'Over there,' replied the assistant, 'beyond fiction.'

ANON: *Financial Times, 9 November 1981*

Economists are people who work with numbers but don't have the personality to be accountants.

ANON

When better business decisions are made, economists won't make them.

ANON

Economists are pessimists: they've predicted eight of the last three depressions.

BARRY ASMUS, American economist and public speaker

But the age of chivalry is gone. That of sophisters, economists, and calculators, has succeeded; and the glory of Europe is extinguished for ever.

EDMUND BURKE (1729–97), British statesman, orator and writer: *Reflections on the Revolution in France*

Of political economy:
Respectable Professors of the Dismal Science.

THOMAS CARLYLE (1795–1881), Scottish essayist and historian: *Latter-Day Pamphlets, 1, 'The Present Time'*

Other Things Being Equal – One of the old-time greats in economics; you can generally tell whether a man is an economist by the number of times he uses this particular phrase.

WILLIAM DAVIS (1933–), author, columnist and broadcaster

In all recorded history there has not been one economist who has had to worry about where the next meal would come from.

PETER F. DRUCKER (1909–2005), American management expert

Ask five economists and you'll get five different explanations (six if one went to Harvard).

EDGAR R. FIEDLER (?1930–2003), American economist: quoted in *Quotations with an Attitude*

All races have produced notable economists, with the exception of the Irish who doubtless can protest their devotion to higher arts.

JOHN KENNETH GALBRAITH (1908–2006), Canadian-born American economist, diplomat, and writer: *The Age of Uncertainty, chapter 1*

It takes a certain brashness to attack the accepted economic legends but none at all to perpetuate them. So they are perpetuated.

JOHN KENNETH GALBRAITH: *The Liberal Hour*

Perhaps it is a sense of history that divides good economics from bad.

JOHN KENNETH GALBRAITH: *The Age of Uncertainty, broadcast version*

There is much of economic theory which is pursued for no better reason than its intellectual attraction; it is a good game. We have no reason to be ashamed of that, since the same would hold for many branches of mathematics.

SIR JOHN RICHARD HICKS (1904–89), British economist: *Causality in Economics*

Please find me a one-armed economist so we will not always hear, 'On the other hand …'

HERBERT (CLARK) HOOVER (1894–1964), American statesman and president (Attributed)

The theory of economics must begin with a correct theory of consumption.

WILLIAM STANLEY JEVONS (1835–82), English economist and logician: *Theory of Political Economy, chapter 3*

Did you ever think that making a speech on economics is a lot like pissing down your leg? It seems hot to you, but it never does to anyone else.

LYNDON B(AINES) JOHNSON (1908–73), American president

If economists were any good at business, they would be rich men instead of advisers to rich men.

KIRK KERKORIAN (1917–): quoted in Robert W. Kent, *Money Talks*

But … do not let us overestimate the importance of the economic problem, or sacrifice to its supposed necessities other matters of greater and more permanent significance. It should be a matter for specialists – like dentistry. If economists could manage to get themselves thought of as humble, competent people, on a level with dentists, that would be splendid!

JOHN MAYNARD KEYNES (1883–1946), English economist: *Essays in Persuasion*, Part 5

The ideas of economists and political philosophers, both when they are right and when they are wrong, are more powerful than is commonly understood. Indeed the world is ruled by little else. Practical men, who believe themselves to be quite exempt from any intellectual influences, are usually the slaves of some defunct economist.

JOHN MAYNARD KEYNES: *General Theory of Employment, book 6*

Economics is a subject that does not greatly respect one's wishes.

NIKITA (SERGEYEVICH) KHRUSHCHEV (1894–1971), Soviet statesman and premier

An economist is an expert who will know tomorrow why the things he predicted yesterday didn't happen today.

DR LAURENCE J. PETER (1919–90), Canadian educator: *Peter's Quotations*

Government's view of the economy could be summed up in a few short phrases: If it moves, tax it. If it keeps moving, regulate it. And if it stops moving, subsidise it.

RONALD REAGAN (1911–2004), American president

If all economists were laid end to end, they would not reach a conclusion.

GEORGE BERNARD SHAW (1856–1950), Irish dramatist and critic (Attributed)

The first lesson of economics is scarcity: There is never enough of anything to satisfy all those who want it. The first lesson of politics is to disregard the first lesson of economics.

THOMAS SOWELL (1930–), American economist and writer

Prime Minister:
Yes. It's all very simple. I want you to abolish economists … Yes, all of them. They never agree on anything. They just fill the heads of politicians with all sorts of curious notions, like the more you spend, the richer you get.

MARGARET (HILDA) THATCHER (1925–), English politician and prime minister: *Yes (Prime) Minister sketch, The National Viewers' and Listeners' Association Award Presentation, 20 January 1984*

The economists are generally right in their predictions, but generally a good deal out in their dates.

SIDNEY (JAMES) WEBB, Baron Passfield (1859–1947), English economist and social historian: *Observer, 'Sayings of the Week', 25 February 1924*

Materialism

Materialism is decadent and degenerate only if the spirit of the nation has withered and if individual people are so unimaginative that they wallow in it.

(JUSTIN) BROOKS ATKINSON (1894–1984), American dramatic critic and essayist: *Once Around the Sun*

No social system will bring us happiness, health and prosperity unless it is inspired by something greater than materialism.

CLEMENT RICHARD ATTLEE, 1st Earl Attlee (1883–1967), English statesman and prime minister

Ye cannot serve God and mammon.

The Bible, Authorised (King James) Version, Matthew 6:24

Our life on earth is, and ought to be, material and carnal. But we have not yet learned to manage our materialism and carnality properly; they are still entangled with the desire for ownership.

E(DWARD) M(ORGAN) FORSTER (1879–1970), English novelist: *Abinger Harvest*

Some men worship rank, some worship heroes, some worship power, some worship God, and over these ideals they dispute – but they all worship money.

MARK TWAIN (Samuel Langhorne Clemens) (1835–1910), American novelist and humorist: *Notebook*

Mathematics

Maths is like love – a simple idea but it can get complicated.

ANON

Of decimal points:
I never could make out what those damned dots meant.

LORD RANDOLPH SPENCER CHURCHILL (1849–95), English statesman: quoted in W. S. Churchill, *Lord Randolph Churchill, volume 1*

As far as the laws of mathematics refer to reality, they are not certain; and as far as they are certain, they do not refer to reality.

ALBERT EINSTEIN (1879–1955), German-Swiss-American physicist

To count is a modern practice, the ancient method was to guess; and when numbers are guessed they are always magnified.

SAMUEL JOHNSON (1709–84), English lexicographer, essayist and poet: *A Journey to the Western Islands of Scotland*

The chief use of pure mathematics in economic questions seems to be in helping a person to write down quickly, shortly and exactly, some of his thoughts for his own use: and make sure that he has enough and only enough premises for his conclusions (i.e. that his equations are neither more nor less in number than his unknowns).

ALFRED MARSHALL (1842–1924), English classical economist: *Principles of Economics*

Mathematics contains much that will neither hurt one if one does not know it nor help one if one does know it.

JOHANN BURKHARD MENCKE (1674–1732), historian: *De charlataneria eruditorum*

Moriarty:
How are you at Mathematics?

H.S.:
I speak it like a native.

SPIKE MILLIGAN (1918–2002), Irish comedian: *The Goon Show, 'Dishonoured'*

Mathematics may be defined as the subject in which we never know what we are talking about, nor whether what we are saying is true.

BERTRAND (ARTHUR WILLIAM) RUSSELL, 3rd Earl Russell (1872–1970), English philosopher and mathematician: *Mysticism and Logic, chapter 4*

Mathematics, rightly viewed, possess not only truth, but supreme beauty – a beauty cold and austere, like that of sculpture.

BERTRAND (ARTHUR WILLIAM) RUSSELL, as above

Politics & Politicians

Being an MP is a good job, the sort of job all working-class parents want for their children – clean, indoors and no heavy lifting. What could be nicer?

DIANE ABBOTT (1953–), British politician: quoted in *A Collection of Quotable Quotes*

Practical politics consists in ignoring facts.
HENRY BROOKS ADAMS (1838–1918), American historian and author

A politician is an animal who can sit on a fence and yet keep both ears to the ground.
ANON

A politician is someone who divides his time between running for office and running for cover.
ANON: quoted in Greg Knight, *Honourable Insults*

Everyone's a socialist – until they're a capitalist.
ANON

The trouble with some of the big guns in politics is that they are of small calibre and are big bores.
ANON: quoted in Greg Knight, *Honourable Insults*

Man is by nature a political animal.
ARISTOTLE (384–322 BC), Greek philosopher and scientist: *Politics*

Nowadays, for the sake of the advantage which is to be gained from the public revenues and from office, men want to be always in office.
ARISTOTLE, as above

To exploit and to govern mean the same thing … Exploitation and government are two inseparable expressions of what is called politics.
MIKHAIL BAKUNIN (1814–76), Russian anarchist and writer: *The Knouto-Germanic Empire and the Social Revolution*

Politics is the art of looking for trouble, finding it whether it exists

or not, diagnosing it incorrectly, and applying the wrong remedy.
SIR ERNEST BENN (1875–1954), British publicist: *Observer, 1930*

Politics:
A strife of interests masquerading as a contest of principles. The conduct of public affairs for private advantage.
AMBROSE (GWINETT) BIERCE (1842–?1914), American journalist and humorist: The Devil's Dictionary

[On John Prescott] John has some great strengths – such as his left hook.
TONY (ANTHONY CHARLES LYNTON) BLAIR (1953–), British prime minister: quoted in *A Collection of Quotable Quotes*

Politics is the art of the possible.
R(ICHARD) A(USTEN) BUTLER, Baron Butler of Saffron Walden (1902–84), British politician: *The Art of the Possible, Epigraph*

If you take yourself seriously in politics, you've had it.
LORD CARRINGTON (1919–), British statesman

I remain just one thing, and one thing only – and that is a clown. It places me on a far higher plane than any politician.
SIR CHARLES CHAPLIN (1889–1977), English comedian, film actor and director: *Observer, 'Sayings of the Week', 17 June 1960*

Political skill:
Of Lord Charles Beresford:
He is one of those orators of whom it was well said, 'Before they get up they do not know what they are going to say; when they are speaking, they do not know what they are saying; and when they sit down, they do not know what they have said.'
SIR WINSTON LEONARD SPENCER CHURCHILL (1874–1965), English statesman, writer and prime minister: *Speech, House of Commons, 20 December 1912*

… is the ability to foretell what is going to happen tomorrow, next week, next month, and next year. And to have the ability afterwards to explain why it didn't happen.

SIR WINSTON LEONARD SPENCER CHURCHILL: quoted in Bill Adler, *The Churchill Wit*

Everything that steel achieves in war can be won in politics by eloquence.

DEMETRIUS OF PHALERUM (345–280 BC), Greek orator and statesman: quoted in *Diogenes Laertius, Lives and Opinions of Eminent Philosophers*

That fabulous animal formally called 'economic policy' and more familiarly called political interference.

G. A. DUNCAN: *Economic Journal, December 1961*

Government has come to be a trade, and is managed solely on commercial principles. A man plunges into politics to make his fortune, and only cares that the world shall last his days.

RALPH WALDO EMERSON (1803–82), American poet, essayist and philosopher: *Letters to Thomas Carlyle, 7 October 1835*

The first mistake in public business is the going into it.

BENJAMIN FRANKLIN (1706–90), American statesman, scientist and author: *Poor Richard's Almanac*

Politics is not the art of the possible. It consists in choosing between the disastrous and the unpalatable.

JOHN KENNETH GALBRAITH (1908–2006), Canadian-born American economist, diplomat and writer: *Ambassador's Journal*

There are times in politics when you must be on the right side and lose.

JOHN KENNETH GALBRAITH: *Observer, 'Sayings of the Year', 29 December 1968*

There are two problems in my life. The political ones are insoluble and the economic ones are incomprehensible.

SIR ALEC DOUGLAS-HOME, Lord Home of Hirsel (1903–95), British statesman and prime minister: *Speech, January 1964*

Green politics is not about being far left or far right, but far-sighted.

DAVID ICKE (1952–), former sportsman and conspiracy theorist

Doing what's right isn't the problem. It's knowing what's right.

LYNDON B(AINES) JOHNSON (1908–73), American statesman and president

There is a holy, mistaken zeal in politics, as well as religion. By persuading others we convince ourselves.

JUNIUS, pseudonym of an anonymous writer to the London Public Advertiser, 1768–1772: *Letter 35, 19 December 1769*

Politicians are the same all over. They promise to build a bridge even when there's no river.

NIKITA (SERGEYEVICH) KHRUSHCHEV (1894–1971), Soviet statesman and premier: *Remark at Glen Cove, New York, 1960*

Politics is who gets what, when, how.

HAROLD LASSWELL (1902–78), American political economist: *Politics: Who Gets What, When, How*

A politician must often talk and act before he has thought and read. He may be very ill-informed respecting a question; all his notions about it may be vague and inaccurate; but speak he must; and if he is a man of talents, of tact, and of intrepidity, he soon finds that, even under such circumstances, it is possible to speak successfully.

THOMAS BABINGTON MACAULAY (1800–59), English historian, essayist and statesman: *Edinburgh Review, April 1839, 'Gladstone on Church and State'*

Politics offers yesterday's answers to today's problems.

(HERBERT) MARSHALL MCLUHAN (1911–80), Canadian educator, author and media expert

When you're abroad, you're a statesman; when you're at home you're just a politician.

SIR (MAURICE) HAROLD MACMILLAN, Earl of Stockton (1894–1986), British statesman and prime minister: *Speech, 1958*

When it comes to the crunch, the trade unions will put their arms around Mr Kinnock's shoulders and say 'Neil'. And he will, he will.

JOHN MAJOR (1943–), British prime minister: quoted in E. Webber, *The Book of Business Quotations*

Lear:
Get thee glass eyes,
And, like a scurvy politician, seem
To see the things thou dost not.

WILLIAM SHAKESPEARE (1564–1616), English dramatist and poet: *King Lear, Act 4*

He knows nothing and he thinks he knows everything. That points clearly to a political career.

GEORGE BERNARD SHAW (1856–1950), Irish dramatist and critic: *Major Barbara*

The first lesson of economics is scarcity: There is never enough of anything to satisfy all those who want it. The first lesson of politics is to disregard the first lesson of economics.

THOMAS SOWELL (1930–), American economist and writer

Politics is perhaps the only profession for which no preparation is thought necessary.

ROBERT LOUIS BALFOUR STEVENSON (1850–94), Scottish writer

Politics, as the word is commonly understood, are nothing but corruptions.

JONATHAN SWIFT: *Thoughts on Various Subjects*

Political principles resemble military tactics; they are usually designed for a war which is over.

R(ICHARD) H(ENRY) TAWNEY (1880–1962), English economic historian: *Equality*

[Prior to 1992 general election] I think Essex man will vote for a Conservative government.

MARGARET (HILDA) THATCHER (1925–), English politician and prime minister

A politician is a man who understands government, and it takes a politician to run a government. A statesman is a politician who's been dead ten or fifteen years.

HARRY S. TRUMAN (1884–1972), American statesman and president: *New York World Telegram and Sun, 12 April 1958*

A week is a long time in politics.

SIR (JAMES) HAROLD WILSON, Lord Wilson of Rievaulx (1916–95), English statesman and prime minister

Socialism

Under capitalism man exploits man; under socialism, it's just the opposite.

ANON

Never confuse socialism with trade unionism.

ANEURIN BEVAN (1897–1960), British statesman: quoted by Paul Johnson, *Observer, 11 September 1977*

Capitalism is using its money; we socialists throw it away.

FIDEL CASTRO (RUZ) (1927–), Cuban statesman: *Observer, 'Sayings of the Year', 27 December 1964*

We are all Socialists nowadays.

KING EDWARD VII (1841–1910): *Speech, Mansion House, London, 1895*

The purpose of the socialist society is the happiness of man, which can be realised only through material and spiritual freedom. Attainment of such freedom depends on the extent of man's ownership of his needs, ownership that is personal and sacredly guaranteed.

MOAMAR AL GADDAFI (1942–), Libyan army officer and statesman: *The Green Book*

The Third Theory is founded upon socialism ... With the Communist system on one side and the capitalist system on the other, we must try to find a 'Third System' which would be equally different from either. For while capitalism, by handing over the reins to the individual without any restraints, has transformed society into a sort of circus, communism's claim to solve economic problems by the total and final abolishing of private property has ended by turning individual human beings into sheep.

MOAMAR AL GADDAFI: quoted in M. Bianco, *Gaddafi, Voice from the Desert, Part 3*

There is a popular cliché, deeply beloved by conservatives, that socialism and communism are the cause of a low standard of living. It is much more nearly accurate to say that a low and simple standard of living makes socialism and communism feasible.

JOHN KENNETH GALBRAITH (1908–2006), Canadian-born American economist, diplomat and writer: *American Capitalism, chapter 12*

The ideal of Socialism is grand and noble; and it is, I am convinced, possible of realization; but such a state of society cannot be manufactured – it must grow. Society is an organism, not a machine.

HENRY GEORGE (1839–97), American economist: *Progress and Poverty*

More socialism means more democracy, openness and collectivism in everyday life.

MIKHAIL GORBACHEV (1931–), Russian politician, Nobel Peace Prize winner 1990

Can you imagine lying in bed on a Sunday morning with the love of your life, a cup of tea and a bacon sandwich, and all you had to read was the Socialist Worker?

DEREK JAMESON (1929–), British journalist and broadcaster

The main tenet of Socialism, namely, the community of goods, must be rejected without qualification, for it would injure those it pretends to benefit, it would be contrary to the natural rights of man, and it would introduce confusion and disorder into the commonwealth.

POPE LEO XIII (Gioacchino Pecci) (1810–1903): *Rerum novarum, 15 May 1891*

The function of socialism is to raise suffering to a higher level.

NORMAN MAILER (1923–), American novelist and playwright

Socialism is simply communism for people without the testosterone to man the barricades.

GARY NORTH (1942–), American writer

To the ordinary working man, the sort you would meet in any pub on Saturday night, Socialism does not mean much more than better wages and shorter hours and nobody bossing you about.

GEORGE ORWELL (Eric Arthur Blair) (1903–50), English novelist and essayist: *The Road to Wigan Pier*

Socialism means equality of income or nothing.

GEORGE BERNARD SHAW (1856–1950), Irish dramatist and critic: *The Intelligent Woman's Guide to Socialism, Capitalism, Sovietism and Fascism, Appendix*

Socialism is nothing but the capitalism of the lower classes.

OSWALD SPENGLER (1880–1936), German philosopher of history

The temporary victory of Socialism in one country alone is possible, but its lasting victory in one country alone is impossible: that demands the victory of the revolution in other lands as well.

JOSEPH STALIN (Iosif Vissarionovich Dzhugashvili) (1879–1953), Soviet premier: *Leninism*

Statistics

Any figure that looks interesting is probably wrong.

ANON

If you just torture the data long enough, they will confess.

ANON

Statistician:
A man who can go directly from an unwarranted assumption to a preconceived conclusion.

ANON

On the reason for the War Office's keeping three sets of figures:

One to mislead the public, another to mislead the Cabinet, and the third to mislead itself.

HERBERT HENRY ASQUITH, 1st Earl of Oxford and Asquith (1852–1928), English statesman and prime minister: quoted in Alastair Home, *The Price of Glory*

Statistics are the triumph of the quantitative method, and the quantitative method is the victory of sterility and death.

(JOSEPH) HILAIRE (PIERRE) BELLOC (1870–1953), Anglo-French author

A witty statesman said, you might prove anything by figures.

THOMAS CARLYLE (1795–1881), Scottish essayist and historian: *Chartism*

Statistics is a science which ought to be honourable, the basis of many most important sciences, but it is not to be carried on by steam, this science, any more than others are; a wise head is requisite for carrying it on. Conclusive facts are inseparable from inconclusive except by a head that already understands and knows.

THOMAS CARLYLE, as above

It is now proved beyond doubt that smoking is one of the leading causes of statistics.

FLETCHER KNEBEL (1911–93), American journalist and writer: quoted in *Reader's Digest, December 1961*

Statistics are like a bikini. What they reveal is suggestive, but what they conceal is vital.

AARON LEVENSTEIN (?1911–86), American business expert

You cannot feed the hungry on statistics.

DAVID LLOYD GEORGE, 1st Earl Lloyd George of Dwyfor (1863–1945), Welsh politician and British prime minister: *Speech, 1904*

There are two kinds of statistics, the kind you look up and the kind you make up.

REX STOUT (1886–1975), American writer: *Death of a Doxy*

There are three kinds of lies: lies, damned lies, and statistics.

MARK TWAIN (Samuel Langhorne Clemens) (1835–1910), American novelist and humorist: *Autobiography*

Trade & Commerce

'The average man finds life very uninteresting as it is. And I think that the reason why … is that he is always waiting for something to happen to him instead of setting to work to make things happen' (A. A. Milne). How can you make the most of opportunities that present themselves? What is the 'established wisdom' on selling? What are the effects of monopoly or competition? In this section we turn to quotations on the market-place: to buying and selling, international trade, and the laws of supply and demand: 'A fair price … is whatever you can get plus ten per cent' (Dr Ali Ahmed Attiga), the proverbial, 'The customer is always right', and 'While the sand is yet on your feet, sell' (The Talmud).

Agriculture

Farming looks mighty easy when your plow is a pencil, and you're a thousand miles from the corn field.
DWIGHT D(AVID) EISENHOWER (1890–1969), American general and president: *Speech, Peoria, Illinois, 25 September 1956*

The agricultural class is the least of all disposed to innovation, and the most peculiarly attached to ancient customs and routine.
JOHN RAMSEY MCCULLOCH (1789–1864), Scottish economist, statistician and writer: *Principles of Political Economy, Part 3*

I know of no pursuit in which more real and important services can be rendered to any country than by improving its agriculture, its breed of useful animals, and other branches of a husbandman's cares.
GEORGE WASHINGTON (1732–99), American statesman and president: *Letter to John Sinclair, 20 July 1794*

Each equal additional quantity of work bestowed on agriculture, yields an actual diminished return.

SIR EDWARD WEST (1782–1828): *Essay on the Application of Capital to Land*

A good farmer is nothing more nor less than a handy man with a sense of humus.

E(LWYN) B(ROOKS) WHITE (1899–1985), American humorist and essayist: *One Man's Meat, 'The Practical Farmer'*

Bargains

Here's the rule for bargains: 'Do other men, for they would do you.' That's the true business precept.

CHARLES (JOHN HUFFAM) DICKENS (1812–70), English novelist: *Martin Chuzzlewit*

A bargain is something you have to find a use for once you have bought it.

BENJAMIN FRANKLIN (1706–90), American statesman, scientist and author (Attributed)

Looking at bargains from a purely commercial point of view, someone is always cheated, but looked at with the simple eye both seller and buyer always win.

DAVID GRAYSON (Ray Stannard Baker) (1870–1946), American journalist, biographer and essayist: *Adventures in Contentment*

Bargains made in speed are commonly repented at leisure.

GEORGE PETTIE (1548–89), English writer: *Petite Palace of Pettie His Pleasure*

A miser and a liar bargain quickly.

PROVERB

Bargain like a gipsy, but pay like a gentleman.

PROVERB

It's a bad bargain where nobody gains.
PROVERB

Buying & Selling

Anyone who has to ask the cost can't afford it.
ANON

As a writer I have always been keenly interested in the very
impressive phenomenon of the big departmental store, regarded
either as a picturesque spectacle, or as a living organism, or as a
sociological portent. I am all in favour of the department store; I
cannot keep my eyes off its window-displays, its crowds of
customers, its army of employees.
(ENOCH) ARNOLD BENNETT (1867–1931), English novelist

There is no such thing as 'soft sell' and 'hard sell'. There is only
'smart sell' and 'stupid sell'.
CHARLES (HENDRICKSON) BROWER (1901–84), American advertising
executive: *News reports, 20 May 1958*

The customer's always right, my boys,
The customer's always right.
The son-of-a-bitch
Is probably rich
So smile with all your might.
SIR NOËL (PIERCE) COWARD (1899–1973), English actor and dramatist: *Sail
Away*

It is well known what a middleman is: he is a man who
bamboozles one party and plunders the other.
BENJAMIN DISRAELI, 1st Earl of Beaconsfield (1804–81), English statesman,
prime minister and novelist: *Speech, 11 April 1845*

A budget tells us what we can't afford, but it doesn't keep us from buying it.

WILLIAM FEATHER (1889–1981), American businessman: *The Business of Life*

A market is never saturated with a good product, but it is very quickly saturated with a bad one.

HENRY FORD (1863–1947), American car manufacturer

Man does not only sell commodities, he sells himself and feels himself to be a commodity.

ERICH FROMM (1900–80), German-born American psychoanalyst and philosopher: *Escape from Freedom*

I'm not asset stripping ... I prefer to think of it as unbundling.

SIR JAMES GOLDSMITH (1933–97): *Financial Times, 'Business Quotes of the Year', 30 December 1989*

When a man is trying to sell you something, don't imagine he is that polite all the time.

EDGAR WATSON HOWE (1853–1937), American journalist, novelist and essayist: *Country Town Sayings*

It will be the unwitting customers who, as always when countries indulge in protectionism, end up having to pay more money.

SIR DIGBY JONES (1955–), trade and investment minister, Director, CBI

The farmer is the only man in our economy who buys everything he buys at retail, sells everything he sells at wholesale, and pays the freight both ways.

JOHN FITZGERALD KENNEDY (1917–63), American statesman and president: *Speech, 22 September 1960*

Give a man a fish and he will eat for a day. Teach a man to fish and he will eat for a lifetime. Teach a man to create an artificial

shortage of fish and he will eat steak.
JAY LENO (1950–), American comedian

People don't want to be 'marketed TO'; they want to be
'communicated WITH'.
FLINT MCGLAUGHLIN, American marketing writer

Caveat emptor.
Let the buyer beware.
MAXIM

I never tell one client that I cannot attend his sales convention
because I have a previous engagement with another client;
successful polygamy depends upon pretending to each spouse
that she is the only pebble on your beach.
DAVID OGILVY (1911–99), British advertising executive

There are more fools among buyers than among sellers.
PROVERB

A man without a smiling face must not open a shop.
CHINESE PROVERB

When you go to buy, don't show your silver.
CHINESE PROVERB

In marketing I've seen only one strategy that can't miss – and
that is to market to your best customers first, your best prospects
second and the rest of the world last.
JOHN ROMERO (1967–), American game designer and programmer

Every one lives by selling something.
ROBERT LOUIS BALFOUR STEVENSON (1850–94), Scottish writer: *Across the Plains*

While the sand is yet on your feet, sell.
The Talmud

Because I cannot 'afford to buy' a thing it does not follow that I have less need of it or less desire to have it than another man who can and does afford it.
PHILIP H. WICKSTEED (1844–1927): *Alphabet of Economic Science*

For every sale you miss because you're too enthusiastic, you will miss a hundred because you're not enthusiastic enough.
ZIG ZIGLAR (1926–), American author and motivational speaker

Choice

The strongest principle of growth lies in human choice.
GEORGE ELIOT (Mary Ann Evans) (1819–90), English novelist: *Daniel Deronda*

It is your own conviction which compels you; that is, choice compels choice.
EPICTETUS (?AD 50–?120), Greek philosopher: *Discourses*

Of the colours available on the Model T Ford car:
Any colour, so long as it's black.
HENRY FORD (1863–1947), American car manufacturer (Attributed)

No choice among stinking fish.
THOMAS FULLER (1654–1734), English physician, writer and compiler: *Gnomologia*

You pays your money and you takes your choice.
Punch, 1846

Partisanship is our great curse. We too readily assume that

everything has two sides and that it is our duty to be on one or the other.

JAMES HARVEY ROBINSON (1863–1936), American historian and educator: *The Mind in the Making*

Commerce is the agency by which the power of choice is obtained.

JOHN RUSKIN (1819–1900), English art critic and social reformer: *Munera pulveris*

Even children learn in growing up that 'both' is not an admissible answer to a choice of 'which one?'

PAUL ANTHONY SAMUELSON (1915–), American economist: *Economics*

Cities

To some extent, if you've seen one city slum you've seen them all.

SPIRO T. AGNEW (1918–96), American vice-president: *Speech, Detroit, 18 October 1968*

A great city is not to be confounded with a populous one.

ARISTOTLE (384–322 BC), Greek philosopher and scientist: *Politics*

The building of cities is one of man's greatest achievements. The form of his city always has been and always will be a pitiless indicator of the state of his civilisation.

EDMUND N. BACON (1910–2005): *Contemporary Architects*

It is much more difficult to develop a city than to send a man to the moon.

PROFESSOR COLIN BUCHANAN (1907–2001), transport and planning consultant: *Observer, 'Sayings of the Decade', 28 December 1969*

Of Los Angeles:
A city with all the personality of a paper cup.

RAYMOND CHANDLER (1888–1959), American thriller writer

If you would be known, and not know, vegetate in a village; if you would know, and not be known, live in a city.
CHARLES CALEB COLTON (?1780–1832), English clergyman and writer: *Lacon*

In great cities men are more callous both to the happiness and the misery of others ... for they are constantly in the habit of seeing both extremes.
CHARLES CALEB COLTON, as above

New York, New York! It's a wonderful town! The west side of the island was rich in facades not unlike the possibilities of a fairy princess with syphilis.
RICHARD CONDON (1915–96), American novelist: *The Manchurian Candidate, chapter 11*

No city should be too large for a man to walk out of in a morning.
CYRIL (VERNON) CONNOLLY (1903–74), English essayist, critic and novelist: *The Unquiet Grave, chapter 1*

Cities give us collision. London and New York take the nonsense out of man.
RALPH WALDO EMERSON (1803–82), American poet, essayist and philosopher: *The Conduct of Life*

'Tis the men, not the houses, that make the city.
THOMAS FULLER (1654–1734), English physician, writer and compiler: *Gnomologia*

Of London:
Crowds without company, and dissipation without pleasure.
EDWARD GIBBON (1737–94), English historian: *Autobiography*

In the country we forget the town, and in town we despise the country.
WILLIAM HAZLITT (1778–1830), English essayist: *Table Talk, 'On Going a Journey'*

Great cities seldom rest: if there be none
T'invade from far, they'll find worse foes at home.

ROBERT HERRICK (1591–1674), English poet: *Hesperides*

You find no man, at all intellectual, who is willing to leave
London. No Sir, when a man is tired of London, he is tired of
life; for there is in London all that life can afford.

SAMUEL JOHNSON (1709–84), English lexicographer, essayist and poet:
quoted in James Boswell, *The Life of Samuel Johnson*

The city has a face, the country a soul.

JACQUES DE LACRETELLE (1888–1985), French novelist: *Idées dans un chapeau*

I have an affection for a great city. I feel safe in the neighborhood
of man, and enjoy the sweet security of the streets.

HENRY WADSWORTH LONGFELLOW (1807–82), American poet and
translator: *Driftwood*

In great cities men are like a lot of stones thrown together in a
bag; their jagged corners are rubbed off till in the end they are as
smooth as marbles.

W(ILLIAM) SOMERSET MAUGHAM (1874–1965), English writer: *The Summing Up*

Towered cities please us then,
And the busy hum of men.

JOHN MILTON (1608–74), English poet: *L'Allegro*

A commuter is one who never knows how a show comes out
because he has to leave early to catch a train to get him back to
the country in time to catch a train to bring him back to the city.

OGDEN NASH (1902–71), American humorous poet: *Versus*, 'The Banker's Special'

Of Los Angeles:
Seventy-two suburbs in search of a city.
DOROTHY (ROTHSCHILD) PARKER (1893–1967), American writer

Any city, however small, is in fact divided into two, one the city of the poor, the other of the rich; these are at war with one another.
PLATO (?427–?347 BC), Greek philosopher: *The Republic*

Cities are the abyss of the human species. At the end of a few generations in them races perish or degenerate, and it is necessary to renew them. This renewal always comes from the country.
JEAN-JACQUES ROUSSEAU (1712–78), Swiss-born French philosopher and writer: *Émile*

The people are the city.
WILLIAM SHAKESPEARE (1564–1616), English dramatist and poet: *Coriolanus, Act 3*

A city is like a magnet – the bigger it is, the greater the drawing power.
SAMUEL TENENBAUM, American academic: *The New York Times, 1971*

Commerce & Trade

Money is the measure of commerce.
NICHOLAS BARBON (?–1698): *Discourse Concerning Coining the New Money Lighter*

The commerce of the world is conducted by the strong, and usually it operates against the weak.
HENRY WARD BEECHER (1813–87), American clergyman, editor and writer: *Proverbs from Plymouth Pulpit*

Commerce:
A kind of transaction in which A plunders from B the goods of C, and for compensation B picks the pocket of D of money belonging to E.

AMBROSE (GWINETT) BIERCE (1842–?1914), American journalist and humorist: *The Devil's Dictionary*

Commerce is the grand panacea, which, like a beneficent medical discovery, will serve to inoculate with the healthy and saving taste for civilisation all the nations of the world.

RICHARD COBDEN (1804–65), English economist and statesman: *England, Ireland and America*

No nation was ever ruined by trade.

BENJAMIN FRANKLIN (1706–90), American statesman, scientist and author: *Thoughts on Commercial Subjects*

Honour sinks where commerce long prevails.

OLIVER GOLDSMITH (?1728–74), Irish dramatist, novelist and poet: *The Traveller*

Commerce is the art of exploiting the need or desire someone has for something.

EDMOND (LOUIS ANTOINE HUOT) DE GONCOURT (1822–96) and JULES (ALFRED HUOT) DE GONCOURT (1830–70), French writers and collaborators: *Journal, July 1864*

Trade could not be managed by those who manage it if it had much difficulty.

SAMUEL JOHNSON (1709–34), English lexicographer, essayist and poet: *Letter to Hester Thrale, 16 November 1779*

Wealth depends upon commerce, and commerce depends upon circulation.

JOHN LAW (1671–1729), Scottish financier: *Money and Trade Considered*

Trade is the mother of money.

PROVERB

In democracies, nothing is more great or more brilliant than commerce: it attracts the attention of the public, and fills the imagination of the multitude; all energetic passions are directed towards it.

ALEX (CHARLES HENRI MAURICE CLÉREL) DE TOCQUEVILLE (1805–59), French politician and political writer: *Democracy in America*

I am a bad Englishman, because I think the advantages of commerce are dearly bought for some by the lives of many more.

HORACE WALPOLE, 4th Earl of Orford (1717–97), English writer and historian: *Letter to Horace Mann, 26 May 1762*

Competition

Free competition tends to give to labor what labor creates, to capitalists what capital creates, and to entrepreneurs what the coordinating function creates.

JOHN BATES CLARK (1847–1938), American economist and professor: *The Distribution of Wealth*

Competition means decentralized planning by many separate persons.

FRIEDRICH AUGUST VON HAYEK (1899–1992), Czechoslovakian economist: *The Use of Knowledge in Society, in Individualism and Economic Order*

Planning and competition can be combined only by planning for competition, but not by planning against competition.

FRIEDRICH AUGUST VON HAYEK: *The Road to Serfdom, chapter 3*

Potter is potter's enemy, and craftsman is craftsman's rival; tramp is jealous of tramp, and singer of singer.

HESIOD (c. 700 BC), Greek poet: *Works and Days*

Price-cutting and rebating, collecting information on the trade of competitors, the operation of companies under other names to obviate prejudice or secure an advantage, or for whatever reason, are all legitimate methods of competition, whatever moral criticism they may justify. There is no rule of fairness or reasonableness which regulates competition.

JOHN G. JOHNSON and JOHN G. MILBURN: *Brief for the Standard Oil Company, filed in the US Circuit Court, St Louis, 1909*

The very essence of competitive commerce is waste; the waste that comes of the anarchy of war.

WILLIAM MORRIS (1834–96), English writer and social reformer: *Art under Plutocracy*

Free competition, though within its limits it is productive of good results, cannot be the ruling principle of the economic world. It is necessary that economic affairs be brought once more into subjection to a true and effective guiding principle.

POPE PIUS XI (Achille Ratti) (1857–1939), Italian ecclesiastic and pope: *Quadragesimo anno, 15 May 1931*

Monopolies, trade unions, political parties, arise out of the very process of competition and prevent it from being effective as a mechanism for ensuring the general good.

JOAN VIOLET ROBINSON (1903–83), English economist: *Marx, Marshall and Keynes*

Consumers & Consumption

The public! How many fools does it take to make a public?

SÉBASTIEN ROCH NICOLAS CHAMFORT (1741–94), French writer

The customer is an object to be manipulated, not a concrete person whose aims the businessman is interested to satisfy.

ERICH FROMM (1900–80), German-born American psychoanalyst and philosopher: *Escape from Freedom*

Consumer wants can have bizarre, frivolous, or even immoral origins, and an admirable case can still be made for a society that seeks to satisfy them. But the case cannot stand if it is the process of satisfying wants that creates the wants.

JOHN KENNETH GALBRAITH (1908–2006), Canadian-born American economist, diplomat and writer: *The Affluent Society*

The urge to consume is fathered by the value system which emphasizes the ability of the society to produce.

JOHN KENNETH GALBRAITH, as above

The root-evil of depressed trade is under-consumption.

JOHN ATKINSON HOBSON (1858–1940), British economist and author: *The Evolution of Modern Capitalism, chapter 11*

The consumer today is the victim of the manufacturer who launches on him a regiment of products for which he must make room in his soul.

MARY (THERESE) MCCARTHY (1912–89), American novelist and critic: *On the Contrary*

Consumption, in the sense in which the word is used in this science, is synonymous with use; and is, in fact, the great end and object of industry.

JOHN RAMSEY MCCULLOCH (1789–1864), Scottish economist, statistician and writer: *Principles of Political Economy, Part 4*

If men ceased to consume, they would cease to produce.

DAVID RICARDO (1772–1823), English economist: *Principles of Political Economy and Taxation, chapter 21*

The consumer, so it is said, is the king ... each is a voter who uses his money as votes to get the things done that he wants done.

PAUL ANTHONY SAMUELSON (1915–), American economist: *Economics*

To found a great empire for the sole purpose of raising up a people of customers may at first sight appear a project fit only for a nation of shopkeepers. It is, however, a project altogether unfit for a nation of shopkeepers; but extremely fit for a nation that is governed by shopkeepers.

ADAM SMITH (1723–90), Scottish economist and philosopher: *The Wealth of Nations*

Corporations

Corporation:
An ingenious device for obtaining individual profit without individual responsibility.

AMBROSE (GWINETT) BIERCE (1842–?1914), American journalist and humorist: *The Devil's Dictionary*

A nearly ideal condition would be that in which, in every department of industry, there should be one great corporation, working without friction and with enormous economy, and compelled to give to the public the full benefit of that economy.

JOHN BATES CLARK (1847–1938), American economist and professor: *The Control of Trusts*

Corporations cannot commit treason, nor be outlawed nor excommunicated, for they have no souls.

SIR EDWARD COKE (1552–1634), English jurist: *Case of Sutton's Hospital*

Corporations are invisible, immortal and have no soul.

ROGER MANWOOD (1525–93), Chief Baron of the English Exchequer
(Attributed)

A corporation is an artificial being, invisible, intangible, and
existing only in contemplation of the law.

JOHN MARSHALL (1755–1835), American jurist and Chief Justice of US
Supreme Court: *Trustees of Dartmouth College v. Woodward, US Supreme Court*

History proves that, owing to a change in social conditions,
functions that were once performed by small bodies can be
performed today only by large corporations. Nevertheless, just as
it is wrong to take from the individual and commit to the
community functions that private enterprise and industry can
perform, so it is an injustice, a grave evil and a violation of right
order for a large organization to arrogate to itself functions
which could be performed efficiently by smaller ones.

POPE PIUS XI (Achille Ratti) (1857–1939), Italian ecclesiastic and pope:
Quadragesimo anno, 15 May 1931

Did you ever expect a corporation to have a conscience, when it
has no soul to be damned, and no body to be kicked?

LORD THURLOW, Edward, 1st Baron of (1731–1806), English lawyer and Lord
Chancellor (Attributed)

Fair Trade

Fair Trade supports some of the most bio-diverse farming
systems in the world. When you visit a Fair Trade coffee grower's
fields, with the forest canopy overhead and the sound of
migratory songbirds in the air, it feels like you're standing in the
rainforest.

MIGUEL ALTIERI, expert and author on agroecology

It hit me very early on that something was terribly wrong, that I would see silos full of food and supermarkets full of food, and kids starving … In Fair Trade, we see ourselves as this infinitesimal part of the world economy. But somebody's got to come up with an alternative model that says children eating is No. 1.

MEDEA BENJAMIN (1952–), American peace and justice activist

It is very important for you to know that fair trade leads to better roads, better health and better lives for farmers not just in Nicaragua, but around the world.

ROSARIO CASTELLÓN, Nicaraguan advocate of fair trade

We should vigorously promote trade and investment liberalization and facilitation on the basis of mutual trust, further reduce restrictions on export of technologies, and remove trade barriers, so as to create a fair, just, reasonable and open environment for trade.

HU JINTAO (1942–), President of the People's Republic of China

When you buy Fairtrade products you can guarantee that the farmers who have worked hard to grow them get a minimum price. Fairtrade is a way of giving regular support – and enjoying delicious high quality foods at the same time.

EMMA THOMPSON (1959–), British actress

International Relations & Free Trade

If we take care of our imports, our exports will take care of themselves.

ANON

Alliance:

In international politics, the union of two thieves who have their hands so deeply inserted in each other's pocket that they cannot separately plunder a third.

AMBROSE (GWINETT) BIERCE (1842–?1914), American journalist and humorist: *The Devil's Dictionary*

Diplomacy:

The patriotic art of lying for one's country.

AMBROSE (GWINETT) BIERCE, as above

The call for free trade is as unavailing as the cry of a spoiled child for the moon. It never has existed; it never will exist.

HENRY CLAY (1777–1852), American statesman: *Speech in the Senate, 2 February 1832*

Conferences at the top level are always courteous. Name-calling is left to the foreign ministers.

W(ILLIAM) AVERELL HARRIMAN (1891–1986), American businessman and diplomat: *News summaries, 1 August 1955*

I am for free commerce with all nations.

THOMAS JEFFERSON (1743–1826), American statesman and president: *Letter to Elbridge Gerry, 1799*

Free trade, one of the greatest blessings which a government can confer on a people, is in almost every country unpopular.

THOMAS BABINGTON MACAULAY (1800–59), English historian, essayist and statesman: *Essay on Mitford's History of Greece*

There are many things which free trade does passably. There are none which it does absolutely well; for competition is as rife in the career of fraudulent practice as in that of real excellence.

JOHN STUART MILL (1806–73), English philosopher and economist: *Dissertations and Discussions, volume 4, 'Endowments'*

Of the United States:
It is not possible for this nation to be at once politically
internationalist and economically isolationist. This is just as
insane as asking one Siamese twin to high dive while the other
plays the piano.

ADLAI (EWING) STEVENSON (1900–68), American statesman: *Speech, New
Orleans, Louisiana, 10 October 1952*

An ambassador is an honest man sent to lie abroad for the
commonwealth.

SIR HENRY WOTTON (1568–1639), English traveller, diplomatist and poet:
Christopher Fleckmore's autograph album

The Market &
Supply & Demand

The market is totally impartial.

ANON

Good ware makes quick markets.

NICOLAS BRETON (?1555–?1625), English poet and satirist: *Crossing of
Proverbs*

Supply-and-demand, – alas! For what noble work was there ever
yet any audible demand in that poor sense? The man of
Macedonia, speaking in vision to an Apostle Paul, 'Come over
and help us,' did not specify what rate of wages he would give.

THOMAS CARLYLE (1795–1881), Scottish essayist and historian: *Past and
Present*

A friend in the market is better than money in the chest.

THOMAS FULLER (1654–1734), English physician, writer and compiler:
Gnomologia

The market is the best garden.

GEORGE HERBERT (1593–1633), English metaphysical poet: *Outlandish Proverbs*

In the usual and ordinary course of things, the demand for all commodities precedes their supply.

DAVID RICARDO (1772–1823), English economist: *Principles of Political, Economy and Taxation, chapter 32*

Free enterprise ended in the United States a good many years ago. Big oil, big steel, big agriculture avoid the open market place. Big corporations fix prices among themselves and drive out the small entrepreneur. In their conglomerate forms, the huge corporations have begun to challenge the legitimacy of the State.

GORE (EUGENE LUTHER) VIDAL (1925–), American novelist and playwright

Monopoly

How come there's only one Monopolies Commission?

ANON

Monopolistic combination is common enough in all parts of the economic system; very much the same motives which drive business men to form rings and cartels drive their employees to form unions. The one, as much as the other, is a natural product of a gregarious animal.

SIR JOHN RICHARD HICKS (1904–89), British economist: *The Theory of Wages, Part 2*

It is better to abolish monopolies in all cases than not to do it in any.

THOMAS JEFFERSON (1743–1826), American statesman and president: *Letter to James Madison, 1788*

A monopoly is a terrible thing until you've got one.
RUPERT MURDOCH (1931–), Australian-born media executive

[Of the board game] Monopoly does a poor job of demonstrating the benefits of mutually advantageous trade in a market economy.
BENJAMIN POWELL, American economist

Like many businessmen of genius he learned that free competition was wasteful, monopoly efficient.
MARIO PUZO (1920–99), American novelist: *The Godfather*

A monopoly granted either to an individual or to a trading company has the same effect as a secret in trade or manufactures. The monopolists, by keeping the market constantly understocked, by never fully supplying the effectual demand, sell their commodities much above the natural price, and raise their emoluments, whether they consist in wages or profit, greatly above their natural rate.
ADAM SMITH (1723–90), Scottish economist and philosopher: *The Wealth of Nations, volume 1*

Monopoly … is a great enemy to good management.
ADAM SMITH, as above

It is not competition, but monopoly, that deprives labor of its product. Wages, inheritance, gifts and gambling aside, every process by which men acquire wealth rests upon a monopoly, a prohibition, a denial of liberty.
BENJAMIN R. TUCKER (1854–1939), American anarchist: *Why I Am an Anarchist*

Opportunities

The gods help them that help themselves.

AESOP (c.620–564 BC), Greek fabulist: *Fables, 'Hercules and the Wagoner'*

I would rather be an opportunist and float than go to the bottom with my principles round my neck.

STANLEY BALDWIN (1867–1947), British statesman (Attributed)

It is always good
When a man has two irons in the fire.

FRANCIS BEAUMONT (1584–1616) and JOHN FLETCHER (1579–1625),
English dramatists: *The Faithful Friends*

You never know till you try to reach them how accessible men are; but you must approach each man by the right door.

HENRY WARD BEECHER (1813–87), American clergyman, editor and writer:
Proverbs from Plymouth Pulpit

Go around asking a lot of damfool questions and taking chances. Only through curiosity can we discover opportunities, and only by gambling can we take advantage of them.

CLARENCE BIRDSEYE (1886–1956), American industrialist

Next to knowing when to seize an opportunity, the most important thing in life is to know when to forego an advantage.

BENJAMIN DISRAELI (1804–81), British politician

It is folly for a man to pray to the gods for that which he has the power to obtain for himself.

EPICURUS (341–270 BC), Greek philosopher: *Vatican Sayings*

There is one disadvantage which the man of philosophical habits of mind suffers, as compared with the man of action. While he is taking an enlarged and rational view of the matter before him, he lets his chance slip through his fingers.

OLIVER WENDELL HOLMES, SR (1809–94), American physician, professor and author: *The Professor at the Breakfast Table*

We are continuously faced by great opportunities brilliantly disguised as insoluble problems.

LEE IACOCCA (1924–), American industrialist

When one door of happiness closes, another opens; but often we look so long at the closed door that we do not see the one which has been opened for us.

HELEN (ADAMS) KELLER (1880–1968), American author and lecturer: *We Bereaved*

All of us do not have equal talent, but all of us should have an equal opportunity to develop our talents.

JOHN FITZGERALD KENNEDY (1917–63), American statesman and president: *Address, San Diego State College, California, 6 June 1963*

In great affairs we ought to apply ourselves less to creating chances than to profiting from those that offer.

FRANÇOIS LA ROCHEFOUCAULD, Duc de la Rochefoucauld (1613–80), French writer: *Maxims*

The average man finds life very uninteresting as it is. And I think that the reason why … is that he is always waiting for something to happen to him instead of setting to work to make things happen.

A(LAN) A(LEXANDER) MILNE (1882–1956), English writer and dramatist: *If I May: The Future*

Make hay while the sun shines.

PROVERB

Opportunity seldom knocks twice.
PROVERB

When one door shuts, another opens.
PROVERB

While we stop to think, we often miss our opportunity.
PUBLILIUS SYRUS (1st c. BC), Latin writer of mimes: *Sententiae*

Flipping burgers is not beneath your dignity. Your grandparents had a different word for burger-flipping; they called it opportunity.
CHARLES SYKES, American radio talk show host and author: *Dumbing Down Our Kids*

I was seldom able to see an opportunity until it had ceased to be one.
MARK TWAIN (Samuel Langhorne Clemens) (1835–1910), American novelist and humorist

Prices & Value

Nothing that costs only a dollar is worth having.
ELIZABETH ARDEN (1884–1966), American cosmetician: *Fortune, 1973*

A fair price for oil is whatever you can get plus ten per cent.
DR ALI AHMED ATTIGA (1931–), Saudi Arabian delegate to OPEC: *Observer, 'Sayings of the Year', 29 December 1974*

But the market is the best judge of value: for by the concourse of buyers and sellers, the quantity of wares, and the occasion for them are best known. Things are just worth so much, as they can be sold for, according to the old rule Valet Quantum Veni Potest.
NICHOLAS BARBON (c. 1640–1698), English economist, physician and financial speculator: *A Discourse of Trade*

That which cost little is less valued.

MIGUEL DE CERVANTES (SAAVEDRA) (1547–1616), Spanish writer: *Don Quixote*

If the choice lies between the production or purchase of two commodities, the value of one is measured by the sacrifice of going without the other.

H. J. DAVENPORT (1862–1931): *Journal of Political Economy*, 'The Formula of Sacrifice'

What is a man if he is not a thief who openly charges as much as he can for the goods he sells?

MAHATMA GANDHI (Mohandas Karamchand Gandhi) (1869–1948), Hindu nationalist leader: *Non-Violence in Peace and War*

The value of a thing is the amount of laboring or work that its possession will save the possessor.

HENRY GEORGE (1839–97), American economist: *The Science of Political Economy*

Question:
What's two and two?

Grade:
Buying or selling?

LORD GRADE (1906–98), British television mogul: *Observer, 1962*

As in other things, so in men, not the seller but the buyer determines the price. For let a man (as most men do) rate themselves at the highest value they can; yet their true value is no more than it is esteemed by others.

THOMAS HOBBES (1588–1679), English political philosopher: *Leviathan*

The value or worth of a man is ... his price – that is to say, so much as would be given for the use of his power.

THOMAS HOBBES, as above

It has long been recognised, by the business world and by economists alike, that a period of rising prices acts as a stimulus to enterprise and is beneficial to business men.

JOHN MAYNARD KEYNES (1883–1946), English economist: *A Tract on Monetary Reform, chapter 1*

Ad valorem.
According to the value.
LATIN PHRASE

[On the earrings his stores sold for 99p.] They cost the same as a prawn sandwich but maybe the prawn sandwich would last longer.

GERALD RATNER (1949–), British businessman: *Speech to Institute of Directors, April 1991*

We also do cut-glass sherry decanters complete with six glasses on a silver-plated tray that your butler can serve you drinks on, all for £4.95. People say, 'How can you sell this for such a low price?' I say, because it's total crap.

GERALD RATNER, as above

Value is the life-giving power of anything; cost, the quantity of labour required to produce it; price, the quantity of labour which its possessor will take in exchange for it.

JOHN RUSKIN (1819–1900), English art critic and social reformer: *Munera pulveris*

Every man has his price.
SAYING

The market price of every particular commodity is regulated by the proportion between the quantity which is actually brought to market and the demand of those who are willing to pay the natural price of the commodity.

ADAM SMITH (1723–90), Scottish economist and philosopher: *The Wealth of Nations, volume 1*

The real price of every thing, what every thing really costs to the man who wants to acquire it, is the toil and trouble of acquiring it.

ADAM SMITH, as above

The word value … has two different meanings, and some-times expresses the utility of some particular object, and sometimes the power of purchasing other goods which the possession of that object conveys. The one may be called 'value in use'; the other, 'value in exchange'.

ADAM SMITH, as above

All those men have their price.

SIR ROBERT WALPOLE, 1st Earl of Orford (1676–1745), English statesman (Attributed)

It is not that pearls fetch a high price because men have dived for them; but on the contrary, men dive for them because they fetch a high price.

BISHOP RICHARD WHATELY (1787–1863), English Archbishop of Dublin: *Introductory Lectures on Political Economy*

Spending

It does seem to be true that the more you get the more you spend.

CHARLES ALLSOP (1940–), broker (Attributed)

Annual income twenty pounds, annual expenditure nineteen nineteen and six, result happiness. Annual income twenty pounds, annual expenditure twenty pounds ought and six, result misery.

CHARLES (JOHN HUFFAM) DICKENS (1812–70), English novelist: *David Copperfield, chapter 12*

Everybody is always in favour of general economy and particular expenditure.

SIR (ROBERT) ANTHONY EDEN, 1st Earl of Avon (1897–1977), British statesman and prime minister: *Observer, 'Sayings of the Week', 17 June 1956*

The workers spend what they get and the capitalists get what they spend.

MICHAL KALECKI (1899–1970), Polish economist (Attributed)

Spend, and God will send.

PROVERB

To a good spender, God is the treasurer.

PROVERB

All decent people live beyond their incomes nowadays, and those who aren't respectable live beyond other people's. A few gifted individuals manage to do both.

SAKI (Hector Hugh Munro) (1870–1916), English novelist and short-story writer: *The Match Maker*

Utility & Expediency

By the principle of utility is meant that principle which approves or disapproves of every action whatsoever according to the tendency which it appears to have to augment or diminish the happiness of the party whose interest is in question.

JEREMY BENTHAM (1748–1832), English philosopher: *The Principles of Morals and Legislation*

A stronger incentive will be required to induce a person to pay a given price for anything if he is poor than if he is rich. A shilling is the measure of less pleasure, or satisfaction of any kind, to a rich man than to a poor one.

ALFRED MARSHALL (1842–1924), English classical economist: *Principles of Economics, book 1*

You can't learn too soon that the most useful thing about a principle is that it can always be sacrificed to expediency.

W(ILLIAM) SOMERSET MAUGHAM (1874–1965), English writer: *The Circle, Act 3*

Actions are right in proportion as they tend to promote happiness; wrong as they tend to produce the reverse of happiness. By happiness is intended pleasure, and the absence of pain; by unhappiness, pain, and the privation of pleasure.

JOHN STUART MILL (1806–73), English philosopher and economist: *Utilitarianism*

No man is justified in doing evil on the ground of expediency.

THEODORE ROOSEVELT (1858–1919), American statesman and president: *The Strenuous Life*

Utility is the great idol of the age, to which all powers must do service and all talents swear allegiance.

(JOHANN CHRISTOPH) FRIEDRICH VON SCHILLER (1759–1805), German playwright, poet and historian: *On the Aesthetic Education of Man*

Human Resources

'To be successful, a woman has to be better at her job than a man' (Golda Meir). 'Management by objectives works if you know the objectives. Ninety per cent of the time you don't' (Peter Drucker). 'I think it's ludicrous that it takes seventeen unions to build a motor car in Britain' (Lord Scanlon). The quotations in this section consider the essential business asset of people. We see widely varying opinions of businessmen and businesswomen, the art of delegation and good management, and the roles of consultants – 'I come from an environment where, if you see a snake, you kill it. At General Motors, if you see a snake, the first thing you do is hire a consultant on snakes' (Ross Perot) – trade unions and public relations. We also trace the path of careers through promotion up to old age and retirement.

Businessmen & Businesswomen

Executive:
An ulcer with authority.
FRED ALLEN (John F. Sullivan) (1894–1956), American comedian

A woman who strives to be like a man lacks ambition.
ANON

If you want something done, give it to a busy man ... and he'll have his secretary do it.
ANON

Speaking to her husband:
Dear, never forget one little point. It's my business. You just work here.

ELIZABETH ARDEN (1884–1966), American cosmetician: quoted in J. Fisk and R. Barren, *Great Business Quotations*

Men of business have a solid judgement – a wonderful guessing power of what is going to happen – each in his own trade; but they have never practised themselves in reasoning out their judgements and in supporting their guesses by argument: probably if they did so some of the finer and correcter parts of their anticipations would vanish.

WALTER BAGEHOT (1826–77), English economist and journalist: *Economic Studies*

No matter who reigns, the merchant reigns.

HENRY WARD BEECHER (1813–87), American clergyman, editor and writer: *Proverbs from Plymouth Pulpit*

When asked the secret of his success with women:
I treat the charwomen like duchesses, and the duchesses like charwomen.

GEORGE BRYAN BRUMMELL (Beau Brummell) (1778–1840), English dandy

Brigands demand your money or your life; women require both.

SAMUEL BUTLER (1835–1902), English author, painter and musician (Attributed)

Few people do business well who do nothing else.

LORD CHESTERFIELD, Philip Dormer Stanhope, 4th Earl of (1694–1773), English statesman and writer: *Letters, 7 August 1749*

A businessman needs three umbrellas – one to leave at the office, one to leave at home and one to leave on the train.

PAUL DICKSON (1939–), American writer: *Playboy, 1978*

The decisive economic contribution of women in the developed industrial society is rather simple ... It is, overwhelmingly, to make possible a continuing and more or less unlimited increase in the sale and use of consumer goods.

JOHN KENNETH GALBRAITH (1908–2006), Canadian-born American economist, diplomat and writer: *Annals of an Abiding Liberal*

These men of the technostructure are the new and universal priesthood. Their religion is business success; their test of virtue is growth and profit. Their bible is the computer printout; their communion bench is the committee room. The sales force carries their message to the world, and a message is what it is often called.

JOHN KENNETH GALBRAITH: *The Age of Uncertainty*

Every director bites the hand that lays the golden egg.

SAMUEL GOLDWYN (1882–1974), American film producer (Attributed)

The appointment of a woman to office is an innovation for which the public is not prepared, nor am I.

THOMAS JEFFERSON (1743–1826), American statesman and president: *Letter to Albert Gallatin, January 1807*

For the female of the species is more deadly than the male.

(JOSEPH) RUDYARD KIPLING (1865–1936), English novelist, poet and short-story writer: *The Female of the Species*

The silliest woman can manage a clever man; but it needs a very clever woman to manage a fool.

(JOSEPH) RUDYARD KIPLING: *Plain Tales from the Hills, 'Three and – an Extra'*

The businessman has the same fundamental psychology as the artist, inventor, or statesman. He has set himself at a certain work and the work absorbs and becomes himself. It is the expression of his personality; he lives in its growth and perfection according to his plans.

FRANK H. KNIGHT (1885–1972), Professor of Economics: *Risk, Uncertainty and Profit*

If a woman is sufficiently ambitious, determined and gifted – there is practically nothing she can't do.

HELEN LAWRENSEN, American journalist: *Esquire, 1971*

Damn the great executives, the men of measured merriment, damn the men with careful smiles, damn the men that run the shops, oh, damn their measured merriment.

(HARRY) SINCLAIR LEWIS (1885–1951), American novelist: *Arrowsmith*

There is only one political career for which women are perfectly suited: diplomacy.

CLARE BOOTHE LUCE (1903–87), American playwright and diplomat

To be successful, a woman has to be better at her job than a man.

GOLDA MEIR (1898–1978), Russian-born Israeli stateswoman and prime minister

Let woman then go on – not asking favours, but claiming as a right the removal of all hindrances to her elevation in the scale of being – let her receive encouragement for the proper cultivation of her powers, so that she may enter profitably into the active business of life.

LUCRETIA MOTT (1793–1880): *Speech, 17 December 1849*

A man in business must put up many affronts if he loves his own quiet.

WILLIAM PENN (1644–1718), English Quaker and founder of Pennsylvania: *Some Fruits of Solitude*

A man who is always ready to believe what is told him will never do well, especially a businessman.

PETRONIUS GAIUS, also known as Petronius Arbiter (? AD–65), Roman writer: *Satyricon*

In their hearts women think that it is men's business to earn money and theirs to spend it.

ARTHUR SCHOPENHAUER (1788–1860), German pessimist philosopher: *Parerga and Paralipomena, 'On Women'*

The business man has failed in politics as he has in citizenship. Why? Because politics is business. That's what's the matter with everything – art, literature, religion, journalism, law, medicine – they're all businesses, and all – as you see them. Make politics a sport, as they do in England, or a profession, as they do in Germany, and we'll have – well, something else than we have now – if we want it, which is another question.

LINCOLN STEFFENS (1866–1936), American writer and editor: *The Shame of the Cities*

Whilst there is a world 'tis woman that will govern it.

SIR JOHN VANBRUGH (1664–1726), English dramatist and Baroque architect: *The Provok'd Wife*

On liberated women:
They have a right to work wherever they want to – as long as they have dinner ready when you get home.

JOHN WAYNE (Marion Michael Morrison) (1907–79), American film star

A great society is a society in which its men of business think greatly of their functions.

ALFRED NORTH WHITEHEAD (1861–1947), English mathematician and philosopher: *Adventures in Ideas*

Even when the path is nominally open – when there is nothing to prevent a woman from being a doctor, a lawyer, a civil servant – there are many phantoms and obstacles, I believe, looming in her way.

(ADELINE) VIRGINIA WOOLF (1882–1941), English novelist and critic: *Women and Wanting*

Careers & Promotion

You've forgotten the grandest moral attribute of a Scotsman, Maggie, that he'll do nothing which might damage his career.

SIR JAMES MATTHEW BARRIE (1860–1937), Scottish novelist and dramatist: *What Every Woman Knows, Act 2*

If you aspire to the highest place, it is no disgrace to stop at the second, or even the third, place.

MARCUS TULLIUS CICERO (106–43 BC), Roman statesman and orator: *On Oratory*

Sir Joseph Porter:
When I was a lad I served a term
As office boy to an Attorney's firm.
I cleaned the windows and I swept the floor,
And I polished up the handle of the big front door.
I polished up that handle so carefullee
That now I am the Ruler of the Queen's Navee!

SIR WILLIAM SCHWENK GILBERT (1836–1911), English parodist and librettist: *HMS Pinafore, Act 1*

Your levellers wish to level down as far as themselves; but they cannot bear levelling up to themselves. They would all have some people under them; why not then have some people above them?

SAMUEL JOHNSON (1709–84), English lexicographer, essayist and poet: quoted in James Boswell, *The Life of Samuel Johnson*

Be nice to people on your way up because you'll meet 'em on your way down.
WILSON MIZNER (1876–1933), American dramatist

The Peter Principle:
In a Hierarchy Every Employee Tends to Rise to his Level of Incompetence. Work is accomplished by those employees who have not yet reached their level of incompetence. Competence, like truth, beauty and contact lenses, is in the eye of the beholder.
DR LAURENCE J. PETER (1919–90), Canadian educator and RAYMOND HULL (1919–): *The Peter Principle*

He who would climb the ladder must begin at the bottom.
PROVERB

Do not despise the bottom rungs in the ascent to greatness.
PUBLILIUS SYRUS (1st c. BC), Latin writer of mimes: *Moral Sayings*

Consultants

The consultant … offers the advantage of generally having had no firsthand experience in the matters of interest, thereby assuring a clear mind uncluttered by any of the facts.
NORMAN R. AUGUSTINE (1935–), American business executive: *Augustine's Laws*

Consult:
To seek another's approval of a course already decided upon.
AMBROSE (GWINETT) BIERCE (1842–?1914), American journalist and humorist: *The Devil's Dictionary*

I come from an environment where, if you see a snake, you kill it. At General Motors, if you see a snake, the first thing you do is hire a consultant on snakes.

ROSS PEROT (1930–), American businessman: *Financial Times, 'Business Quotes of the Year', 24 December 1988*

Consultants are people who borrow your watch and tell you what time it is and then walk off with the watch.

ROBERT TOWNSEND (1957–), American company director

Delegation

And Moses chose able men out of all Israel, and made them heads over the people, rulers of thousands, rulers of hundreds, rulers of fifties, and rulers of tens. And they judged the people at all seasons: the hard causes they brought unto Moses, but every small matter they judged themselves.

The Bible, Authorised (King James) Version, Exodus 18:25–26

What is worth doing is worth the trouble of asking somebody to do it.

AMBROSE (GWINETT) BIERCE (1842–?1914), American journalist and humorist: *The Devil's Dictionary*

Life is too short to do anything for oneself that one can pay others to do for one.

W(ILLIAM) SOMERSET MAUGHAM (1874–1965), English writer: *The Summing Up*

If you want a thing done well, do it yourself.

NAPOLEON I (Napoleon Bonaparte) (1769–1821), French emperor and general: *Maxims*

Nothing is impossible for the man who doesn't have to do it himself.

A. H. WEILER (1909–43), American newspaperman and editor: *The New York Times, 1968, privately circulated memorandum*

Executives

So the question is, do corporate executives, provided they stay within the law, have responsibilities in their business activities other than to make as much money for their stockholders as possible? And my answer to that is, no they do not.

MILTON FRIEDMAN (1912–2006), American economist, interview in *Chemtech, February 1974*: quoted in *Respectfully Quoted*

Take our twenty best people away, and I will tell you that Microsoft would become an unimportant company.

BILL GATES (1955–), American businessman and philanthropist

There is no quicker way for two executives to get out of touch with each other than to retire to the seclusion of their offices and write each other notes.

R. ALEC MACKENZIE, American management consultant: *The Time Trap*

The best executive is the one who has sense enough to pick good men to do what he wants done, and self-restraint enough to keep from meddling with them while they do it.

THEODORE ROOSEVELT (1858–1919), American statesman and president

Today's adaptive executives … must be experts not in bureaucracy, but in the co-ordination of ad-hocracy. They must adjust to immediate pressures – yet think in terms of long-term goals.

ALVIN TOFFLER (1928–), American writer: *The Adaptive Corporation*

Lesson for stockholders and directors: If the chief executive doesn't retire gracefully after five or six years – throw the rascal out.

ROBERT TOWNSEND (1957–), American company director

Industrial Relations

Strike while your employer has a big contract.
ANON

There is no right to strike against the public safety by anybody, anywhere, anytime.
(JOHN) CALVIN COOLIDGE (1872–1933), American president: *Telegram to the president of the American Federation of Labor, 14 September 1919*

Of Stanley Baldwin:
His motto in the fierce crises in industrial relations was 'not to fire the first shot'. That did not prevent him from firing the last, but it was, at worst, only designed to graze.
SIR COLIN R. COOTE: quoted in Frank S. Pepper, *Contemporary Biographical Quotations*

Industrial relations are like sexual relations. It's better between two consenting parties.
LORD VIC FEATHER (1908–76), General Secretary of the TUC: *Guardian Weekly, 8 August 1976*

An occasional strike is an indication that countervailing power is being employed in a sound context where the costs of any wage increase cannot readily be passed along to someone else. It should be an occasion for mild rejoicing in the conservative press. The Daily Worker, eagerly contemplating the downfall of capitalism, should regret this manifestation of the continued health of the system.
JOHN KENNETH GALBRAITH (1908–2006), Canadian-born American economist, diplomat and writer: *American Capitalism, chapter 9*

Communication in Britain is often about what people don't say, rather than what they do. Uniquely in our country, a manager can interpret his subordinate's silence as assent, while they see it as their ultimate protest.

SIR JOHN HARVEY-JONES (1924–), former chairman of ICI: *Managing to Survive*

Industrial relations are human relations.

EDWARD (RICHARD GEORGE) HEATH (1916–2005), British statesman and prime minister (Attributed)

Without credible communication, and a lot of it, employee hearts and minds are never captured.

JOHN P. KOTTER, American authority on leadership: *Leading Change*

Another fact of life that will not have escaped you is that, in this country, the twenty-four-hour strike is like the twenty-four-hour flu. You have to reckon on it lasting at least five days.

DENIS NORDEN (1922–), British humorist: *You Can't Have Your Kayak and Heat It*, 'Great Expectations'

It's not the sanity of the picket lines that bothers me, it's the sanity of human life.

JOHN PRESCOTT (1938–), British politician: *Guardian, 15 November 2002*

Industrial relations are much more like a marriage relationship than anything else. You do not want the courts. When you do it means you are finished.

GEORGE WOODCOCK (1904–79), General secretary of the TUC: *Observer, 'Sayings of 1968', 29 December 1968*

Leadership & Management

Here is a paradox for the management theorists: any boss who cannot outmanoeuvre a system designed to keep him under control is probably not worth having.

ANON: *The Economist*

Management is the art of getting other people to do all the work.
ANON

Leaders walk their talk; in true leaders, there is no gap between the theories they espouse and their practice.
WARREN BENNIS (1925–), American scholar, organisational consultant and author

The art of leadership is saying no, not yes. It is very easy to say yes.
TONY (ANTHONY CHARLES LYNTON) BLAIR (1953–), British prime minister

The Leaders of Industry, if Industry is ever to be led, are virtually the Captains of the World … Captains of Industry are the true Fighters, henceforth recognisable as the only true ones.
THOMAS CARLYLE (1795–1881), Scottish essayist and historian: *Past and Present, book 4*

British management doesn't seem to understand the importance of the human factor.
CHARLES, Prince of Wales (1948–): *Speech, Parliamentary and Scientific Committee lunch, 21 February 1979*

The man who commands efficiently must have obeyed others in the past, and the man who obeys dutifully is worthy of being some day a commander.
MARCUS TULLIUS CICERO (106–43 BC), Roman statesman and orator: *De Legibus*

Management by objectives works if you know the objectives. Ninety per cent of the time you don't.
PETER F. DRUCKER (1909–2005), American management expert

So much of what we call management consists in making it difficult for people to work.
PETER F. DRUCKER, as above

The function which distinguishes the manager above all others is his educational one. The one contribution he is uniquely expected to make is to give others vision and ability to perform. It is vision and moral responsibility that, in the last analysis, define the manager.

PETER F. DRUCKER, as above

I tell you, sir, the only safeguard of order and discipline in the modern world is a standardized worker with interchangeable parts. That would solve the entire problem of management.

JEAN GIRAUDOUX (1882–1944), French dramatist: *The Madwoman of Chaillot*

It is very seldom that you are fired for your own inadequacy. More often than not you are fired because your managers got it wrong.

SIR JOHN HARVEY-JONES (1924–), former chairman of ICI: *Managing to Survive*

Leadership is the priceless gift that you earn from the people who work for you. I have to earn the right to that gift and have to continuously re-earn that right.

SIR JOHN HARVEY-JONES, as above

The first myth of management is that it exists. The second myth of management is that success equals skill.

ROBERT HELLER (1919–), American writer: *The Great Executive Dream*

The very essence of leadership is that you have to have a vision.

THEODORE HESBURGH (1917–), American priest

You don't have to be intellectually bright to be a competent leader.

SIR EDMUND HILLARY (1919–), New Zealand explorer and mountaineer

If you can keep your head when all about you are losing theirs, it's just possible you haven't grasped the situation.

JEAN KERR (1923–2003), American essayist and playwright: *Please Don't Eat the Daisies*

Chief executives repeatedly fail to recognize that for communication to be effective, it must be two-way: there has to be feedback to ascertain the extent to which the message has been understood, believed, assimilated, and accepted. This is a step few companies ever take (perhaps because they fear to learn how little of the message has actually been transmitted).

ROBERT N. MCMURRY (1901–): *Harvard Business Review, 1965, 'Clear Communications for Chief Executives'*

The ordinary man is involved in action, the hero acts. An immense difference.

HENRY MILLER (1891–1980), American writer: *The Books in My Life*

The real leader has no need to lead – he is content to point the way.

HENRY MILLER: *The Wisdom of the Heart*

Be willing to make decisions. That's the most important quality in a good leader.

GEORGE S. PATTON (1885–1945), American general

People ask the difference between a leader and a boss … The leader works in the open, and the boss in covert. The leader leads, and the boss drives.

THEODORE ROOSEVELT (1858–1919), American statesman and president: *Speech, New York, 24 October 1910*

Leaders must be seen to be up front, up to date, up to their job and up early in the morning.

LORD SIEFF (1899–1972), former chairman, Marks & Spencer: quoted in Helen Exley, *The Best of Business Quotations*

Top management must know how good or bad employees' working conditions are. They must eat in the employees' restaurants, see whether the food is well cooked, visit the washroom and lavatories; if they are not good enough for those in charge, they are not good enough for anyone.
LORD SIEFF

'Top' management is supposed to be a tree full of owls hooting when management heads into the wrong part of the forest. I'm still unpersuaded they even know where the forest is.
ROBERT TOWNSEND (1957–), American company director

There is a chance that you will carry on doing the job you did before so that your successor is not able to do anything. Do not become a big tree under which nothing can grow.
Windsor Leadership Trust Consultation Meeting, July 2007

Public Relations

Some are born great, some achieve greatness, and some hire public relations officers.
DANIEL J. BOORSTIN (1914–2004), American educator and writer: *The Image*

Public relations specialists make flower arrangements of the facts, placing them so that the wilted and less attractive petals are hidden by sturdy blooms.
ALAN HARRINGTON (1919–97), American writer: *Life in the Crystal Palace*

There are a million definitions of public relations. I have found it to be the craft of arranging the truth so that people will like you.
ALAN HARRINGTON, as above

Of Anthony Eden:
They asked for a leader and were given a public relations officer;
here is the news and this is Anthony Eden reading it.
MALCOLM MUGGERIDGE (1903–90), English editor and writer: *Tread Softly for You Tread on My Jokes*

Next to doing the right thing, the most important thing is to let
people know you are doing the right thing.
JOHN D. ROCKEFELLER (1839–1937), American industrialist and philanthropist

Retirement & Old Age

Retirement means twice as much husband on half as much money.
ANON

There is no such thing as 'on the way out'. As long as you are still
doing something interesting and good, you're in business because
you're still breathing.
(DANIEL) LOUIS ARMSTRONG, nickname Satchmo (1900–71), American
jazz trumpeter and bandleader

Age will not be defied.
FRANCIS BACON, 1st Baron Verulam, Viscount St Albans (1561–1626),
English writer, philosopher and statesman: *Essays, 'Of Regiment of Health'*

The old repeat themselves and the young have nothing to say.
The boredom is mutual.
JACQUES BAINVILLE (1879–1936), French historian, journalist and essayist:
Lectures, 'Charme de la conversation'

I will never be an old man. To me, old age is always fifteen years
older than I am.
BERNARD MANNES BARUCH (1870–1965), American financier and
statesman: *Observer, 'Sayings of the Week', 21 August 1955*

In the morning, we carry the world like Atlas; at noon, we stoop and bend beneath it; and at night, it crushes us flat to the ground.

HENRY WARD BEECHER (1813–87), American clergyman, editor and writer: *Proverbs from Plymouth Pulpit*

They shall not grow old, as we that are left grow old: Age shall not weary them, nor the years condemn. At the going down of the sun and in the morning. We will remember them.

LAURENCE ROBERT BINYON (1869–1943), English poet: *For the Fallen (1914–18)*

Retirement at sixty-five is ridiculous. When I was sixty-five, I still had pimples.

GEORGE BURNS (1896–1996), American comedian

'You are old, Father William,' the young man said,
'And your hair has become very white;
And yet you incessantly stand on your head –
Do you think at your age, it is right?'

LEWIS CARROLL (Charles Lutwidge Dodgson) (1832–98), English writer and **mathe**matician: *Alice's Adventures in Wonderland, chapter 5*

I prefer old age to the alternative.

MAURICE CHEVALIER (1888–1972), French singer and film actor: *Remark, 1962*

The role of a retired person is no longer to possess one.

SIMONE DE BEAUVOIR (1908–86), French existentialist novelist and feminist: *The Coming of Age*

Youth is a blunder; manhood a struggle; old age a regret.

BENJAMIN DISRAELI, 1st Earl of Beaconsfield (1804–81), English statesman, prime minister and novelist: *Coningsby*

I grow old … I grow old …
I shall wear the bottoms of my trousers rolled.

T(HOMAS) S(TEARNS) ELIOT (1888–1965), American-born British poet,
dramatist and critic: *The Love Song of J. Alfred Prufrock*

Si jeunesse savait; si vieillesse pouvait.
If only youth knew; if only age could.

HENRI ESTIENNE (1528–98), French scholar and editor: *Les prémices*

In general we must reduce and eventually remove subsidies of all
kinds which distort the relative cost of different forms of energy,
and which stimulate wasteful consumption … But the best way
to help pensioners is to increase pensions, not to sell fuel to
everybody far below its cost.

DENIS (WINSTON) HEALEY (1917–), English politician: *Budget Speech,
House of Commons, 12 November 1974*

Retirement is the ugliest word in the language.

ERNEST HEMINGWAY (1899–1961), American novelist and short-story
writer

I don't feel eighty. In fact I don't feel anything till noon. Then it's
time for my nap.

BOB HOPE (1903–2003), English-born American comedian and comic actor

You know you're getting old when the candles cost more than the
cake.

BOB HOPE, as above

Whenever a man's friends begin to compliment him about
looking young, he may be sure that they think he is growing old.

WASHINGTON IRVING (1783–1859), American essayist, biographer and
historian: *Bracebridge Hall, 'Bachelors'*

Pension:
An allowance made to anyone without an equivalent. In England it is generally understood to mean pay given to a state hireling for treason to his country.

SAMUEL JOHNSON (1709–84), English lexicographer, essayist and poet: *Dictionary of the English Language*

The first years of man must make provision for the last.

SAMUEL JOHNSON: *Rasselas*

The love of retirement has, in all ages, adhered closely to those minds which have been enlarged by knowledge, or elevated by genius.

SAMUEL JOHNSON: *The Rambler, 10 April 1750*

I am Retired Leisure. I am to be met within trim gardens. I am already come to be known by my vacant face and careless gesture, perambulating at no fixed pace nor with any settled purpose. I walk about; not to and from.

CHARLES (ELIA) LAMB (1775–1834), English essayist: *Last Essays of Elia, 'The Superannuated Man'*

Old age has its pleasures, which, though different, are not less than the pleasures of youth.

W(ILLIAM) SOMERSET MAUGHAM (1874–1965), English writer: *The Summing Up*

Few men of action have been able to make a graceful exit at the appropriate time.

MALCOLM MUGGERIDGE (1903–90), English editor and writer, *The Most of Malcolm Muggeridge, 'Twilight of Greatness'*

One of the many pleasures of old age is giving things up.

MALCOLM MUGGERIDGE

I have made noise enough in the world already, perhaps too much, and am now getting old, and want retirement.

NAPOLEON I (Napoleon Bonaparte) (1769–1821), French emperor and general: *To Barry E. O'Meara at St Helena, 1 October 1816*

My second fixed idea is the uselessness of men above 60 years of age, and the incalculable benefit it would be in commercial, political and professional life if, as a matter of course, men stopped work at this age.

SIR WILLIAM OSLER (1849–1919), Canadian physician: *Speech, Baltimore, 22 February 1905*

If you wish good advice, consult an old man.

PROVERB

It is better to wear out than to rust out.

PROVERB

Old age comes stealing on.

PROVERB

Young men think old men fools, and old men know young men to be so.

PROVERB

So little done, so much to do.

CECIL JOHN RHODES (1853–1902), English colonial financier and statesman in South Africa: *Last words*

Every parting gives a foretaste of death; every coming together again a foretaste of the resurrection. This is why even people who were indifferent to each other rejoice so much if they come together again after twenty or thirty years' separation.

ARTHUR SCHOPENHAUER (1788–1860), German pessimist philosopher: *Parerga and Paralipomena, 'Further Psychological Observations'*

Jacques:
All the world's a stage,
And all the men and women merely players;
They have their exits and their entrances;
And one man in his time plays many parts,
His acts being seven ages.

WILLIAM SHAKESPEARE (1564–1616), English dramatist and poet: *As You Like It, Act 2*

The pension system is only an alternative to paying a higher salary to those rendering existing services and leaving them subsequently to look after their own superannuation allowance.

SIR JOSIAH STAMP (1880–1941): *Wealth and Taxable Capacity, chapter 2*

[When asked what she wanted to be remembered for] Everything.

MAE WEST (1892–1980), American stage and film actress (Attributed)

Trade Unions

Trade unions are islands of anarchy in a sea of chaos.

ANEURIN BEVAN (1897–1960), British statesman

Not a penny off the pay,
not a second on the day.

ARTHUR COOKE (1885–1931), English trade unionist: *Slogan before miners' strike of 1926*

With all their faults, trade unions have done more for humanity than any other organization of men that ever existed. They have done more for decency, for honesty, for education, for the betterment of the race, for the developing of character in man, than any other association of men.

CLARENCE SEWARD DARROW (1857–1938), American lawyer, reformer and writer: *The Railroad Trainman, November 1909*

If trade unionists failed to register their protest by striking, their silence would be regarded as an admission that they acquiesced in the pre-eminence of economic forces over human welfare. Such acquiescence would be a recognition of the right of the middle classes to exploit the workers when business was flourishing and to let the workers go hungry when business was slack.

FRIEDRICH ENGELS (1820–95), German socialist leader and political philosopher: *The Condition of the Working Class in England in 1844, chapter 9*

A whole new way of life started after the dispute with the government in 1971. It seemed as if trade unions suddenly became aware of their position and their potential. Whereas in the 1960s, we in the Trade Union movement used to bemoan our inertia. I remember us complaining, 'Well, we are really passive.' 'We observe only from the sidelines.' 'We do not affect politics very much.' Now all that has changed!

LORD GORMLEY, Joseph, Lord of Ashton-in-Makefield (1917–93), British trade unionist: quoted in Cary L. Cooper and Peter Hingley, *The Change Makers*

Trade unions are the only means by which workmen can protect themselves from the tyranny of those who employ them. But the moment that trade unions become tyrants in their turn they are engines for evil: they have no right to prevent people from working on any terms that they choose.

MR JUSTICE (NATHANIEL) LINDLEY: *Judgment in Lyons v. Wilkins, 1896*

Trade unionism has enabled skilled artisans, and even many classes of unskilled workers, to enter into negotiations with their employers with the same gravity, self-restraint, dignity and forethought as are observed in the diplomacy of great nations. It has led them generally to recognise that a simply aggressive policy is a foolish policy, and that the chief use of military resources is to preserve an advantageous peace.

ALFRED MARSHALL (1842–1924), English classical economist: *Principles of Economics, book 6*

In the first place, trade unions are about individuals, and the right of a man to answer back to his boss.

LIONEL (LEN) MURRAY, Baron Murray of Epping Forest (1922–2004), British trade unionist

It is one of the characteristics of a free and democratic modern nation that it have free and independent labor unions.

FRANKLIN DELANO ROOSEVELT (1882–1945), American statesman and president: *Address, Teamsters' Union convention, Washington DC, 11 September 1940*

It is essential that there should be organizations of labor. This is an era of organization. Capital organizes and therefore labor must organize.

THEODORE ROOSEVELT (1858–1919), American statesman and president: *Speech, Milwaukee, 14 October 1912*

I think it's ludicrous that it takes seventeen unions to build a motor car in Britain.

LORD SCANLON, Hugh (1913–2004), British trade unionist: *Observer, 'Sayings of the Week', 30 July 1979*

All too often miners, and indeed other trade unionists, underestimate the economic strength they have.

ARTHUR SCARGILL (1938–), British trades union leader

There's a feeling that strength is determined by the size of a union. That clearly is nonsense.

ARTHUR SCARGILL

Workers' control means the castration of the trade union movement.

ARTHUR SCARGILL: *Observer, 'Sayings of 1978', 31 December 1978*

Facts show that politically independent trade unions do not exist anywhere. There have never been any. Experience and theory say that there will never be any.

LEON TROTSKY (Lev Davidovich Bronstein) (1879–1940), Russian revolutionary and Communist theorist: *Communism and Syndicalism, 1929*

Workers & The People

FISH: First In, Still Here.

ANON

Human labour is not an end but a means.

FRÉDÉRIC BASTIAT (1801–50): *Sophistries économiques, chapter 2*

The people are the masters.

EDMUND BURKE (1729–97), British statesman, orator and writer: *Speech on the Economical Reform, 11 February 1780*

We are all special cases.

ALBERT CAMUS (1913–60), French philosopher and writer

I am for people. I can't help it.

Sir CHARLES CHAPLIN (1889–1977), English comedian, film actor and director: *Observer, 'Sayings of the Week', 28 September 1952*

Mankind is not a tribe of animals to which we owe compassion. Mankind is a club to which we owe our subscription.

G(ILBERT) K(EITH) CHESTERTON (1874–1936), English essayist, novelist, poet and critic: *Daily News, 10 April 1906*

I got disappointed in human nature as well and gave it up because I found it too much like my own.

JAMES PATRICK DONLEAVY (1926–), American-born Irish novelist: *Fairy Tales of New York*

No man is an island, entire of itself; every man is a piece of the Continent, a part of the main.

JOHN DONNE (1573–1631), English metaphysical poet and preacher: *Devotions, 12*

Jack of all trades and master of none.

MARIA EDGEWORTH (1767–1849), English novelist: *Popular Tales*

The world is full of willing people: some willing to work, the rest willing to let them.

ROBERT FROST (1874–1963), American poet

We cannot safely leave politics to politicians, or political economy to college professors. The people themselves must think, because the people alone can act.

HENRY GEORGE (1839–97), American economist: *Social Problems*

Getting results through people is a skill that cannot be learned in the classroom.

J(EAN) PAUL GETTY (1892–1976), American financier

I don't want any yes-men around me. I want everybody to tell me the truth even if it costs them their jobs.

SAMUEL GOLDWYN (1882–1974), American film producer (Attributed)

Every thing in the world is purchased by labour.

DAVID HUME (1711–76), Scottish philosopher and historian: *Essays, 'Of Commerce'*

It is a shameful and inhuman thing to treat men as mere chattels for profit, or to regard them as simply so much muscle power.

POPE LEO XIII (Gioacchino Pecci) (1810–1903): *Rerum novarum, 15 May 1891*

Labor is prior to, and independent of, capital. Capital is only the fruit of labor, and could never have existed if labor had not first existed. Labor is the superior of capital, and deserves much the higher consideration.

ABRAHAM LINCOLN (1809–65), American statesman and president: *Message to Congress, 3 December 1861*

You can fool some of the people all the time and all the people some of the time; but you can't fool all the people all the time.

ABRAHAM LINCOLN (Attributed)

The power of population is indefinitely greater than the power in the earth to produce subsistence for man. Population, when unchecked, increases in a geometrical ratio. Subsistence only increases in an arithmetical ratio. A slight acquaintance with numbers will show the immensity of the first power in comparison with the second.

THOMAS ROBERT MALTHUS (1766–1834), English economist: *An Essay on the Principle of Population, chapter 1*

The people, and the people alone, are the motive force in the making of world history.

MAO TSE-TUNG (Mao Zedong) (1893–1976), Chinese Communist leader: *Quotations from Chairman Mao Tse-Tung*

The workers have nothing to lose but their chains. They have a world to gain. Workers of the world, unite!

KARL MARX (1818–83), German founder of modern communism and FRIEDRICH ENGELS (1820–95), German socialist leader: *The Communist Manifesto, closing words*

I've always been interested in people, but I've never liked them.

W(ILLIAM) SOMERSET MAUGHAM (1874–1965), English writer: *Observer, 'Sayings of the Week', 28 August 1949*

A small group of thoughtful people could change the world. Indeed, it's the only thing that ever has.

MARGARET MEAD (1901–78), American cultural anthropologist

The bad workmen who form the majority of the operatives in many branches of industry are decidedly of the opinion that bad workmen ought to receive the same wages as good.

JOHN STUART MILL (1806–73), English philosopher and economist: *On Liberty*

When white-collar people get jobs, they sell not only their time and energy, but also their personalities as well. They sell by the week, or month, their smiles and their kindly gestures, and they must practice that prompt repression of resentment and aggression.

C(HARLES) WRIGHT MILLS (1916–62), American sociologist: *White Collar*

Subordinates multiply at a fixed rate regardless of the amount of work produced.

C(YRIL) NORTHCOTE PARKINSON (1909–93), English historian and journalist: *Parkinson's Law*

Labour, like all other things which are purchased and sold, and which may be increased or diminished in quantity, has its natural and its market price. The natural price of labour is that price which is necessary to enable the labourers, one with another, to subsist and perpetuate the race, without either increase or diminution.

DAVID RICARDO (1772–1823), English economist: *On the Principles of Political Economy and Taxation, chapter 1*

We are an indispensable team; you are overmanned; they are redundant.

ANTHONY SAMPSON (1926–), English journalist and biographer: *Observer, 1981*

I love mankind, it's people I can't stand.

CHARLES (MONROE) SCHULZ (1922–2000), American cartoonist: *Go Fly a Kite, Charlie Brown*

Hamlet:
What a piece of work is a man! How noble in reason! How infinite in faculties! in form and moving, how express and admirable! in action, how like an angel! in apprehension, how like a god! the beauty of the world! the paragon of animals! And yet, to me, what is this quintessence of dust? Man delights not me – no, nor woman neither.

WILLIAM SHAKESPEARE (1564–1616), English dramatist and poet: *Hamlet, Act 2*

People are always blaming their circumstances for what they are. I don't believe in circumstances. The people who get on in this world are the people who get up and look for the circumstances they want, and, if they can't find them, make them.

GEORGE BERNARD SHAW (1856–1950), Irish dramatist and critic: *Mrs Warren's Profession*

You're not a man, you're a machine.

GEORGE BERNARD SHAW: *Arms and the Man, Act 3*

The greatest improvement in the productive powers of labour, and the greater part of the skill, dexterity and judgement with which it is any where directed, or applied, seem to have been the effects of the division of labour.

ADAM SMITH (1723–90), Scottish economist and philosopher: *The Wealth of Nations, volume 1*

Be nice to nerds. Chances are you'll end up working for one.

CHARLES SYKES, American radio talk show host and author: *Dumbing Down Our Kids*

The really efficient laborer will be found not to crowd his day with work, but will saunter to his task surrounded by a wide halo of ease and leisure.

HENRY DAVID THOREAU (1817–62), American essayist and poet: *Journal, 1841*

You can fool too many of the people too much of the time.

JAMES (GROVER) THURBER (1894–1961), American humorist and cartoonist: *The Thurber Carnival*

Lord Darlington:
It is absurd to divide people into good and bad. People are either charming or tedious.

OSCAR WILDE (1856–1900), Irish poet, dramatist and wit: *Lady Windermere's Fan, Act 1*

Time

Very often life seems to be a battle against time. There are too many things to fit into the day. The quotations here remind us that 'Time is money', but their scope is much wider than this. We see what can be learnt from the past, and also how to plan for – and cope with – the future, while not forgetting John Maynard Keynes' famous quote, 'In the long run we are all dead'. And since our time isn't just spent working, we consider how we occupy our time off, at home or on holiday ... although, as Noël Coward puts it, 'Work is much more fun than fun'.

Future & Planning

Forecasting is very difficult, especially if it is about the future.
ANON

If life is eternal, why are you hurrying?
ANON

The future is not what it was.
ANON

The future is ... black.
JAMES (ARTHUR) BALDWIN (1924–87), American novelist and essayist:
Observer, 'Sayings of the Week', 25 August 1963

In developing our industrial strategy for the period ahead, we have had the benefit of much experience. Almost everything has been tried at least once.
TONY (ANTHONY NEIL WEDGWOOD) BENN (1925–), English politician:
Observer, 'Sayings of the Week', 17 March 1974

Future:
That period of time in which our affairs prosper, our friends are true and our happiness is assured.

AMBROSE (GWINETT) BIERCE (1842–?1914), American journalist and humorist: *The Devil's Dictionary*

You can never plan the future by the past.

EDMUND BURKE (1729–97), British statesman, orator and writer: *Letter to a Member of the National Assembly*

A trend is a trend is a trend
But the question is, will it bend?
Will it alter its course
Through some unforeseen force
And come to a premature end?

SIR ALEC CAIRNCROSS (1911–98), Scottish economist: *Economic Journal, December 1969, 'Economic Forecasting'*

You never reach the promised land. You can march towards it.

(LEONARD) JAMES CALLAGHAN (1912–2005), English statesman and prime minister: *Observer, 'Sayings of 1978', 31 December 1978*

Red Queen:
The rule is, jam tomorrow and jam yesterday – but never jam today.

LEWIS CARROLL (Charles Lutwidge Dodgson) (1832–98), English writer and mathematician: *Through the Looking-Glass, chapter 5*

It is a mistake to look too far ahead. Only one link of the chain of destiny can be handled at a time.

SIR WINSTON LEONARD SPENCER CHURCHILL (1874–1965), English statesman, writer and prime minister: *Speech, House of Commons, 27 February 1945*

It is always wise to look ahead, but difficult to look further than you can see.

SIR WINSTON LEONARD SPENCER CHURCHILL: *Observer, 'Sayings of the Week', 27 July 1952*

There is a perverse failure to make the actual demand of yesterday a basis for the production of today, or to make the demand of last year a basis for the production of this year.

JOHN BATES CLARK (1847–1938), American economist and professor: *K. Rodbertus, Overproduction and Crises*

Study the past, if you would divine the future.

CONFUCIUS (Kong Zi) (551–479 BC), Chinese philosopher: *Analects*

I never think of the future. It comes soon enough.

ALBERT EINSTEIN (1879–1955), German-Swiss-American physicist: *Interview, 1930*

If a man carefully examine his thoughts, he will be surprised to find how much he lives in the future. His well-being is always ahead.

RALPH WALDO EMERSON (1803–82), American poet, essayist and philosopher: *Journals, 1827*

Remember that the future is neither ours nor wholly not ours, so that we may neither count on it as sure to come nor abandon hope of it as certain not to be.

EPICURUS (341–270 BC), Greek philosopher: *Letter to Menoeceus*

The danger of the past was that men became slaves. The danger of the future is that men may become robots.

ERICH FROMM (1900–80), German-born American psychoanalyst and philosopher: *The Sane Society*

He that fears not the future may enjoy the present.

THOMAS FULLER (1654–1734), English physician, writer and compiler: *Gnomologia*

You cannot fight against the future. Time is on our side.

WILLIAM EWART GLADSTONE (1809–98), British statesman and prime minister: *Speech on Reform Bill, 1866*

Excessive forethought and too great solicitude for the future are often productive of misfortune; for the affairs of the world are subject to so many accidents that seldom do things turn out as even the wisest predicted; and whoever refuses to take advantage of present good from fear of future danger, provided the danger be not certain and near, often discovers to his annoyance and disgrace that he has lost opportunities full of profit and glory, from dread of dangers which have turned out to be wholly imaginary.

FRANCESCO GUICCIARDINI (1483–1540), Florentine statesman and historian: *Storia d'Italia*

In an ideal world I would like to be alive until I am dead.

SIR JOHN HARVEY-JONES (1924–   ), former chairman of ICI: quoted in *Wrinklies' Wit & Wisdom Forever*

The best preparation for good work tomorrow is to do good work today.

ELBERT (GREEN) HUBBARD (1856–1915), American businessman, writer and printer: *The Note Book*

The world community can continue to pursue the arms race and build ever-larger and more deadly weapons, or it can shift and move deliberately and urgently towards the provision of the basic needs of our global family. It cannot do both. Either we invest in arms and death, or we invest in life and the future development of the people of the world.

CARDINAL (GEORGE) BASIL HUME (1923–99), English Roman Catholic Benedictine monk, Archbishop of Westminster

I like the dreams of the future better than the history of the past.

THOMAS JEFFERSON (1743–1826), American statesman and president: *Letter to John Adams*

The importance of money essentially flows from its being a link between the present and the future.

JOHN MAYNARD KEYNES (1883–1946), English economist: *The General Theory of Employment, Interest and Money, book 5*

This long run is a misleading guide to current affairs. In the long run we are all dead. Economists set themselves too easy, too useless a task if in tempestuous seasons they can only tell us that when the storm is long past the ocean is flat again.

JOHN MAYNARD KEYNES: *A Tract on Monetary Reform, chapter 3*

Optimists and pessimists differ only on the date of the end of the world.

STANISLAW (JERZY) LEC (1909–66), Polish poet and aphorist

The earth we abuse and the living things we kill will, in the end, take their revenge; for in exploiting their presence we are diminishing our future.

MARYA MANNES (1904–90), American essayist and journalist: *More in Anger*

We are all in favour of the future.

REGINALD MAUDLING (1917–79), British politician: *Observer, 'Sayings of 1964', 27 December 1964*

If you want a picture of the future, imagine a boot stamping on the human face – forever.

GEORGE ORWELL (Eric Arthur Blair) (1903–50), English novelist and essayist

He who plants a walnut tree expects not to eat of the fruit.

PROVERB

The wise man looks ahead.
PROVERB

He who can see three days ahead will be rich for three thousand years.
JAPANESE PROVERB

The only limit to our realization of tomorrow will be our doubts of today.
FRANKLIN DELANO ROOSEVELT (1882–1945), American statesman and president

Looking forward into an empty year strikes one with a certain awe, because one finds therein no recognition. The years behind have a friendly aspect, and they are warmed by the fires we have kindled, and all their echoes are the echoes of our own voices.
ALEXANDER SMITH (1830–67), Scottish poet and essayist: *Dreamthorp*

I consider the world as made for me, not me for the world. It is my maxim therefore to enjoy it while I can, and let futurity shift for itself.
TOBIAS GEORGE SMOLLETT (1721–71), British novelist: *Roderick Random, chapter 45*

Anyone who talks five-year plans talks crap.
SIR ALAN SUGAR (1947–), British entrepreneur

Future shock is the disorientation that affects an individual, a corporation or a country when he or it is overwhelmed by change and the prospect of change. It is the consequence of having to make too many decisions about too many new and unfamiliar problems in too short a time. Future shock is more than a metaphor. It is a form of personal and social breakdown. We are in collision with tomorrow. Future shock has arrived.
ALVIN TOFFLER (1928–), American academic: *Observer, 1972*

The Shape of Things to Come.

H(ERBERT) G(EORGE) WELLS (1866–1946), English novelist, journalist and
social philosopher: *Title of book*

We are leaving the period of money fever that was the Eighties
and entering a period of moral fever.

TOM WOLFE (1931–), American writer

History

History is the sum total of the things that could have been
avoided.

KONRAD ADENAUER (1876–1967), Chancellor of West Germany

History:
An account mostly false, of events mostly unimportant, which
are brought about by rulers mostly knaves, and soldiers mostly
fools.

AMBROSE (GWINETT) BIERCE (1842–?1914), American journalist and
humorist: *The Devil's Dictionary*

History is philosophy teaching by examples.

DIONYSUS OF HALICARNASSUS (?40–8 BC), Greek historian and
rhetorician: *Ars rhetorica*

The historical sense involves a perception, not only of the
pastness of the past but of its presence.

T(HOMAS) S(TEARNS) ELIOT (1888–1965), American-born British poet,
dramatist and critic

The materialist conception of history starts from the proposition
that the production of the means to support human life and,
next to production, the exchange of things produced, is the basis
of all social structure … From this point of view the final causes

of all social changes and political revolutions are to be sought …
in changes in the modes of production and exchange.

FRIEDRICH ENGELS (1820–95), German socialist leader and political
philosopher: *Socialism, Utopian and Scientific*

History is more or less bunk. It's tradition. We don't want
tradition. We want to live in the present and the only history that
is worth a tinker's dam is the history we make today.

HENRY FORD (1863–1947), American car manufacturer: *Chicago Tribune, 1916*

The marriage of economics and history produces a hybrid which
regularly combines the inadequacies of both.

JOHN KENNETH GALBRAITH (1908–2006), Canadian-born American
economist, diplomat and writer: *The Liberal Hour*

We have all passed a lot of water since then.

SAMUEL GOLDWYN (1882–1974), American film producer: quoted in Philip
French, *The Movie Moguls*

What experience and history teach is this – that people and
governments never have learned anything from history, or acted
on principles deduced from it.

GEORG WILHELM FRIEDRICH HEGEL (1770–1831), German philosopher:
Philosophy of History

What we know of the past is mostly not worth knowing. What is
worth knowing is mostly uncertain. Events in the past may
roughly be divided into those which probably never happened
and those which do not matter.

WILLIAM RALPH INGE (1860–1954), English theologian: *Assessments and
Anticipations, 'Prognostications'*

It takes a great deal of history to produce a little literature.

HENRY JAMES (1843–1916), American-born British novelist: *Life of Nathaniel
Hawthorne, chapter 1*

History, Stephen said, is a nightmare from which I am trying to awake.

JAMES (AUGUSTINE ALOYSIUS) JOYCE (1882–1941), Irish novelist and short-story writer: *Ulysses*

The great events of history are often due to secular changes in the growth of population and other fundamental economic causes, which, escaping by their gradual character the notice of contemporary observers, are attributed to the follies of statesmen or the fanaticism of atheists.

JOHN MAYNARD KEYNES (1883–1946), English economist: *The Economic Consequences of the Peace, chapter 2*

Those who cannot remember the past are condemned to repeat it.

GEORGE SANTAYANA (1863–1952), American philosopher and poet: *The Life of Reason*

History gets thicker as it approaches recent times.

A(LAN) J(OHN) P(ERCIVALE) TAYLOR (1906–90), English historian: *English History 1914–1945*

Anything but history, for history must be false.

SIR ROBERT WALPOLE, 1st Earl of Orford (1676–1745), English statesman: *Walpoliana*

Honesty is the best policy, but he who acts on that principle is not an honest man.

BISHOP RICHARD WHATELY (1787–1863), English Archbishop of Dublin: *Apothegms*

Holidays & Leisure

Sunday clears away the rust of the whole week.

JOSEPH ADDISON (1672–1719), English essayist and dramatist: *Spectator, 9 July 1711*

There can be no high civilization where there is not ample leisure.

HENRY WARD BEECHER (1813–87), American clergyman, editor and writer: *Proverbs from Plymouth Pulpit*

Life's too short for chess.

HENRY JAMES BYRON (1834–84), English dramatist: *Our Boys, Act 1*

A single sentence will suffice for modern man: he fornicated and read the papers.

ALBERT CAMUS (1913–60), French philosopher and writer: *The Fall*

Sunburn is very becoming – but only when it is even – one must be careful not to look like a mixed grill.

SIR NOËL (PIERCE) COWARD (1899–1973), English actor and dramatist: *The Lido Beach*

Work is much more fun than fun.

SIR NOËL (PIERCE) COWARD: *Observer, 'Sayings of the Week', 21 June 1963*

What is this life if, full of care,
We have no time to stand and stare?

W(ILLIAM) H(ENRY) DAVIES (1871–1940), Welsh-born English poet: *Leisure*

Rat:
There is nothing – absolutely nothing – half so much worth doing as simply messing about in boats.

KENNETH GRAHAME (1859–1932), Scottish writer: *The Wind in the Willows, chapter 1*

Of cricket:
It's more than a game. It's an institution.

THOMAS HUGHES (1822–96), English novelist: *Tom Brown's Schooldays*

Summer afternoon – summer afternoon; to me those have always been the two most beautiful words in the English language.

HENRY JAMES (1843–1916), American-born British novelist: *A Backward Glance (Edith Wharton), chapter 10*

Holidays are often overrated disturbances of routine, costly and uncomfortable, and they usually need another holiday to correct their ravages.

E(DWARD) V(ERRALL) LUCAS (1868–1938), English novelist, poet and essayist

I must confess that I am interested in leisure in the same way that a poor man is interested in money.

PRINCE PHILIP, Duke of Edinburgh (1921–)

A good holiday is one spent among people whose notions of time are vaguer than yours.

J(OHN) B(OYNTON) PRIESTLEY (1894–1984), English author

Idle folks have the least leisure.

PROVERB

To be able to fill leisure intelligently is the last product of civilization.

BERTRAND (ARTHUR WILLIAM) RUSSELL, 3rd Earl Russell (1872–1970), English philosopher and mathematician: *The Conquest of Happiness*

Prince:
If all the year were playing holidays.
To sport would be as tedious as to work.

WILLIAM SHAKESPEARE (1564–1616), English dramatist and poet: *Henry the Fourth, Part One, Act 1*

What the banker sighs for, the meanest clown may have, – leisure and a quiet mind.

HENRY DAVID THOREAU (1817–62), American essayist and poet: *Journal, 18 January 1841*

Home & Family Life

There's a way of transferring funds that is even faster than electronic banking. It's called marriage.

ANON

Work is where Daddy goes to get tired.

ANON

I can't be a wife. I'm not that sort of person. Wives have to compromise all the time.

SARAH BRIGHTMAN (1960–), English singer, actress and dancer

I'm a father; that's what matters most. Nothing matters more.

GORDON BROWN (1951–), British prime minister

Families is where our nation finds hope, where wings take dream.

GEORGE W. BUSH (1946–), American president

You are a king by your own fire-side, as much as any monarch in his throne.

MIGUEL DE CERVANTES (SAAVEDRA) (1547–1616), Spanish writer: *Don Quixote*

A man's house is his castle.

SIR EDWARD COKE (1552–1634), English jurist: *Institutes*

Accidents will happen in the best-regulated families.

CHARLES (JOHN HUFFAM) DICKENS (1812–70), English novelist: *David Copperfield*

A man builds a fine house; and now he has a master, and a task for life; he is to furnish, watch, show it, and keep it in repair the rest of his days.

RALPH WALDO EMERSON (1803–82), American poet, essayist and philosopher: *Society and Solitude*

Blood's thicker than water, and when one's in trouble
Best to seek out a relative's open arms.

EURIPIDES (?480–406 BC), Greek tragic dramatist: *Andromache*

Marry, and with luck
It may go well. But when a marriage fails
Then those who marry live at home in hell.

EURIPIDES: *Orestes*

Charity begins at home, but should not end there.

THOMAS FULLER (1654–1734), English physician, writer and compiler:
Gnomologia

What children hear at home soon flies abroad.

THOMAS FULLER, as above

What's the good of a home, if you are never in it?

GEORGE GROSSMITH (1847–1912), English comedian and singer and
WALTER WEEDON GROSSMITH, his brother: *The Diary of a Nobody*,
chapter 1

Home life ceases to be free and beautiful as soon as it is founded
on borrowing and debt.

HENRIK IBSEN (1828–1906), Norwegian dramatist and poet: *A Doll's
House*

To be happy at home is the ultimate result of all ambition, the
end to which every enterprise and labour tends, and of which
every desire prompts the prosecution.

SAMUEL JOHNSON (1709–84), English lexicographer, essayist and poet: *The
Rambler*

A house is a machine for living in.

(CHARLES ÉDOUARD JEANNERET) LE CORBUSIER (1887–1965), Swiss
architect: *Towards an Architecture*

There is no more lovely, friendly and charming relationship, communion or company than a good marriage.

MARTIN LUTHER (1483–1546), German leader of Protestant Reformation: *Table Talk*

The days just prior to marriage are like a snappy introduction to a tedious book.

WILSON MIZNER (1876–1933), American playwright

Marriage is an insult and women shouldn't touch it.

JENNI MURRAY (1950–), British broadcaster

There's no place like home.

JOHN HOWARD PAYNE (1791–1852), American writer: *Home Sweet Home*

Home is the girl's prison and the woman's workhouse.

GEORGE BERNARD SHAW (1856–1950), Irish dramatist and critic: *Man and Superman, Maxims for Revolutionists*

Everybody's always talking about people breaking into houses … but there are more people in the world who want to break out of houses.

THORNTON (NIVEN) WILDER (1897–1975), American novelist and playwright: *The Matchmaker*

Time

Time is the greatest innovator.

FRANCIS BACON, 1st Baron Verulam, Viscount St Albans (1561–1626), English writer, philosopher and statesman: *'Of Innovations'*

To choose time is to save time.

FRANCIS BACON: *Essays, 'Of Dispatch'*

Time is a great teacher, but unfortunately it kills all its pupils.

HECTOR BERLIOZ (1803–69), French composer: *Almanach des lettres françaises*

Year:
A period of three hundred and sixty-five disappointments.

AMBROSE (GWINETT) BIERCE (1842–?1914), American journalist and humorist: *The Devil's Dictionary*

I recommend you to take care of the minutes; for hours will take care of themselves.

LORD CHESTERFIELD, Philip Dormer Stanhope, 4th Earl of (1694–1773), English statesman and writer: *Letters to his son, 6 November 1747*

It is an undoubted truth, that the less one has to do, the less time one finds to do it in. One yawns, one procrastinates, one can do it when one will, and therefore one seldom does it at all.

LORD CHESTERFIELD

There is time enough for everything in the course of the day if you do but one thing at once; but there is not time enough in the year if you will do two things at a time.

LORD CHESTERFIELD: *Letters to his son, 14 April 1747*

One of the great disadvantages of hurry is that it takes such a long time.

G(ILBERT) K(EITH) CHESTERTON (1874–1936), English essayist, novelist, poet and critic: *All Things Considered*

I felt as if I were walking with destiny, and that all my past life had been but a preparation for this hour and this trial.

SIR WINSTON LEONARD SPENCER CHURCHILL (1874–1965), English statesman, writer and prime minister: *The Gathering Storm, chapter 38*

The to-do list has become a tyrant, pushing us to do more instead of helping us to do better and to do right.

MARSHALL COOK, American professor of journalism and communications

Time is a great manager: it arranges things well.

PIERRE CORNEILLE (1606–84), French tragic dramatist: *Sertorius*

The supply of time is totally inelastic. Time is totally perishable and cannot be stored. Time is totally irreplaceable ... there is no substitute for time.

PETER F. DRUCKER (1909–2005), American management expert: *The Effective Manager*

All my possessions for a moment of time.

ELIZABETH I (1533–1603), Queen of England: *Last words*

Can anybody remember when the times were not hard, and money not scarce?

RALPH WALDO EMERSON (1803–82), American poet, essayist and philosopher: *Society and Solitude, 'Works and Days'*

Do not squander time, for that is the stuff life is made of.

BENJAMIN FRANKLIN (1706–90), American statesman, scientist and author: *The Way to Wealth*

Lost time is never found again.

BENJAMIN FRANKLIN: *Poor Richard's Almanac*

Remember that time is money.

BENJAMIN FRANKLIN: *Advice to Young Tradesmen*

Most people work the greater part of their time for a mere living; and the little freedom which remains to them so troubles them that they use every means of getting rid of it.

JOHANN WOLFGANG VON GOETHE (1749–1832), German poet, scientist and writer: *The Sorrows of Young Werther*

The hours we pass with happy prospects in view are more pleasing than those crowned with fruition.

OLIVER GOLDSMITH (?1728–74), Irish dramatist, novelist and poet: *The Hermit*

Time goes by; reputation increases, ability declines.

DAG HAMMARSKJÖLD (1905–61), Swedish statesman and secretary-general of the United Nations: *Markings, '1945–1949: Towards new shores – ?'*

No amount of 'tricks of the trade' will avoid the need to set some sort of priority when allocating one's time.

SIR JOHN HARVEY-JONES (1924–), former chairman of ICI: *Making It Happen*

Old time, in whose banks we deposit our notes,
Is a miser who always wants guineas for groats;
He keeps all his customers still in arrears
By lending them minutes and charging them years.

OLIVER WENDELL HOLMES, SR (1809–94), American physician, professor and author: *Our Banker*

Carpe diem.
Seize the day.

HORACE (Quintus Horatius Flaccus) (65–8 BC), Roman poet and satirist: *Ars poetica, 1:11:8*

We must use time as a tool not as a couch.

JOHN FITZGERALD KENNEDY (1917–63), American statesman and president: *Observer, 'Sayings of the Week', 10 December 1961*

Those who make the worst use of their time are the first to complain of its brevity.

JEAN DE LA BRUYÈRE (1645–96), French moralist: *Characters*

Lives of great men all remind us
We can make our lives sublime.
And, departing, leave behind us
Footprints on the sands of time.

HENRY WADSWORTH LONGFELLOW (1807–82), American poet and translator: *A Psalm of Life*

Time has no divisions to mark its passage, there is never a thunderstorm or blare of trumpets to announce the beginning of a new month or year. Even when a new century begins it is only we mortals who ring bells and fire off pistols.

THOMAS MANN (1875–1955), German novelist and essayist: *The Magic Mountain*

Time ... is the centre of the chief difficulty of almost every economic problem.

ALFRED MARSHALL (1842–1924), English classical economist: *Principles of Economics*

Tempus fugit.
Time flies.

OVID (Publius Ovidius Naso) (43 BC–?17 AD), Roman poet: *Fasti*

An hour in the morning is worth two in the evening.

PROVERB

Lose an hour in the morning and you'll be all day hunting for it.

PROVERB

Punctuality is the soul of business.

PROVERB

Take time by the forelock.
PROVERB

Time lost cannot be recalled.
PROVERB

What greater crime than loss of time?
PROVERB

Who waits for time, loses time.
PROVERB

Half our life is spent trying to find something to do with the
time we have rushed through life trying to save.
WILL(IAM PENN ADAIR) ROGERS (1879–1935), American actor and
humorist: *The Autobiography of Will Rogers*

Better three hours too soon than a minute too late.
WILLIAM SHAKESPEARE (1564–1616), English dramatist and poet: *The
Merry Wives of Windsor, Act 2*

Macbeth:
Tomorrow, and tomorrow, and tomorrow,
Creeps in this petty pace from day to day
To the last syllable of recorded time,
And all our yesterdays have lighted fools
The way to dusty death. Out, out, brief candle!
Life's but a walking shadow, a poor player,
That struts and frets his hour upon the stage,
And then is heard no more; it is a tale
Told by an idiot, full of sound and fury,
Signifying nothing.
WILLIAM SHAKESPEARE: *Macbeth, Act 5*

Time's the king of men,
He's both their parent, and he is their grave,
And gives them what he will, not what they crave.
WILLIAM SHAKESPEARE: *Pericles, Act 2*

We burn daylight.
WILLIAM SHAKESPEARE: *The Merry Wives of Windsor, Act 2*

If Winter comes, can Spring be far behind?
PERCY BYSSHE SHELLEY (1792–1822), English poet: *Ode to the West Wind*

Time: that which man is always trying to kill, but which ends in killing him.
HERBERT SPENCER (1820–1903), English philosopher: *Definitions*

Fugit irreparabile tempus.
When time flies it cannot be recalled.
VIRGIL (Publius Vergilius Maro) (70–19 BC), Roman poet: *Georgics*

He was always late on principle, his principle being that **punct**uality is the thief of time.
OSCAR WILDE (1856–1900), Irish poet, dramatist and wit: *The Picture of Dorian Gray*

Time is waste of money.
OSCAR WILDE: *Phrases and Philosophies for the Use of the Young*

Procrastination is the thief of time.
EDWARD YOUNG (1683–1765), English poet and dramatist: *Night Thoughts*

Business Facts of Life

The quotations in this section reveal differing attempts to come to terms with such realities of life as failure, poverty, bankruptcy, debt and unemployment. On the one hand we see an approach that looks objectively at the problems, trying to find a solution, for example the Arabic proverb 'Man learns little from success, but much from failure'. On the other hand there's an approach that tries to raise morale by touches of gentle humour – for example Errol Flynn's 'If there's anyone listening to whom I owe money, I'm prepared to forget it if you are'.

Assertiveness

The basic difference between being assertive and being aggressive is how our words and behaviour affect the rights and well-being of others.
SHARON ANTHONY BOWER, American writer

To know oneself, one should assert oneself.
ALBERT CAMUS (1913–60), French philosopher and writer

Assertiveness is not what you do, it's who you are!
SHAKTI GAWAIN (1948–), author (Attributed)

To exercise power costs effort and demands courage. That is why so many fail to assert rights to which they are perfectly entitled – because a right is a kind of power but they are too lazy or too cowardly to exercise it.
FRIEDRICH WILHELM NIETZSCHE (1844–1900), German philosopher, poet and critic

Bankruptcy

Pull off a coup and you're a national hero, fail and you're an evil criminal; in business it's the same difference between bankruptcy and making a fortune.

JEFFREY ARCHER (1940–), British politician and author: *A Quiver Full of Arrows*

A beggar can never be bankrupt.

JOHN CLARKE (1609–76), English writer and pioneer settler of Rhode Island: *Paroemiologia Anglo-Latina*

Micawber:
Annual income twenty pounds, annual expenditure nineteen nineteen and six, result happiness. Annual income twenty pounds, annual expenditure twenty pounds ought and six, result misery.

CHARLES (JOHN HUFFAM) DICKENS (1812–70), English novelist: *David Copperfield, chapter 12*

It has long been my deliberate judgement that all bankrupts, of whatsoever denomination, civil or religious, ought to be hanged.

CHARLES (ELIA) LAMB (1775–1834), English essayist: *Letter to Bernard Barton, 8 December 1829*

If the nation is living within its income its credit is good. If in some crisis it lives beyond its income for a year or two it can usually borrow temporarily on reasonable terms. But if, like the spendthrift, it throws discretion to the winds, is willing to make no sacrifice at all in spending, extends its taxing up to the limit of the people's power to pay, and continues to pile up deficits, it is on the road to bankruptcy.

FRANKLIN DELANO ROOSEVELT (1882–1945), American statesman and president: *Speech, Pittsburgh, 19 October 1932*

All decent people live beyond their incomes nowadays, and those who aren't respectable live beyond other people's. A few gifted individuals manage to do both.

SAKI (Hector Hugh Monro) (1870–1916), English novelist and short-story writer: *The Match Maker*

Solvency is entirely a matter of temperament and not of income.

LOGAN PEARSALL SMITH (1865–1946), American-born Englishman of letters: *All Trivia*

He was a gentleman who was generally spoken of as having nothing a-year, paid quarterly.

ROBERT SMITH SURTEES (1803–64), English sporting writer: *Mr Sponge's Sporting Tour, chapter 24*

Crime

I think crime pays. The hours are good, you travel a lot.

WOODY ALLEN (Allen Stewart Konigsberg) (1935–), American film comedian, screenwriter and director: *Take the Money and Run*

Poverty is the parent of revolution and crime.

ARISTOTLE (384–322 BC), Greek philosopher and scientist: *Politics*

Be sure your sin will find you out.

The Bible, Authorised (King James) Version, Numbers 32:23

Crime … is an act committed or omitted in violation of a public law either forbidding or commanding it.

SIR WILLIAM BLACKSTONE (1723–80), English jurist: *Commentaries on the Laws of England*

How many crimes committed merely because their authors could not endure being wrong!

ALBERT CAMUS (1913–60), French philosopher and writer: *The Fall*

Stolen sweets are best.

COLLEY CIBBER (1671–1757), English actor, dramatist and poet laureate: *The Rival Fools*

Of Professor Moriarty:

He is the Napoleon of crime.

SIR ARTHUR CONAN DOYLE (1859–1930), English writer: *The Final Problem*

No man who commits a crime in secret can ever be sure that he will not be detected, even though he has escaped 10,000 times in the past.

EPICURUS (341–270 BC), Greek philosopher: *Aphorisms*

There are three ways by which an individual can get wealth – by work, by gift, and by theft. And, clearly, the reason why the workers get so little is that the beggars and thieves get so much.

HENRY GEORGE (1839–97), American economist: *Social Problems*

Mikado:

My object all sublime

I shall achieve in time –

To let the punishment fit the crime –

The punishment fit the crime.

SIR WILLIAM SCHWENK GILBERT (1836–1911), English parodist and librettist: *The Mikado, Act 2*

Men are not hanged for stealing Horses, but that Horses may not be stolen.

HALIFAX, 1st Marquis of, Sir George Savile (1633–95), English statesman, writer and orator: *Political Thoughts and Reflections: Of Punishment*

I am not a crook.

RICHARD MILHOUS NIXON (1913–94), American politician and president: *Remark, 17 November 1973*

Property is theft.

PIERRE JOSEPH PROUDHON (1809–65), French political theorist: *Qu'est-ce que la propriété?, chapter I*

Crime is a logical extension of the sort of behavior that is often considered perfectly respectable in legitimate business.

ROBERT RICE (1916–), American criminologist: *The Business of Crime*

The faults of the burglar are the qualities of the financier.

GEORGE BERNARD SHAW (1856–1950), Irish dramatist and critic: *Major Barbara*

A crowded police court docket is the surest of all signs that trade is brisk and money plenty.

MARK TWAIN (Samuel Langhorne Clemens) (1835–1910), American novelist and humorist: *Roughing It*

I came to the conclusion many years ago that almost all crime is due to the repressed desire for aesthetic expression.

EVELYN (ARTHUR ST JOHN) WAUGH (1903–66), English novelist: *Decline and Fall*

Debt

Running into debt isn't so bad. It's running into creditors that hurts.

ANON

It is better to pay a creditor than to give to a friend.

ARISTOTLE (384–322 BC), Greek philosopher and scientist: *Nicomachean Ethics*

Debt:
An ingenious substitute for the chain and whip of the slave-driver.

AMBROSE (GWINETT) BIERCE (1842–?1914), American journalist and humorist: *The Devil's Dictionary*

Jubilee 2000 is a broad coalition [to cancel third-world debt] which has moved the earth.

GORDON BROWN (1951–), British prime minister

Debt is a prolific mother of folly and of crime.

BENJAMIN DISRAELI, 1st Earl of Beaconsfield (1804–81), English statesman, prime minister and novelist

Always pay; for first or last you must pay your entire debt.

RALPH WALDO EMERSON (1803–82), American poet, essayist and philosopher: *Essays, 'Compensation'*

If there's anyone listening to whom I owe money, I'm prepared to forget it if you are.

ERROL FLYNN (1909–59), Australian-born American film star

Debt is the worst poverty.

THOMAS FULLER (1654–1734), English physician, writer and compiler: *Gnomologia*

Sins and debts are always more than we think them to be.

THOMAS FULLER, as above

I must say, I never expected to see the day where I would be talking about anything other than reducing the debt; I'm running into the tyranny of zero, which is where you can't reduce (the debt) any more.

ALAN GREENSPAN (1926–), American businessman

Small debts are like small shot; they are rattling on every side, and can scarcely be escaped without a wound: great debts are like cannon; of loud noise, but little danger.

SAMUEL JOHNSON (1709–84), English lexicographer, essayist and poet: *Letter to Joseph Simpson, 1759*

Debt is better than death.
PROVERB

Say nothing of my debts unless you mean to pay them.
PROVERB

The debtor is always in the wrong.
PROVERB

Debt is the slavery of the free.
PUBLILIUS SYRUS (1st c. BC), Latin writer of mimes

A promise made is a debt unpaid.
ROBERT W(ILLIAM) SERVICE (1874–1958), English-born Canadian writer:
The Cremation of Sam McGee

Stephano:
He that dies pays all debts.
WILLIAM SHAKESPEARE (1564–1616), English dramatist and poet: *The
Tempest, Act 3*

He who promises runs in debt.
The Talmud

The payment of debts is necessary for social order. The non-
payment is quite equally necessary for social order. For centuries
humanity has oscillated, serenely unaware, between these two
contradictory necessities.
SIMONE WEIL (1909–43), French philosopher

Equality & Inequality

Equality is a myth – women are better.
ANON

When quarrels and complaints arise, it is when people who are equal have not got equal shares, or vice versa.

ARISTOTLE (384–322 BC), Greek philosopher and scientist: *Nicomachean Ethics*

'The removal of all social and political inequalities' is a very dubious phrase with which to replace 'the removal of all class distinctions'. There will always be certain inequalities in the standard of life in different countries, provinces and places. They can be reduced to a minimum, but they can never be removed.

FRIEDRICH ENGELS (1820–95), German socialist leader and political philosopher: *Letter to August Bebel, 28 March 1875*

Just as the modern mass production requires the standardization of commodities, so the social process requires standardization of man, and this standardization is called 'equality'.

ERICH FROMM (1900–80), German-born American psychoanalyst and philosopher: *The Art of Loving, chapter 2*

Though all men were made of one metal, yet they were not cast all in the same mould.

THOMAS FULLER (1654–1734), English physician, writer and compiler: *Gnomologia*

The grocery store is the great equalizer where mankind comes to grips with the facts of life like toilet tissue.

JOSEPH GOLDBERG (1915–), American grocer: quoted in Jonathon Green, *A Dictionary of Contemporary Quotations*

That all men are equal is a proposition to which, at ordinary times, no sane individual has ever given his assent.

ALDOUS (LEONARD) HUXLEY (1894–1963), English novelist and essayist: *Proper Studies*

We hold these truths to be self-evident: that all men are created equal; that they are endowed by their Creator with inalienable rights; that among these are life, liberty, and the pursuit of happiness.

THOMAS JEFFERSON (1743–1826), American statesman and president: *The Declaration of Independence*

So far is it from being true that men are naturally equal, that no two people can be half an hour together, but one shall acquire an evident superiority over the other.

SAMUEL JOHNSON (1709–84), English lexicographer, essayist and poet: quoted in James Boswell, *The Life of Samuel Johnson*

We need inequality in order to eliminate poverty.

SIR KEITH JOSEPH (1918–94), British politician: quoted in Audrey Hilton, *This England, 74–78*

All of us do not have equal talent, but all of us should have an equal opportunity to develop our talents.

JOHN FITZGERALD KENNEDY (1917–63), American statesman and president: *Speech, 1963*

I have cherished the ideal of a democratic and free society in which all persons live together in harmony and with equal opportunities.

NELSON MANDELA (1918–), South African statesman and president

I shrug my shoulders in despair at women who moan at the lack of opportunities and then take two weeks off work as a result of falling out with their boyfriends.

SOPHIE MIRMAN (1956–), British businesswoman

All animals are equal but some animals are more equal than others.

GEORGE ORWELL (Eric Arthur Blair) (1903–50), English novelist and essayist: *Animal Farm, chapter 10*

At a round table, there's no dispute of place.
PROVERB

The only real equality is in the cemetery.
PROVERB

The nature of things continually tends to the destruction of equality.
JEAN-JACQUES ROUSSEAU (1712–78), Swiss-born French philosopher and writer: *Du central social*

The yearning after equality is the offspring of covetousness, and there is no possible plan for satisfying that yearning which can do aught else than rob A to give to B; consequently all such plans nourish some of the meanest vices of human nature, waste capital, and overthrow civilization.
WILLIAM SUMNER (1840–1910), American political economist and sociologist: *What Social Classes Owe to Each Other*

Inequality … leads to the misdirection of production. For, since the demand of one income of £50,000 is as powerful a magnet as the demand of 500 incomes of £100, it diverts energy from the creation of wealth to the multiplication of luxuries.
R(ICHARD) H(ENRY) TAWNEY (1880–1962), English economic historian: *The Acquisitive Society*

So far as the natural law is concerned, all men are equal.
ULPIAN (Domitius Ulpianus) (?AD 170–?228), Roman jurist: *Liber singularis regularum*

The most dramatic thing is that, even when you look at women who are working full time outside the home … when it comes to ironing and cleaning, 60 or 70 per cent of that work is still done by the women.
MALCOLM WICKS, British politician

Everybody should have an equal chance – but they shouldn't have a flying start.

SIR (JAMES) HAROLD WILSON, Lord Wilson of Rievaulx (1916–95), English statesman and prime minister: *Observer*, 'Sayings of the Year', 1963

Failure

Failure is a temporary detour, not a dead-end street.

ANON

There is much to be said for failure. It is more interesting than success.

SIR MAX BEERBOHM (1872–1956), English writer and caricaturist: *Mainly on the Air*, 'A Small Boy Seeing Giants'

The world is made of people who never quite get into the first team and who just miss the prizes at the flower show.

JACOB BRONOWSKI (1908–74), English scientist and writer: *The Face of Violence*, chapter 6

He that is down needs fear no fall.

JOHN BUNYAN (1628–88), English preacher and writer: *Pilgrim's Progress*

[On being asked to name the biggest mistake he had made] I wish you'd have given me this written question ahead of time so I could plan for it … I'm sure something will pop into my head here in the midst of this press conference, with all the pressure of trying to come up with answer, but it hadn't yet … I don't want to sound like I have made no mistakes. I'm confident I have. I just haven't – you just put me under the spot here, and maybe I'm not as quick on my feet as I should be in coming up with one.

GEORGE W. BUSH (1946–), American president

What worries me is that we are going to end up as a fourth-rate country.

CHARLES, Prince of Wales (1948–): *Observer, 'Sayings of the Year',* 29 December 1985

It is a law of human nature that in victory even the coward may boast of his prowess, while defeat injures the reputation even of the brave.

GAIUS SALLUSTIUS CRISPUS (1st c. AD), Roman historian and politician

Would you ever buy a used car from me?

JOHN DELOREAN (1925–2005), American motor-car entrepreneur: *Observer, 'Sayings of the Year',* 30 December 1984

I have not failed. I've just found 10,000 ways that won't work.

THOMAS ALVA EDISON (1847–1931), American inventor

If at first you don't succeed, try again. Then quit. No use being a damn fool about it.

W(ILLIAM) C(LAUDE) FIELDS (William Claude Dukenfield) (1880–1946), American actor and comedian

Only those who dare to fail greatly can ever achieve greatly.

ROBERT FRANCIS KENNEDY (1925–68), American statesman

It's a good thing to make mistakes so long as you're found out quickly.

JOHN MAYNARD KEYNES (1883–1946), English economist (Attributed)

Men fall from great fortune because of the same shortcomings that led to their rise.

JEAN DE LA BRUYÈRE (1645–96), French moralist: *Characters*

If we had no faults of our own, we would not take so much

pleasure in noticing those of others.
FRANÇOIS LA ROCHEFOUCAULD, Duc de La Rochefoucauld (1613–80),
French writer: *Reflections*

Great men too make mistakes, and many among them do it so
often that one is almost tempted to call them little men.
GEORG CHRISTOPH LICHTENBERG (1742–99), German physicist and
writer: *Aphorisms*

Many of the job failures, nervous breakdowns, and 'battles with
the bottle' almost certainly have their causes in vocational
misplacement and subsequent mishandling by well-intentioned
but often unqualified personnel people.
ROBERT N. MCMURRY (1901–   ): *Howard Business Review, 1965, 'Clear
Communications for Chief Executives'*

Failure makes people bitter and cruel. Success improves the
character of the man.
W(ILLIAM) SOMERSET MAUGHAM (1874–1965), English writer: *The
Summing Up*

Of a bankrupt:
Failure has gone to his head.
WILSON MIZNER (1876–1933), American dramatist (Attributed)

The man who makes no mistakes does not usually make anything.
EDWARD JOHN PHELPS (1822–1900), American lawyer and diplomat: *Speech,
Mansion House, London, 24 January 1899*

To err is human, to forgive, divine.
ALEXANDER POPE (1688–1744), English poet and satirist: *An Essay on
Criticism*

A miss is as good as a mile.
PROVERB

Failure teaches success.
PROVERB

You win some, you lose some.
PROVERB

Man learns little from success, but much from failure.
ARABIC PROVERB

There is no formula for success. But there is a formula for failure, and that is trying to please everybody.
NICHOLAS RAY (1911–79), American film director: quoted in Jonathon Green, *A Dictionary of Contemporary Quotations*

Fortune's not content with knocking a man down; she sends him spinning head over heels, crash upon crash.
MARCUS or Lucius ANNAEUS SENECA (The Elder) (?55 BC–?AD 39), Roman writer on oratory and history: *Letters to Lucilius*

I would prefer even to fail with honour than win by cheating.
SOPHOCLES (?496–406 BC), Greek dramatist: *Philoctetes*

Once we realise that imperfect understanding is the human condition, there is no shame in being wrong, only in failing to correct our mistakes.
GEORGE SOROS (1930–), Hungarian-born businessman and philanthropist

It's a British cultural thing to look at what's gone wrong.
JOHN SUFFOLK, British Government Chief Information Officer

Experience is the name everyone gives to their mistakes.
OSCAR WILDE (1856–1900), Irish poet, dramatist and wit: *Lady Windermere's Fan*

The Haves & The Have-Nots

The Third World is not a reality, but an ideology.
HANNAH ARENDT (1906–75), American writer: *On Violence*

The unfortunate need people who will be kind to them; the prosperous need people to be kind to.
ARISTOTLE (384–322 BC), Greek philosopher and scientist: *Nicomachean Ethics*

You cannot sift out the poor from the community. The poor are indispensable to the rich.
HENRY WARD BEECHER (1813–87), American clergyman, editor and writer: *Proverbs from Plymouth Pulpit*

There are only two families in the world, my old grandmother used to say, The Haves and The Have-Nots.
MIGUEL DE CERVANTES (SAAVEDRA) (1547–1616), Spanish writer: *Don Quixote*

The rich man may never get into heaven, but the pauper is already serving his term in hell.
ALEXANDER CHASE (1926–), American journalist: *Perspectives*

The honest poor can sometimes forget poverty. The honest rich can never forget it.
G(ILBERT) K(EITH) CHESTERTON (1874–1936), English essayist, novelist, poet and critic: *All Things Considered, 'Cockneys and Their Jokes'*

If rich, it is easy enough to conceal our wealth; but if poor, it is not quite so easy to conceal our poverty. It is less difficult to hide a thousand guineas than one hole in our coat.
CHARLES CALEB COLTON (?1780–1832), English clergyman and writer: *Lacon*

I was told that the Privileged and the People formed Two Nations.
BENJAMIN DISRAELI, 1st Earl of Beaconsfield (1804–82), English statesman, prime minister and novelist: *Sybil, book 4*

Two nations between whom there is no intercourse and no sympathy; who are as ignorant of each other's habits, thoughts and feelings, as if they were dwellers in different zones or inhabitants of different planets ... the rich and the poor.
BENJAMIN DISRAELI: *Sybil, book 2*

At the end of this century when we look back on the great tragedies and movements of our age, certainly this famine, which potentially will kill 100 million people, is one of the shameful things of our time and I find it an indictment of us and of a pathetic way of living that a piece of plastic seven inches across with a hole in the middle is the price of someone's life this year.
BOB GELDOF (1954–), Irish rock star: *BBC News, Review of the Year, 29 December 1985*

So long as all the increased wealth which modern progress brings goes but to build up great fortunes, to increase luxury and make sharper the contrast between the House of Have and the House of Want, progress is not real and cannot be permanent.
HENRY GEORGE (1839–97), American economist: *Progress and Poverty*

Development in the Third World usually means the overdevelopment of objects and the under-development of people.
RICHARD GOTT (1938–), British journalist: *Guardian, 30 November 1976*

If a free society cannot help the many who are poor, it cannot save the few who are rich.
JOHN FITZGERALD KENNEDY (1917–63), American statesman and president: *Inaugural address, 20 January 1961*

The concessions of the privileged to the unprivileged are seldom brought about by any better motive than the power of the unprivileged to extort them.

JOHN STUART MILL (1806–73), English philosopher and economist: *The Subjugation of Women*

God help the rich; the poor can beg.

PROVERB

There's one law for the rich, and another for the poor.

PROVERB

The rich man thinks of the future, the poor man thinks of today.

CHINESE PROVERB

The poor man is ruined as soon as he begins to ape the rich.

PUBLILIUS SYRUS (1st c. BC), Latin writer of mimes: *Moral Sayings*

As long as there are rich people in the world, they will be desirous of distinguishing themselves from the poor.

JEAN-JACQUES ROUSSEAU (1712–78), Swiss-born French philosopher and writer: *Discourse on Political Economy*

Who made your millions for you? Me and my like. Whats kep us poor? Keepin you rich.

GEORGE BERNARD SHAW (1856–1950), Irish dramatist and critic: *Major Barbara, Act 2*

The world will not live in harmony so long as two-thirds of its inhabitants find difficulty in living at all.

U THANT (1909–74), Burmese diplomat, secretary-general of United Nations: *Observer, 'Sayings of the Decade', 28 December 1969*

There is only one class in the community that thinks more about money than the rich, and that is the poor.

OSCAR WILDE (1856–1900), Irish poet, dramatist and wit: *The Soul of Man Under Socialism*

Inflation

Inflation means that your money won't buy as much today as it did when you didn't have any.

ANON

When I first started working I used to dream of the day when I might be earning the salary I'm starving on now.

ANON

Inflation is one form of taxation that can be imposed without legislation.

MILTON FRIEDMAN (1912–2006), American economist

Inflation does not lubricate trade but by rescuing traders from their errors of optimism or stupidity.

JOHN KENNETH GALBRAITH (1908–2006), Canadian-born American economist, diplomat and writer: *Money, chapter 2*

We are obviously all hurt by inflation. Everybody is hurt by inflation. If you really wanted to examine who percentage-wise is hurt the most in their incomes, it is the Wall Street brokers. I mean their incomes have gone down the most.

ALAN GREENSPAN (1926–), American businessman: quoted in *Respectfully Quoted*

Inflation is like sin; every government denounces it and every government practises it.

SIR FREDERICK LEITH-ROSS (1887–1968): *Observer, 30 June 1957*

Justice & Injustice

Justice is a certain rectitude of mind whereby a man does what he ought to do in the circumstances confronting him.

SAINT THOMAS AQUINAS (1225–74), Italian theologian, scholastic philosopher and Dominican friar: *Summa theologiae*

A false balance is abomination to the Lord: but a just weight is his delight.

The Bible, Authorised (King James) Version, Proverbs 11:1

Is not this the fast that I have chosen? to loose the bands of wickedness, to undo the heavy burdens, and to let the oppressed go free, and that ye break every yoke? Is it not to deal thy bread to the hungry, and that thou bring the poor that are cast out to thy house? when thou seest the naked, that thou cover him; and that thou hide not thyself from thine own flesh? Then shall thy light break forth as the morning, and thine health shall spring forth speedily: and thy righteousness shall go before thee; the glory of the Lord shall be thy reward.

As above, Isaiah 58:6-8

The labourer is worthy of his hire.

As above, Luke 10:7

The fundamentals of justice are that no one shall suffer wrong, and that the public good be served.

MARCUS TULLIUS CICERO (106–43 BC), Roman statesman and orator: *De officiis*

Let justice be done, though the world perish.

FERDINAND I (1503–64), Holy Roman Emperor (Attributed)

Justice is the end of government. It is the end of civil society. It ever has been and ever will be pursued until it be obtained, or until liberty be lost in the pursuit.

ALEXANDER HAMILTON (?1757–1804), American Federalist politician: *The Federalist*

Justice should not only be done, but should manifestly and undoubtedly be seen to be done.

GORDON HEWART, Lord Hewart (1870–1943), British lawyer and statesman: *The Chief (R. Jackson)*

If you study the history and records of the world you must admit that the source of justice was the fear of injustice.

HORACE (Quintus Horatius Flaccus) (65–8 BC), Roman poet and satirist: *Satires*

The three fundamental rules of justice, the stability of possession, its transference by consent, and the performance of promises, are duties of princes as well as of subjects … Where possession has no stability, there must be perpetual war. Where property is not transferred by consent, there can be no commerce. Where promises are not observed, there can be no leagues or alliances.

DAVID HUME (1711–76), Scottish philosopher and historian: *A Treatise of Human Nature, book 3*

Love of justice in the generality of man is only the fear of suffering from injustice.

FRANÇOIS LA ROCHEFOUCAULD, Duc de La Rochefoucauld (1613–80), French writer: *Maxims*

Justice without force is impotent, force without justice is tyranny … Not being able to make what is just strong, we make what was strong just.

BLAISE PASCAL (1623–62), French philosopher, mathematician and physicist: *Pensées*

Every one loves justice in the affairs of another.
PROVERB

Poverty

A true test of a civilisation is the way it treats its poor.
ANON

God loves the poor, and that is why he made so many of them.
ANON

What fun it would be to be poor, as long as one was excessively poor! Anything in excess is most exhilarating.
JEAN ANOUILH (1910–87), French dramatist: *Ring Round the Moon, Act 2*

Poverty is the parent of revolution and crime.
ARISTOTLE (384–322 BC), Greek philosopher and scientist: *The Politics, book 2*

Poverty is an anomaly to rich people. It is very difficult to make out why people who want dinner do not ring the bell.
WALTER BAGEHOT (1826–77), English economist and journalist: *Literary Studies*

Poverty is not a misfortune to the poor only who suffer it, but it is more or less a misfortune to all with whom he deals.
HENRY WARD BEECHER (1813–87), American clergyman, editor and writer: *Speech, 16 October 1863*

For the poor always ye have with you.
The Bible, Authorised (King James) Version, John 12:8

We spend more on cows than the poor.
GORDON BROWN (1951–), British prime minister

To be poor and independent is very nearly an impossibility.

WILLIAM COBBETT (1762–1835), English farmer, social reformer and writer: *Advice to Young Men*

Poverty is the symptom; slavery the disease.

G(EORGE) D(OUGLAS) H(OWARD) COLE (1889–1959), English economist and historian: *Self-Government in Industry*

The poor man is happy: he expects no change for the worse.

DEMETRIUS OF PHALERUM (?345–280 BC), Greek orator and statesman: *Fragment*

Sam Weller:
Poverty and oysters always seem to go together.

CHARLES (JOHN HUFFAM) DICKENS (1812–70), English novelist: *Pickwick Papers*

Poverty consists in feeling poor.

RALPH WALDO EMERSON (1803–82), American poet, essayist and philosopher: *Society and Solitude*

There's no scandal like rags, nor any crime so shameful as poverty.

GEORGE FARQUHAR (1678–1707), Irish dramatist: *The Beaux' Stratagem*

I used to think I was poor. Then they told me I wasn't poor, I was needy. Then they told me it was self-defeating to think of myself as needy. I was deprived. Then they told me that underprivileged was overused. I was disadvantaged. I still don't have a dime. But I have a great vocabulary.

JULES FEIFFER (1929–), American cartoonist: *Village Voice, 1965*

Poverty often deprives a man of all spirit and virtue.

BENJAMIN FRANKLIN (1706–90), American statesman, scientist and author: *Poor Richard's Almanac*

He is not poor that hath not much, but he that craves much.
THOMAS FULLER (1654–1734), English physician, writer and compiler:
Gnomologia

It is but a truism that labor is most productive where its wages
are largest. Poorly paid labor is inefficient labor, the world over.
HENRY GEORGE (1839–97), American economist: *Progress and Poverty, book 9*

Poverty is a great enemy to human happiness; it certainly
destroys liberty, and it makes some virtues impracticable, and
others extremely difficult.
SAMUEL JOHNSON (1709–84), English lexicographer, essayist and poet:
quoted in James Boswell, *The Life of Samuel Johnson*

Our purpose is not to buy friends or hire allies. Our purpose is
to defeat poverty ... Our goal is to again influence history instead
of merely observing it.
JOHN FITZGERALD KENNEDY (1917–63), American statesman and
president: *Saturday Review, 7 December 1963, 'Ideas, Attitudes, Purposes from His
Speeches and Writings'*

In other countries poverty is a misfortune – with us it is a crime.
EDWARD GEORGE EARLE LYTTON BULWER-LYTTON, 1st Baron Lytton
(1803–73), English novelist, dramatist and statesman: *England and the English*

If you are poor today you will always be poor. Only the rich now
acquire riches.
MARTIAL (Marcus Valerius Martialis) (?AD 40–?104), Spanish-born
epigrammatist and poet: *Epigrams*

Beggars should be abolished entirely! Verily, it is annoying to give
to them and it is annoying not to give to them.
FRIEDRICH WILHELM NIETZSCHE (1844–1900), German philosopher, poet
and critic: *Thus Spoke Zarathustra, 'On the Pitying'*

Work for the elimination of concrete evils rather than for the realisation of abstract goods. Do not aim at establishing happiness by political means. Rather, aim at the elimination of poverty by direct means.

SIR KARL POPPER (1902–94), Austrian-born English philosopher and biochemist: *Conjectures and Refutations, 'Utopia and Violence'*

Better die a beggar than live a beggar.

PROVERB

He who is content in his poverty, is wonderfully rich.

PROVERB

If you have no money, be polite.

PROVERB

Poverty is not a vice.

PROVERB

Poverty is the mother of crime.

PROVERB

The poor sit on the front benches in Paradise.

PROVERB

I can't talk religion to a man with bodily hunger in his eyes.

GEORGE BERNARD SHAW (1856–1950), Irish dramatist and critic: *Major Barbara, Act 1*

Lack of money is the root of all evil.

GEORGE BERNARD SHAW: *Man and Superman*

The greatest of our evils and the worst of our crimes is poverty, and ... our first duty, to which every other consideration should

be sacrificed, is not to be poor.
GEORGE BERNARD SHAW: *Major Barbara*

No complaint … is more common than that of a scarcity of money.
ADAM SMITH (1723–90), Scottish economist and philosopher: *The Wealth of Nations, volume 1*

No society can surely be flourishing and happy, of which the far greater part of the members are poor and miserable.
ADAM SMITH, as above

Poverty is no disgrace to a man, but it is confoundedly inconvenient.
SYDNEY SMITH (1771–1845), English journalist, clergyman and wit: *His Wit and Wisdom*

Redundancy

We have corporate CEOs who raise their pay 20 per cent or more in years when they lay off thousands of people. It's obscene.
CHARLES HANDY (1932–), Irish author and philosopher

You're fired!
SIR ALAN SUGAR (1947–), British entrepreneur: *The Apprentice, BBC television*

When two men in a business always agree one of them is unnecessary.
WILLIAM WRIGLEY, JR (1861–1932), American businessman

Taxes

His horse went dead, and his mule went lame,
And he lost six cows in a poker game;

Then a hurricane came on a Summer day,
And blew the house where he lived away;
An earthquake came when that was gone,
And swallowed the land the house stood on.
And then the tax collector came around,
And charged him up with the hole in the ground.
ANON

Taxman:
The position is that if I don't have one thousand pounds from you soon, you're going to jail.

Businessman:
Now you're talking. Here's one thousand pounds in used notes.

Taxman:
Let me give you a receipt.

Businessman:
What, a thousand nicker in cash and you're going to put it through the books?

ANON: quoted in Fred Metcalf, *The Penguin Dictionary of Modern Humorous Quotations*

Render unto Caesar the things which are Caesar's; and unto God the things that are God's.

The Bible, Authorised (King James) Version, Matthew 22:21

Tariff:
A scale of taxes on imports, designed to protect the domestic producer against the greed of his consumer.

AMBROSE (GWINETT) BIERCE (1842–?1914), American journalist and humorist: *The Devil's Dictionary*

There is just one thing I can promise you about the outer-space

program – your tax dollar will go further.
WERNHER VON BRAUN (1912–77), German-born American rocket engineer

The really rich people figure out how to dodge taxes anyway.
GEORGE W. BUSH (1946–), American president

There is no such thing as a good tax.
SIR WINSTON LEONARD SPENCER CHURCHILL (1874–1965), English statesman, writer and prime minister: *Observer, 'Sayings of the Week', 6 June 1937*

The art of taxation consists in so plucking the goose as to obtain the largest amount of feathers with the least possible amount of hissing.
JEAN BAPTISTE COLBERT (1619–83), French statesman (Attributed)

You should go and see the Millennium Dome. Apparently they've got an exhibition in there that shows you how VAT works.
KEN DODD (1927–), English comedian

The hardest thing in the world to understand is the income tax.
ALBERT EINSTEIN (1879–1955), German-Swiss-American physicist (Attributed)

The Treasury has a vested interest in trying to sustain the process by which people are encouraged to get lung cancer.
MICHAEL FOOT (1913–), English politician: *Observer, 'Sayings of the Year', 27 December 1964*

A government big enough to give us everything we want would be big enough to take from us everything we have.
GERALD FORD (1913–2006), American president

In this world nothing can be said to be certain, except death and taxes.
BENJAMIN FRANKLIN (1706–90), American statesman, scientist and author: *Letter to Jean Baptiste Le Roy, 13 November 1789*

The amount paid by those who drink and smoke was £715,000,000, very nearly a pre-war Budget, whereas the taxation paid by those who did not drink and smoke, on tea, coffee, and so on, was £25,000,000. Yet those citizens expect and receive precisely the same protections from the Fleet, the Army, and the police.

(SIR) A(LAN) P(ATRICK) HERBERT (1890–1971), English writer and MP: *House of Commons, 29 November 1945*

A tax is a payment exacted by authority from part of the community for the benefit of the whole.

SAMUEL JOHNSON (1709–84), English lexicographer, essayist and poet: *Taxation No Tyranny*

Tariffs today are no longer a means of safeguarding growing capitalist production against mature competitors, but a weapon in the struggle of one nationalist block against another. They do not assist industry to grow and capture the domestic market, but merely serve the cartelisation of industry, i.e. assist the struggle of capitalist producers against consumers … Thus a policy of tariffs is in fact no more than a means of casting feudal interests in capitalist form.

ROSA LUXEMBURG (1871–1919), Polish-born German socialist revolutionary: *Social Reform or Revolution*

He who builds a better mousetrap these days runs into material shortages, patent-infringement suits, work stoppages, collusive bidding, discount discrimination – and taxes.

H. E. MARTZ, quoted in *Quotations with an Attitude*

A country cannot be expected to renounce the power of taxing foreigners, unless foreigners will in return practise towards itself the same forbearance. The only mode in which a country can save itself from being a loser by the duties imposed by other countries on its commodities, is to impose corresponding duties on theirs.

JOHN STUART MILL (1806–73), English philosopher and economist: *Essays on Some Unsettled Questions of Political Economy*

The men who collect taxes are working in one of the oldest professions known. Archaeological evidence dating from 1900 BC includes a clay tablet recording a tax for public works and a papyrus scroll which reveals that even 4000 years ago, taxpayers had some complaints.

Optimist Magazine

Taxation without representation is tyranny.

JAMES OTIS (1725–83), American revolutionary leader: *Speech to the Superior Court of Massachusetts, February 1761*

The entire graduated income tax structure was created by Karl Marx.

RONALD REAGAN (1911–2004), American president: quoted in J. Charlton, *The Executive's Quotation Book*

Almost all taxes on production fall finally on the consumer.

DAVID RICARDO (1772–1823), English economist: *On Protection to Agriculture*

Taxes, after all, are the dues that we pay for the privileges of membership in an organized society.

FRANKLIN DELANO ROOSEVELT (1882–1945), American statesman and president: *Speech, Worcester, Massachusetts, 21 October 1936*

The greatest, the most important power entrusted to the government is the right to tax the citizens; it is from this right that all the others flow.

CLAUDE HENRI SAINT-SIMON, Comte de (1760–1825), French political economist: *Politics*

High taxes, sometimes by diminishing the consumption of the tax commodities, and sometimes by encouraging smuggling, frequently afford a smaller revenue to government than what might be drawn from more modest taxes.

ADAM SMITH (1723–90), Scottish economist and philosopher

The subjects of every state ought to contribute towards the support of the government, as nearly as possible, in proportion to their respective abilities; that is, in proportion to the revenue which they respectively enjoy under the protection of the state.
ADAM SMITH: *The Wealth of Nations*

My accountants have told me that I can have one foot in Jersey, my left earlobe in the Isle of Man and my right foot in Zurich and pay little or no tax.
SIR ALAN SUGAR (1947–), British entrepreneur

Unemployment

FIFO: First In, First Out.
ANON

'I quit because the boss used repulsive language.'
'What did he say?'
'He said, "You're fired!"'
ANON

LIFO: Last In, First Out.
ANON

The rate of unemployment is 100 per cent if it is you that is unemployed.
ANON

Unemployment is capitalism's way of getting you to plant a garden.
ORSON SCOTT CARD (1951–), American author

A man willing to work, and unable to find work, is perhaps the

saddest sight that fortune's inequality exhibits under this sun.
THOMAS CARLYLE (1795–1881), Scottish essayist and historian: *Chartism*

When a great many people are unable to find work,
unemployment results.
CALVIN COOLIDGE (1872–1933), American president

In order to mitigate unemployment attending business
depression, we urge the enactment of legislation authorizing that
construction and repair of public works be initiated in periods of
acute unemployment.
US Democratic National Platform, 1924

During a tour of unemployment areas in South Wales:
Something must be done.
EDWARD VIII (1894–1972)

Unemployment is of vital importance, particularly to the
unemployed.
EDWARD (RICHARD GEORGE) HEATH (1916–2005), British statesman and
prime minister: *Observer, 'Sayings of 1980', 28 December 1980*

It took me three months to find someone who would repair the
gate in my garden – in a country with three million unemployed.
NORMAN TEBBIT (1931–), British politician

War

[On terrorists] They never stop thinking about new ways to
harm our country and our people, and neither do we.
GEORGE W. BUSH (1946–), American president

[On the 1991 Gulf War] War is never cheap or easy.
GEORGE W. BUSH (1946–), American president

Endless money forms the sinews of war.

MARCUS TULLIUS CICERO (106–43 BC), Roman statesman and orator: *Philippics*

War is the trade of kings.

JOHN DRYDEN (1631–1700), English poet and dramatist: *King Arthur*

Do you want to know the cause of war? It is capitalism, greed, the dirty hunger for dollars. Take away the capitalist and you will sweep war from the earth.

HENRY FORD (1836–1947), American car manufacturer: *Interview, Detroit News*

Non-violence is not a garment to be put on and off at will. Its seat is in the heart, and it must be an inseparable part of our very being.

MAHATMA GANDHI (Mohandas Karamchand Gandhi) (1869–1948), Hindu nationalist leader: *Non-Violence in Peace and War*

Frankly, I'd like to see the government get out of war altogether and leave the whole field to private industry.

JOSEPH HELLER (1923–99), American novelist: *Catch-22*

The most shocking fact about war is that its victims and its instruments are individual human beings, and that these individual beings are condemned by the monstrous conventions of politics to murder or be murdered in quarrels not their own.

ALDOUS (LEONARD) HUXLEY (1894–1963), English novelist and essayist: *The Olive Tree*

At the conclusion of a ten years' war, how are we recompensed for the death of multitudes and the expense of millions but by contemplating the sudden glories of paymasters and agents, contractors and commissaries, whose equipages shine like meteors, and whose palaces rise like exhalations?

SAMUEL JOHNSON (1709–84), English lexicographer, essayist and poet: *Thoughts Respecting Falkland's Islands*

Mankind must put an end to war or war will put an end to mankind.

JOHN FITZGERALD KENNEDY (1917–63), American statesman and president: *Address, United Nations General Assembly, 25 September 1961*

War will exist until that distant day when the conscientious objector enjoys the same reputation and prestige that the warrior does today.

JOHN FITZGERALD KENNEDY

[Asked if he would have gone to war against Saddam Hussein if he refused to disarm] You bet we might have.

JOHN KERRY (1943–), American senator

In a war of ideas it is people who get killed.

STANISLAW (JERZY) LEC (1909–66), Polish poet and aphorist

Though fraud in other activities be detestable, in the management of war it is laudable and glorious, and he who overcomes an enemy by fraud is as much to be praised as he who does so by force.

NICCOLÒ MACHIAVELLI (1469–1527), Italian statesman and political philosopher: *Discorsi*

War can only be abolished through war, and in order to get rid of the gun it is necessary to take up the gun.

MAO TSE-TUNG (Mao Zedong) (1893–1976), Chinese Communist leader: *Quotations from Chairman Mao Tse-Tung*

All are not soldiers that go to war.

PROVERB

All is fair in love and war.
PROVERB

I have seen war. I have seen war on land and sea. I have seen
blood running from the wounded. I have seen men coughing out
their gassed lungs. I have seen the dead in the mud. I have seen
cities destroyed. I have seen 200 limping, exhausted men come
out of the line – the survivors of a regiment of 1000 that went
forward 48 hours before. I have seen children starving. I have
seen the agony of mothers and wives. I hate war.
FRANKLIN DELANO ROOSEVELT (1882–1945), American statesman and
president: *Speech, Chautauqua, New York, 14 August 1936*

As you know, you go to war with the army you have, not the
army you might want or wish to have at a later time.
DONALD RUMSFELD (1932–), American Defense Secretary

Guerre d mort.
War to the death.
FRENCH SAYING

[Referring to Bosnia-Herzegovina] The region is undergoing
ethnic cleansing.
Serbian radio, 1992

In the midst of the most destructive foreign war ... the greater
part of manufacturers may frequently flourish greatly, and, on
the contrary, they may decline on the return to peace.
ADAM SMITH (1723–90), Scottish economist and philosopher: *The Wealth of
Nations, volume 1*

Let him who desires peace, prepare for war.
VEGETIUS (Flavius Vegetius Renatus) (c. AD 374), Latin writer: *Epitoma rei
militaris*

God is always on the side of the heaviest battalions.

VOLTAIRE (François Marie Arouet) (1694–1778), French writer, philosopher and historian: *Letter to M. de Riche, 6 February 1770*

To be prepared for war is one of the most effectual means of preserving peace.

GEORGE WASHINGTON (1732–99), American statesman and president: *Speech, 8 January 1790*

Asking for a declaration of war:
The world must be made safe for democracy.

(THOMAS) WOODROW WILSON (1856–1924), American statesman and president: *Speech to Congress, 2 April 1917*

Business Qualities

What qualities lead to success in business? Does prosperity come from years of hard work or one 'lucky break', from ruthlessly pursuing a goal, asserting your rights and exploiting others, or just being in the right place at the right time?

The quotations in this final section also tackle such questions as: 'Is honesty always the best policy?', 'Do fame and wealth lead to happiness?', 'Do qualities such as loyalty still have a place in the modern business world?', and 'How do you cope with power and fame when you have reached the top?'

Ability

Let every man practise the profession that he knows best.
MARCUS TULLIUS CICERO (106–43 BC), Roman statesman and orator:
Tusculanae disputationes

It is not enough to have a good mind; the main thing is to use it well.
RENÉ DESCARTES (1596–1650), French philosopher and mathematician:
Discourse on Method

Genius is one percent inspiration and ninety-nine percent perspiration.
THOMAS ALVA EDISON (1847–1931), American inventor: *Life*

The same man cannot well be skilled in everything; each has his special excellence.
EURIPIDES (?480–406BC), Greek tragic dramatist: *Rhesus*

One good head is better than a hundred strong hands.
THOMAS FULLER (1654–1734), English physician, writer and compiler: *Gnomologia*

'Tis skill, not strength that governs a ship.
THOMAS FULLER, as above

The winds and waves are always on the side of the ablest navigators.
EDWARD GIBBON (1737–94), English historian: *Decline and Fall of the Roman Empire*

Few great men could pass Personnel.
PAUL GOODMAN (1911–72), American writer: quoted in Jonathon Green, *A Dictionary of Contemporary Quotations*

Some men are born mediocre, some men achieve mediocrity, and some men have mediocrity thrust upon them. With Major Major it had been all three.
JOSEPH HELLER (1923–99), American novelist: *Catch-22, chapter 9*

If you want work well done, select a busy man: the other kind has no time.
ELBERT (GREEN) HUBBARD (1856–1915), American businessman, writer and printer: *The Note Book*

There is no substitute for talent. Industry and all the virtues are of no avail.
ALDOUS (LEONARD) HUXLEY (1894–1963), English novelist and essayist: *Point Counter Point*

A man who qualifies himself well for his calling never fails of employment.
THOMAS JEFFERSON (1743–1826), American statesman and president

The greatest ability is dependability.
BOB JONES (1883–1968), American evangelist

It is a great ability to be able to conceal one's ability.
FRANÇOIS LA ROCHEFOUCAULD, Duc de La Rochefoucauld (1613–80), French writer: *Maxims*

The height of ability in the least able consists in knowing how to submit to the good leadership of others.

FRANÇOIS LA ROCHEFOUCAULD, as above

We have more ability than will power, and it is often an excuse to ourselves that we imagine that things are impossible.

FRANÇOIS LA ROCHEFOUCAULD, as above

From each according to his ability, to each according to his needs!

KARL MARX (1818–83), German founder of modern communism: *Critique of the Gotha Programme*

It takes no more actual sagacity to carry on the everyday hawking and haggling of the world, or to ladle out its normal doses of bad medicine and worse law, than it takes to operate a taxicab or fry a pan offish.

HENRY LOUIS MENCKEN (1880–1956), American philologist, editor and satirist: *In Defense of Women, 'The Feminine Mind'*

I think I can recognise a real entrepreneur at 300 yards on a misty day! Like an actor he is full of self-confidence and vanity … He feels alone and knows that what he says matters, so being able to make and carry through his own decisions is crucial to him. Above all he has this drive to succeed and get things done.

SIR PETER PARKER (1924–2002), former chairman of British Rail: quoted in Cary L. Cooper and Peter Hingley, *The Change Makers*

Competence, like truth, beauty and contact lenses, is in the eye of the beholder.

DR LAURENCE J. PETER (1919–90), Canadian educator and RAYMOND HULL (1919–): *The Peter Principle, chapter 3*

If you have great talents, industry will improve them: if you have but moderate abilities, industry will supply then-deficiency.

SIR JOSHUA REYNOLDS (1723–92), English portrait painter: *Discourses*

Democracy substitutes election by the incompetent many for appointment by the corrupt few.

GEORGE BERNARD SHAW (1856–1950), Irish dramatist and critic: *Man and Superman, Maxims for Revolutionists*

The price of ability does not depend on merit, but on supply and demand.

GEORGE BERNARD SHAW: *The Fortnightly Review, April 1894, 'Socialism and Superior Brains'*

Experto credite.
Always believe the expert.

VIRGIL (Publius Vergilius Maro) (70–19 BC), Roman poet: *Aeneid*

They are able because they think they are able.

VIRGIL, as above

Luck is not something you can mention in the presence of self-made men.

E(LWYN) B(ROOKS) WHITE (1899–1985), American humorist and essayist: *One Man's Meat*

Intelligence is quickness to apprehend as distinct from ability, which is capacity to act wisely on the thing apprehended.

ALFRED NORTH WHITEHEAD (1861–1947), English mathematician and philosopher: *Dialogues*

An expert is a man who has stopped thinking. Why should he think? He is an expert.

FRANK LLOYD WRIGHT (1869–1959), American architect: *Daily Express, 1959*

Ambition

Ambition:
An overmastering desire to be vilified by enemies while living and made ridiculous by friends when dead.

AMBROSE (GWINETT) BIERCE (1842–?1914), American journalist and humorist: *The Devil's Dictionary*

Ambition, having reached the summit, longs to descend.

PIERRE CORNEILLE (1606–84), French tragic dramatist: *Cinna*

At the age of six I wanted to be a cook. At seven I wanted to be Napoleon. And my ambition has been growing steadily ever since.

SALVADOR DALI (1904–89), Spanish painter

A big man has no time really to do anything but just sit and be big.

FRANCIS SCOTT (KEY) FITZGERALD (1896–1940), American novelist: *This Side of Paradise*

Who never climbed high never fell low.

THOMAS FULLER (1654–1734), English physician, writer and compiler: *Gnomologia*

Great ambition, unchecked by principle or the love of glory, is an unruly tyrant.

ALEXANDER HAMILTON (?1757–1804), American Federalist politician: *Letter to James Bayard, 16 January 1801*

A wise man is cured of ambition by ambition itself; his aim is so exalted that riches, office, fortune, and favour cannot satisfy him.

SAMUEL JOHNSON (1709–84), English lexicographer, essayist and poet: *Characters*

Ambition makes more trusty slaves than need.

BEN JONSON (1573–1637), English playwright and poet: *Sejanus*

We often pass from love to ambition, but we hardly ever return from ambition to love.

FRANÇOIS LA ROCHEFOUCAULD, Duc de La Rochefoucauld (1613–80), French writer: *Maxims*

Most people would succeed in small things, if they were not troubled with great ambitions.

HENRY WADSWORTH LONGFELLOW (1807–52), American poet and translator: *Driftwood, 'Table-Talk'*

Ambition is so powerful a passion in the human breast, that however high we reach we are never satisfied.

NICCOLÒ MACHIAVELLI (1469–1527), Italian statesman and political philosopher

A man's worth is no greater than the worth of his ambitions.

MARCUS AURELIUS ANTONINUS (AD 121–180), Roman emperor and Stoic philosopher: *Meditations*

Men may be popular without being ambitious; but there is rarely an ambitious man who does not try to be popular.

LORD NORTH, Frederick, 2nd Earl of Guilford (1732–92), English statesman and prime minister: *House of Commons, March 1769*

He who would leap high must take a long run.

PROVERB

Ambition is a vice, but it may be the father of virtue.

QUINTILIAN, Marcus Fabius Quintilianus (?AD 35–?96), Roman rhetorician and teacher: *De institutione oratorio*

Ambition often puts men upon doing the meanest offices: so climbing is performed in the same posture with creeping.

JONATHAN SWIFT (1667–1745), Anglo-Irish satirist and churchman: *Thoughts on Various Subjects*

Ambition is the last refuge of the failure.

OSCAR WILDE (1856–1900), Irish poet, dramatist and wit: *Phrases and Philosophies for the Use of the Young*

Caution

Better one safe way than a hundred on which you cannot reckon.

AESOP (c. 620–564 BC), Greek fabulist: *Fables, 'The Fox and the Cat'*

'Tis the part of a wise man to keep himself today for tomorrow, and not venture all his eggs in one basket.

MIGUEL DE CERVANTES (SAAVEDRA) (1547–1616), Spanish writer: *Don Quixote*

Delay always breeds danger.

MIGUEL DE CERVANTES (SAAVEDRA), as above

The cautious seldom err.

CONFUCIUS (Kong Zi) (551–479 BC), Chinese philosopher: *The Confucian Analects*

He who is not a bird should not build his nest over abysses.

FRIEDRICH WILHELM NIETZSCHE (1844–1900), German philosopher, poet and critic: *Thus Spoke Zarathustra*

It is well to moor your ship with two anchors.

PUBLILIUS SYRUS (1st c. BC), Latin writer of mimes: *Moral Sayings*

It is a characteristic of wisdom not to do desperate things.

HENRY DAVID THOREAU (1817–62), American essayist and poet: *Walden*

Confidence & Self-Determination

Some men are just as firmly convinced of what they think as

others are of what they know.
ARISTOTLE (384–322 BC), Greek philosopher and scientist: *Nicomachean Ethics*

The ancient Romans had a tradition: whenever one of their engineers constructed an arch, as the capstone was hoisted into place, the engineer assumed accountability for his work in the most profound way possible: he stood under the arch.
MICHAEL ARMSTRONG (1938–), American business executive: *Speech*

We have got to take the gloves off and have a bare-knuckle fight on some of the things we have to do, because we have to have an effective and prosperous industry.
SIR TERENCE BECKETT (1923–), Director General, CBI: *CBI conference, 1980*

And though hard be the task, 'Keep a stiff upper lip.'
PHOEBE CARY (1824–71), American poet: *Keep a Stiff Upper Lip*

The most important thing in the Olympic Games is not winning but taking part … The essential thing in life is not conquering but fighting well.
BARON PIERRE DE COUBERTIN (1863–1937), French founder of the modern Olympic Games: *Speech, Banquet to Officials of Olympic Games, London, 24 July 1908*

The perfection preached in the Gospels never yet built an empire. Every man of action has a strong dose of egotism, pride, hardness, and cunning.
CHARLES ANDRÉ JOSEPH MARIE DE GAULLE (1890–1970), French general and statesman: *The New York Times Magazine, 12 May 1968*

Neither a wise man nor a brave man lies down on the tracks of history to wait for the train of the future to run over him.
DWIGHT D(AVID) EISENHOWER (1890–1969), American general and president: *Time, 6 October 1952*

Nothing great was ever achieved without enthusiasm.
RALPH WALDO EMERSON (1803–82), American poet, essayist and philosopher: *Essays, 'Circles'*

Boldness in business is the first, second, and third thing.
THOMAS FULLER (1654–1734), English physician, writer and compiler: *Gnomologia*

You ought to take the bull between the teeth.
SAMUEL GOLDWYN (1882–1974), American film producer (Attributed)

He who would make serious use of his life must always act as though he had a long time to live and must schedule his time as though he were about to die.
(MAXIMILIEN PAUL) ÉMILE LITTRÉ (1801–81), French scholar and lexicographer: *Dictionnaire de la langue française*

He who overcomes others is strong; but he who overcomes himself is mightier.
JOHN HENRY PATTERSON (1844–1922), American industrialist

Just at this moment we are suffering a national defeat comparable to any lost military campaign, and what is more it is self-inflicted ... I think it is about time we pulled our finger out.
PRINCE PHILIP, Duke of Edinburgh (1921–): *Speech to businessmen, 17 October 1961*

How to be one up – how to make the other man feel that something has gone wrong, however slightly.
STEPHEN POTTER (1900–69), English writer and radio producer: *Lifemanship*

Between saying and doing many a pair of shoes is worn out.
PROVERB

Every man is the architect of his own fortune.
PROVERB

Every man is the son of his own works.
PROVERB

In our complex world, there cannot be fruitful initiative without government, but unfortunately there can be government without initiative.
BERTRAND (ARTHUR WILLIAM) RUSSELL, 3rd Earl Russell (1872–1970), English philosopher and mathematician: *Authority and the Individual,* 'Control and Initiative'

Self-determination is not a mere phrase. It is an imperative principle of action, which statesmen will henceforth ignore at their peril.
(THOMAS) WOODROW WILSON (1856–1924), American statesman and president: *Speech to Congress, 11 February 1918*

Courtesy

Politeness:
The most acceptable hypocrisy.
AMBROSE (GWINETT) BIERCE (1842–?1914), American journalist and humorist: *The Devil's Dictionary*

Be polite. Write diplomatically. Even in a declaration of war one observes the rules of politeness.
OTTO (EDOUARD LEOPOLD) VON BISMARCK (1815–98), German statesman

Manners are of more importance than laws. Upon them, in a great measure, the laws depend. The law touches us but here and there, and now and then. Manners are what vex or soothe, corrupt or purify, exalt or debase, barbarize or refine us, by a constant, steady, uniform, insensible operation, like that of the air we breathe in.
EDMUND BURKE (1729–97), British statesman, orator and writer: *Letters on a Regicide Peace*

Manners maketh man. Yes, but they make woman still more.

SAMUEL BUTLER (1835–1902), English author, painter and musician: *Notebooks*

Red Queen:
It isn't etiquette to cut anyone you've been introduced to.

LEWIS CARROLL (Charles Lutwidge Dodgson) (1832–98), English writer and mathematician: *Through the Looking Glass, chapter 9*

Politeness is the chief sign of culture.

BALTASAR GRACIÁN (1601–58), Spanish prose writer and Jesuit priest: *The Art of Worldly Wisdom*

A commercial society whose members are essentially ascetic and indifferent in social ritual has to be provided with blueprints and specifications for evoking the right tone for every occasion.

(HERBERT) MARSHALL MCLUHAN (1911–80), Canadian educator, author and media expert: *The Mechanical Bride*

Impropriety is the soul of wit.

W(ILLIAM) SOMERSET MAUGHAM (1874–1965), English writer: *The Moon and Sixpence, chapter 4*

Manners make the man.

PROVERB

Efficiency

Our wages are lower, our holidays are shorter, our working hours are longer – simply because we produce less per man employed. Unless we put this right we risk becoming the peasants of the Western world.

SIR MICHAEL CLAPHAM (1912–2002), President, CBI: *Observer, 'Sayings of the Year', 30 December 1973*

Desire to have things done quickly prevents their being done thoroughly.

CONFUCIUS (Kong Zi) (551–479 BC), Chinese philosopher: *Analects*

Watch out for the fellow who talks about putting things in order! Putting things in order always means getting other people under your control.

DENIS DIDEROT (1713–84), French philosopher: *Supplement to Bougainville's 'Voyage'*

Nothing is more central to an organization's effectiveness than its ability to transmit accurate, relevant, understandable information among its members. All the advantages of organizations – economy of scale, financial and technical resources, diverse talents, and contacts – are of no practical value if the organisation's members are unaware of what other members require of them and why.

SAUL GELLERMAN (1929–2003), American author: *The Management of Human Resources*

Celerity is the mother of good fortune. He has done much who leaves nothing over till tomorrow.

BALTASAR GRACIÁN (1601–58), Spanish prose writer and Jesuit priest: *The Art of Worldly Wisdom*

To find men capable of managing business efficiently and secure to them the positions of responsible control is perhaps the most important single problem of economic organization on the efficiency scale.

FRANK H. KNIGHT (1885–1972), Professor of Economics

The efficiency of industry may be expected to be great, in proportion as the fruits of industry are insured to the person exerting it.

JOHN STUART MILL (1806–73), English philosopher and economist: *Principles of Political Economy, book 1*

An ounce of image is worth a pound of performance.

DR LAURENCE J. PETER (1919–90), Canadian educator: *Peter's Quotations*

To do two things at once is to do neither.

PUBLILIUS SYRUS (1st c. BC), Latin writer of mimes: *Moral Sayings*

There are only two qualities in the world: efficiency and inefficiency, and only two sorts of people: the efficient and the inefficient.

GEORGE BERNARD SHAW (1856–1950), Irish dramatist and critic: *John Bull's Other Island, Act 4*

Excellence and size are fundamentally incompatible.

ROBERT TOWNSEND (1957–), American company director

Exploitation

If you allow men to use you for your own purposes, they will use you for theirs.

AESOP (c. 620–564 BC), Greek fabulist: *Fables, 'The Hone, Hunter, and Stag'*

Under capitalism man exploits man; under socialism, it's just the opposite.

ANON

The history of all past society has consisted in the development of class antagonisms, antagonisms that assumed different forms at different epochs. But whatever form they may have taken, one fact is common to all past ages, viz., die exploitation of one part of society by the other.

KARL MARX (1818–83), German founder of modern communism and FRIEDRICH ENGELS (1820–95), German socialist leader: *The Communist Manifesto*

Extravagance

We deny that it is fun to be saving. It is fun to be prodigal. Go to the butterfly, thou parsimonious sluggard; consider her ways and get wise.

FRANKLIN P. ADAMS (1881–1960), American journalist and humorist: *Nods and Becks*

The road of excess leads to the palace of Wisdom.

WILLIAM BLAKE (1757–1827), English poet, painter and engraver: *The Marriage of Heaven and Hell, 'Proverbs of Hell'*

To go beyond is as wrong as to fall short.

CONFUCIUS (Kong Zi) (551–479 BC), Chinese philosopher: *Analects*

My problem lies in reconciling my gross habits with my net income.

ERROL FLYNN (1909–59), Australian-born American film star

I have not been afraid of excess: excess on occasion is exhilarating. It prevents moderation from acquiring the deadening effect of a habit.

W(ILLIAM) SOMERSET MAUGHAM (1874–1965), English writer: *The Summing Up*

The biggest waste of water in the country by far. You spend half a pint and flush two gallons.

PRINCE PHILIP, Duke of Edinburgh (1921–): *Speech, 1965*

Enough is as good as a feast.

PROVERB

He who gives his milk to his cat must drink water.

PROVERB

He who buys what he needs not, sells what he needs.
JAPANESE PROVERB

A glut is an evil. It generally implies production without profit, and sometimes without even the return of the capital employed.
DAVID RICARDO (1772–1823), English economist: *Works, volume 2*

Nothing in excess.
SOLON (?638–?559 BC), Athenian statesman

Lord Illingworth:
Moderation is a fatal thing, Lady Hunstanton. Nothing succeeds like excess.
OSCAR WILDE (1856–1900), Irish poet, dramatist and wit: *A Woman of No Importance, Act 3*

Fame

A celebrity is a person who works hard all his life to become known, then wears dark glasses to avoid being recognised.
FRED ALLEN (John F. Sullivan) (1894–1956), American comedian: *Treadmill to Oblivion*

The desire for fame tempts even noble minds.
SAINT AUGUSTINE (AD 354–430), Early Christian church father and philosopher: *The City of God*

All men desire fame. I have never known a single exception to that rule, and I doubt if anyone else has.
(JOSEPH) HILAIRE (PIERRE) BELLOC (1870–1953), Anglo-French author: *The Silence of the Sea*

Famous:
Conspicuously miserable.
AMBROSE (GWINETT) BIERCE (1842–?1914), American journalist and humorist: *The Devil's Dictionary*

The celebrity is a person who is known for his well-knownness.

DANIEL J. BOORSTIN (1914–2004), American educator and writer: *The Image, chapter 2*

Celebrity:
The advantage of being known by those who don't know you.

SÉBASTIEN ROCH NICOLAS CHAMFORT (1741–94), French writer and wit: *Maximes et pensées*

I have often thought of forming a Society for The Prevention of Cruelty to Celebrities. Apparently for certain individuals, men and women in the public eye are fair game to be knocked off their balance occasionally and made to look foolish. You know, a central figure at a social function isn't always as happy as he looks.

SIR NOËL (PIERCE) COWARD (1899–1973), English actor and dramatist (Attributed)

People that seem so glorious are all show; Underneath they're like anybody else.

EURIPIDES (?480–406 BC), Greek tragic dramatist: *Andromache*

If I'm such a legend, then why am I so lonely? … let me tell you, legends are all very well if you've got somebody around who loves you.

JUDY GARLAND (1922–69), American singer and film star

Nothing arouses ambition so much in the heart as the trumpet-clang of another's fame.

BALTASAR GRACIÁN (1601–58), Spanish prose writer and Jesuit priest: *The Art of Worldly Wisdom*

What is fame? An empty bubble.

JAMES GRAINGER (?1721–66), English physician and man of letters: *Solitude*

No really great man ever thought himself so.

WILLIAM HAZLITT (1778–1830), English essayist: *The Plain Speaker*

Nothing is so common-place as to wish to be remarkable.

OLIVER WENDELL HOLMES, SR (1809–94), American physician, professor and author: *The Autocrat of the Breakfast Table*

We're more popular than Jesus Christ now.

JOHN LENNON (1940–80), English rock musician and songwriter: *The Beatles Illustrated Lyrics*

Fame is the spur that the clear spirit doth raise … To scorn delights, and live laborious days.

JOHN MILTON (1608–74), English poet: *Lycidas*

Would you be known by everybody? Then you know nobody.

PUBLILIUS SYRUS (1st c. BC), Latin writer of mimes: *Moral Sayings*

The first test of a truly great man is his humility.

JOHN RUSKIN (1819–1900), English art critic and social reformer: *Modern Painters*

Malvolio:
Some are born great, some achieve greatness, and some have greatness thrust upon 'em.

WILLIAM SHAKESPEARE (1564–1616), English dramatist and poet: *Twelfth Night, Act 2*

Fame and rest are utter opposites.

SIR RICHARD STEELE (1672–1729), Irish-born British dramatist and essayist: *The Funeral*

Fame is a vapor, popularity an accident; the only earthly certainty is oblivion.

MARK TWAIN (Samuel Langhorne Clemens) (1835–1910), American novelist and humorist: *Notebook*

Greed

The world has enough for everyone's need, but not enough for everyone's greed.

MAHATMA GANDHI (Mohandas Karamchand Gandhi) (1869–1948), Hindu nationalist leader (Attributed)

Avarice, or the desire of gain, is a universal passion, which operates at all times, at all places, and upon all persons.

DAVID HUME (1711–76), Scottish philosopher and historian: *Essays*

Avarice, the spur of industry.

DAVID HUME, as above

Avarice and luxury have been the ruin of every great state.

LIVY (Titus Livius) (59 BC–17 AD), Roman historian: *History of Rome*

Excess of wealth is cause of covetousness.

CHRISTOPHER MARLOWE (1564–93), English dramatist and poet: *The Jew of Malta, Act I*

Avarice has so seized upon mankind that their wealth seems rather to possess them than they to possess their wealth.

PLINY THE YOUNGER (Gaius Plinius Caecilius Secundus) (?AD 62–?113), Roman writer and administrator: *Letters*

Accursed greed for gold,
To what dost thou not drive the heart of man?

VIRGIL (Publius Vergilius Maro) (70–19 BC), Roman poet: *Aeneid*

Happiness

Different men seek after happiness in different ways and by different means, and so make for themselves different modes of life and forms of government.

ARISTOTLE (384–322 BC), Greek philosopher and scientist: *Politics*

Happiness seems to require a modicum of external prosperity.

ARISTOTLE: *Nicomachean Ethics*

The greatest happiness of the greatest number is the foundation of morals and legislation.

JEREMY BENTHAM (1748–1832), English philosopher: *The Commonplace Book*

Happiness:
An agreeable sensation arising from contemplating the misery of another.

AMBROSE (GWINETT) BIERCE (1842–?1914), American journalist and humorist: *The Devil's Dictionary*

In every adversity of fortune, to have been happy is the most unhappy kind of misfortune.

ANICIUS MANLIUS SEVERINUS BOETHIUS (c. 475–524 AD), Roman statesman and philosopher: *De consolatione philosophiae*

Who is content with nothing possesses all things.

NICOLAS BOILEAU (-DESPRÉAUX) (1636–1711), French poet and critic: *Épîtres*

Happiness is a mystery like religion, and should never be rationalized.

G(ILBERT) K(EITH) CHESTERTON (1874–1936), English essayist, novelist, poet and critic: *Heretics, chapter 7*

To fill the hour – that is happiness.

RALPH WALDO EMERSON (1803–82), American poet, essayist and philosopher: *Experience*

Modern man's happiness consists in the thrill of looking at the

shop windows, and in buying all that he can afford to buy, either for cash or on instalments.
ERICH FROMM (1900–80), German-born American psychoanalyst and philosopher: *The Art of Loving*

Well, I've had a happy life.
WILLIAM HAZLITT (1778–1830), English essayist: *Last words*

It's pretty hard to tell what does bring happiness; poverty and wealth have both failed.
FRANK MCKINNEY ('KIN') HUBBARD (1868–1930): *Abe Martin's Broadcast*

Happiness is like coke – something you get as a by-product in the process of making something else.
ALDOUS (LEONARD) HUXLEY (1894–1963), English novelist and essayist: *Point Counter Point*

There is nothing of permanent value (putting aside a few human affections), nothing that satisfies quiet reflection, except the sense of having worked according to one's capacity and light to make things clear and get rid of cant and shams of all sorts.
THOMAS HENRY HUXLEY (1825–95), English biologist, teacher and writer: *To W. Platt Ball, 27 October 1890*

Human life is every where a state in which much is to be endured, and little to be enjoyed.
SAMUEL JOHNSON (1709–84), English lexicographer, essayist and poet: *Rasselas, chapter 11*

It is better that some should be unhappy, than that none should be happy, which would be the case in a general state of equality.
SAMUEL JOHNSON: quoted in James Boswell, *The Life of Samuel Johnson*

The great source of pleasure is variety.
SAMUEL JOHNSON: *Lives of the English Poets, 'Butler'*

Nothing is surely a waste of time when one enjoys the day.
ARTHUR KOESTLER (1905–83), Hungarian-born British writer

We are never so happy nor so unhappy as we imagine.
FRANÇOIS LA ROCHEFOUCAULD, Duc de La Rochefoucauld (1613–80),
French writer: *Reflections*

Happy is the man with a wife to tell him what to do and a
secretary to do it.
LORD MANCROFT (1914–87), British politician: *Observer, 1966*

Few people would assert that a man with fifty thousand a year is likely
to have a very much happier life than if he had only a thousand.
ALFRED MARSHALL (1942–1924), English classical economist: *Economic
Journal, March 1907, 'The Social Possibilities of Economic Chivalry'*

It is only in a very imperfect state of the world's arrangements
that any one can best serve the happiness of others by the
absolute sacrifice of his own.
JOHN STUART MILL (1806–73), English philosopher and economist:
Utilitarianism, chapter 2

The true way to render ourselves happy is to love our work and
find in it our pleasure.
FRANÇOISE DE MOTTEVILLE (1621–89), French writer

Our object in the construction of the state is the greatest
happiness of the whole, and not that of any one class.
PLATO (?427–?347 BC), Greek philosopher: *Republic*

Few people can be happy unless they hate some other person,
nation or creed.
BERTRAND (ARTHUR WILLIAM) RUSSELL, 3rd Earl Russell (1872–1970),
English philosopher and mathematician (Attributed)

If there were in the world today any large number of people who desired their own happiness more than they desired the unhappiness of others, we could have a paradise in a few years.

BERTRAND (ARTHUR WILLIAM) RUSSELL: *Observer, 'Sayings of the Decade', 28 December 1969*

To be without some of the things you want is an indispensable part of happiness.

BERTRAND (ARTHUR WILLIAM) RUSSELL: *The Conquest of Happiness*

Happiness is the only sanction of life; where happiness fails, existence remains a mad and lamentable experiment.

GEORGE SANTAYANA (1863–1952), American philosopher and poet: *The Life of Reason*

The heart is great which shows moderation in the midst of prosperity.

MARCUS or LUCIUS ANNAEUS SENECA (The Elder) (?55 BC–?39 AD), Roman writer on oratory and history: *Suasoriae orlando*

How bitter a thing it is to look into happiness through another man's eyes!

WILLIAM SHAKESPEARE (1564–1616), English dramatist and poet: *As You Like It, Act 5*

A lifetime of happiness! No man alive could bear it: it would be hell on earth.

GEORGE BERNARD SHAW (1856–1950), Irish dramatist and critic: *Man and Superman*

The most decisive mark of the prosperity of any country is the increase of the number of inhabitants.

ADAM SMITH (1723–90), Scottish economist and philosopher: *The Wealth of Nations, volume 1*

There is more felicity on the far side of baldness than young men can possibly imagine.

LOGAN PEARSALL SMITH (1865–1946), American-born Englishman of letters: *All Trivia*

Call no man happy until he dies; he is at best fortunate.

SOLON (?638–?559 BC), Athenian statesman: *Histories (Herodotus)*

It is not the level of prosperity that makes for happiness but the kinship of heart to heart and the way we look at the world. Both attitudes are within our power, so that a man is happy so long as he chooses to be happy, and no one can stop him.

ALEXANDER ISAYEVICH SOLZHENITSYN (1918–), Russian novelist: *Cancer Ward, Part 1*

There is no duty we so much underrate as the duty of being happy.

ROBERT LOUIS BALFOUR STEVENSON (1850–94), Scottish writer: *Virginibus Puerisque, An Apology for Idlers*

Good friends, good books and a sleepy conscience: this is the ideal life.

MARK TWAIN (Samuel Langhorne Clemens) (1835–1910), American novelist and humorist: *Notebook*

Grief can take care of itself, but to get the full value of joy you must have somebody to divide it with.

MARK TWAIN, as above

Employment gives health, sobriety, and morals. Constant employment and well-paid labor produce, in a country like ours, general prosperity, content, and cheerfulness.

DANIEL WEBSTER (1782–1852), American statesman and orator: *Speech, the Senate, 25 July 1846*

After you have exhausted what there is in business, politics, conviviality, and so on – have found that none of these finally satisfy, or permanently wear – what remains? Nature remains.

WALT(ER) WHITMAN (1819–92), American poet, journalist and essayist: *Specimen Days, 'New Themes Entered Upon'*

Give me the luxuries of life and I will willingly do without the necessities.

FRANK LLOYD WRIGHT (1869–1959), American architect: quoted in his obituary

Health

Mr Woodhouse:
Nobody is healthy in London, nobody can be.

JANE AUSTEN (1775–1817), English novelist: *Emma, chapter 12*

Never go to a doctor whose office plants have died.

ERMA BOMBECK (1927–96), American humorist

The trouble about always trying to preserve the health of the body is that it is so difficult to do without destroying the health of the mind.

G(ILBERT) K(EITH) CHESTERTON (1874–1936), English essayist, novelist, poet and critic: *Come to Think of It*

The poorest man would not part with health for money, but the richest would gladly part with all their money for health.

CHARLES CALEB COLTON (?1780–1832), English clergyman and writer: *Lacon*

Our health is our sound relation to external objects; our sympathy with external being.

RALPH WALDO EMERSON (1803–82), American poet, essayist and philosopher: *Journals*

Study sickness while you are well.

THOMAS FULLER (1654–1734), English physician, writer and compiler: *Gnomologia*

Anybody who goes to see a psychiatrist ought to have his head examined.

SAMUEL GOLDWYN (1882–1974), American film producer (Attributed)

All in all, if one sought to design a life style which was destructive of the individual, the way that business has structured itself would seem to be almost ideal.

SIR JOHN HARVEY-JONES (1924–), former chairman of ICI: *Making It Happen*

If you mean to keep as well as possible, the less you think about your health the better.

OLIVER WENDELL HOLMES, SR (1809–94), American physician, professor and author: *Over the Teacups*

Health is worth more than learning.

THOMAS JEFFERSON (1743–1826), American statesman and president: *Letter to John Garland Jefferson*

We are under-exercised as a nation. We look instead of play. We ride instead of walk. Our existence deprives us of the minimum of physical activity essential for healthy living.

JOHN FITZGERALD KENNEDY (1917–63), American statesman and president: *Speech, New York City, 5 December 1961*

How sickness enlarges the dimensions of a man's self to himself! He is his own exclusive object. Supreme selfishness is inculcated upon him as his only duty.

CHARLES (ELIA) LAMB (1775–1834), English essayist: *Last Essays of Elia*

If the nineteenth century was the age of the editorial chair, ours is the century of the psychiatrist's couch.

(HERBERT) MARSHALL MCLUHAN (1911–80), Canadian educator, author and media expert: *Understanding the Media*

Life is not living, but living in health.

MARTIAL (Marcus Valerius Martialis) (?AD 44–?104), Spanish-born epigrammatist and poet: *Epigrams*

For exercise, I wind my watch.

ROBERT MAXWELL (1923–91), Czechoslovakian-born media owner

Health is better than wealth.

PROVERB

By medicine life may be prolonged, yet death
Will seize the doctor too.

WILLIAM SHAKESPEARE (1564–1616), English dramatist and poet:
Cymbeline, Act 5

I enjoy convalescence. It is the part that makes the illness worth while.

GEORGE BERNARD SHAW (1856–1950), Irish dramatist and critic: *Back to Methuselah*

Early to rise and early to bed makes a male healthy and wealthy and dead.

JAMES (GROVER) THURBER (1894–1961), American humorist and cartoonist: *Fables for Our Time, 'The Shrike and the Chipmunks'*

Look to your health; and if you have it, praise God, and value it next to a good conscience; for health is the second blessing that we mortals are capable of; a blessing that money cannot buy.

IZAAK WALTON (1593–1683), English writer: *The Compleat Angler*

Lord Illingworth:
One knows so well the popular idea of health. The English country gentleman galloping after a fox – the unspeakable in full pursuit of the uneatable.

OSCAR WILDE (1856–1900), Irish poet, dramatist and wit: *A Woman of No Importance, Act 1*

Honesty

Rules that are hard to follow are hardly ever followed.

ANON

For the merchant, even honesty is a financial speculation.

CHARLES PIERRE BAUDELAIRE (1821–67), French poet

We underpay all our public servants and we little deserve the honesty and integrity we get.

SIR FREDERICK CATHERWOOD (1925–), British politician and writer

An honest man's word is as good as his bond.

MIGUEL DE CERVANTES (SAAVEDRA) (1547–1616), Spanish writer: *Don Quixote*

Of Mr Baldwin:
It is a fine thing to be honest but it is also very important to be right.

SIR WINSTON LEONARD SPENCER CHURCHILL (1874–1965), English statesman, writer and prime minister (Attributed)

The best measure of a man's honesty isn't his income tax return. It's the zero adjust on his bathroom scale.

ARTHUR C. CLARKE (1917–), British science-fiction author

Would that the simple maxim, that honesty is the best policy, might be laid to heart; that a sense of the true aim of life might elevate the tone of politics and trade till public and private honor became identical.

(SARA) MARGARET MARCHESA OSSOLI FULLER (1810–50), American editor, essayist, poet and teacher: *Summer on the Lakes*

It is difficult but not impossible to conduct strictly honest business. What is true is that honesty is incompatible with the amassing of a large fortune.

MAHATMA GANDHI (Mohandas Karamchand Gandhi) (1869–1948), Hindu nationalist leader: *Non-Violence in Peace and War*

Do not seek dishonest gains: dishonest gains are losses.

HESIOD (c. 700 BC), Greek poet: *Works and Days*

It is always the best policy to speak the truth, unless of course you are an exceptionally good liar.

JEROME K(LAPKA) JEROME (1859–1927), English humorous writer: *The Idler*

There is one way to find out if a man is honest – ask him. If he says 'Yes', you know he is crooked.

GROUCHO MARX (1895–1977), American film comedian

When you steal from one author, it's plagiarism. If you steal from many, it's research.

WILSON MIZNER (1876–1933), American playwright

Put a rogue in the limelight and he will act like an honest man.

NAPOLEON I (Napoleon Bonaparte) (1769–1821), French emperor and general: *Maxims*

It is annoying to be honest to no purpose.

OVID (Publius Ovidius Naso) (43 BC–?17 AD), Roman poet: *Ex ponto*

Honesty is for the most part less profitable than dishonesty.
PLATO (?427–?347 BC), Greek philosopher: *The Republic*

You cannot make people honest by Act of Parliament.
PROVERB

Verges:
I thank God I am as honest as any man living that is an old man and no honester than I.
WILLIAM SHAKESPEARE (1564–1616), English dramatist and poet: *Much Ado about Nothing, Act 3*

It's better to be quotable than to be honest.
TOM STOPPARD (1937–), Czechoslovakian-born British playwright: *Guardian, 1973*

If you tell the truth you don't have to remember anything.
MARK TWAIN (Samuel Langhorne Clemens) (1835–1910), American novelist and humorist: *Notebook*

In modern business it is not the crook who is to be feared most; it is the honest man who doesn't know what he is doing.
WILLIAM WORDSWORTH (1770–1850), British poet

It is not the crook in modern business that we fear, but the honest man who does not know what he is doing.
OWEN D. YOUNG (1874–1962), American lawyer and corporation executive

Humanitarianism

It is easy to perform a good action, but not easy to acquire a settled habit of performing such actions.
ARISTOTLE (384–322 BC), Greek philosopher and scientist: *Nicomachean Ethics*

A man of humanity is one who, in seeking to establish himself, finds a foothold for others and who, desiring attainment for himself, helps others to attain.

CONFUCIUS (Kong Zi) (551–479 BC), Chinese philosopher: *Analects*

Philanthropy is commendable, but it must not cause the philanthropist to overlook the circumstances of economic injustice which make philanthropy necessary.

MARTIN LUTHER KING, JR (1929–68), American Baptist minister and civil rights leader: *Strength to Love*

If you give a hungry man a fish, he will be hungry again tomorrow, but if you teach him how to fish, he will never be hungry again.

CHINESE PROVERB

There is no higher religion than human service. To work for the common good is the greatest creed.

ALBERT SCHWEITZER (1875–1965), Franco-German medical missionary, organist and philosopher

Of philanthropy:
A good part … arises in general from mere vanity and love of distinction, gilded over to others and to themselves with some show of benevolent sentiment.

SIR WALTER SCOTT (1771–1832), Scottish novelist and poet: *Journal, 20 February 1828*

Do not do unto others as you would they should do unto you. Their tastes may not be the same.

GEORGE BERNARD SHAW (1856–1950), Irish dramatist and critic: *Man and Superman, Maxims for Revolutionists*

No benevolent man ever lost altogether the fruits of his
benevolence.

ADAM SMITH (1723–90), Scottish economist and philosopher: *The Theory of
Moral Sentiments, Part 6*

Humour

I hope life isn't a big joke … because I don't get it.

ANON

The most wasted day is that in which we have not laughed.

SÉBASTIEN ROCH NICOLAS CHAMFORT (1741–94), French writer and wit:
Maximes et pensées

Wit is so shining a quality that everybody admires it; most
people aim at it, all people fear it, and few love it unless in
themselves.

LORD CHESTERFIELD, Philip Dormer Stanhope, 4th Earl of (1694–1773),
English statesman and writer: *Letters to his godson*

No mind is thoroughly well organized that is deficient in a sense
of humour.

SAMUEL TAYLOR COLERIDGE (1772–1834), English poet, philosopher and
critic: *Table Talk*

Total absence of humour renders life impossible.

SIDONIE GABRIELLE CLAUDINE COLETTE (1873–1954), French novelist:
Chance Acquaintances

There is nothing in which people more betray their character
than in what they laugh at.

JOHANN WOLFGANG VON GOETHE (1749–1832), German poet, scientist
and writer: *Elective Affinities*

A jest often decides matters of importance more effectually and happily than seriousness.

HORACE (Quintus Horatius Flaccus) (65–8 BC), Roman poet and satirist: *Satires*

Of Lord Chesterfield:
This man I thought had been a Lord among wits; but, I find, he is only a wit among Lords.

SAMUEL JOHNSON (1709–84), English lexicographer, essayist and poet: quoted in James Boswell, *The Life of Samuel Johnson*

And we should consider every day lost on which we have not danced at least once. And we should call every truth false which was not accompanied by at least one laugh.

FRIEDRICH WILHELM NIETZSCHE (1844–1900), German philosopher, poet and critic

Everything is funny, as long as it's happening to somebody else.

WILL(IAM PENN ADAIR) ROGERS (1879–1935), American actor and humorist

The Illiterate Digest
There's no life without humour. It can make the wonderful moments of life truly glorious, and it can make tragic moments bearable.

RUFUS WAINWRIGHT (1973–), Canadian-American singer and songwriter

Humour is the weapon of unarmed people: it helps people who are oppressed to smile at the situation that pains them.

SIMON WIESENTHAL (1908–2005), Austrian-Jewish engineer and Holocaust survivor

The beauty of the world has two edges, one of laughter, one of anguish, cutting the heart asunder.

(ADELINE) VIRGINIA WOOLF (1882–1941), English novelist and critic

Impartiality

What people call impartiality may simply mean indifference, and what people call partiality may simply mean mental activity.

G(ILBERT) K(EITH) CHESTERTON (1874–1936), English essayist, novelist, poet and critic: *All Things Considered*

The human soul is hospitable, and will entertain conflicting sentiments and contradictory opinions with much impartiality.

GEORGE ELIOT (Mary Ann Evans) (1819–80), English novelist

I am free of all prejudice. I hate everyone equally.

W(ILLIAM) C(LAUDE) FIELDS (William Claude Dukenfield) (1880–1946), American actor and comedian (Attributed)

Impartiality is the life of justice, as justice is of all good government.

JOHANN WOLFGANG VON GOETHE (1749–1832), German poet, scientist and writer

Neutrality consists in having the same weights and measures for each.

NAPOLEON I (Napoleon Bonaparte) (1769–1821), French emperor and general: *Maxims*

Heaven is impartial.

CHINESE PROVERB

Justice is impartiality. Only strangers are impartial.

GEORGE BERNARD SHAW (1856–1950), Irish dramatist and critic: *Back to Methuselah*

We all decry prejudice, yet are all prejudiced.

HERBERT SPENCER (1820–1903), English philosopher: *Social Statics*

The man who sees both sides of a question is a man who sees absolutely nothing at all.

OSCAR WILDE (1856–1900), Irish poet, dramatist and wit: *The Critic as Artist, Part 2*

Integrity

Integrity is doing the right thing, even if nobody is watching.

ANON

It's not what we eat but what we digest that makes us strong; not what we gain but what we save that makes us rich; not what we read but what we remember that makes us learned; and not what we profess but what we practice that gives us integrity.

FRANCIS BACON, 1st Baron Verulam, Viscount St Albans (1561–1626), English writer, philosopher and statesman

We ought to see far enough into a hypocrite to see even his sincerity.

G(ILBERT) K(EITH) CHESTERTON (1874–1936), English essayist, novelist, poet and critic: *Heretics, chapter 5*

Perhaps it is better to be irresponsible and right than to be responsible and wrong.

SIR WINSTON LEONARD SPENCER CHURCHILL (1874–1965), English statesman, writer and prime minister: *Party Political Broadcast, 26 August 1950*

What is morally wrong cannot be politically right.

ANTHONY ASHLEY COOPER, 3rd Earl of Shaftesbury (1671–1713), English politician and philosopher (Attributed)

Ethics stays in the prefaces of the average business science book.

PETER F. DRUCKER (1909–2005), American management expert

Integrity is the essence of everything successful.

R(ICHARD) BUCKMINSTER FULLER (1895–1983), American author and inventor

All truth is not to be told at all times.

THOMAS FULLER (1654–1734), English physician, writer and compiler: *Gnomologia*

A 'No' uttered from deepest conviction is better and greater than a 'Yes' merely uttered to please, or what is worse, to avoid trouble.

MAHATMA GANDHI (Mohandas Karamchand Gandhi) (1869–1948), Hindu nationalist leader

What is moral is what you feel good after and what is immoral is what you feel bad after.

ERNEST HEMINGWAY (1899–1961), American novelist and short-story writer: *Death in the Afternoon*

Integrity without knowledge is weak and useless, and knowledge without integrity is dangerous and dreadful.

SAMUEL JOHNSON (1709–84), English lexicographer, essayist and poet: *Rasselas*

Integrity is praised, and starves.

JUVENAL (Decimus Junius Juvenalis) (?AD 60–?140), Roman satirist: *Satires*

It's a matter of having principles. It's easy to have principles when you're rich. The important thing is to have principles when you're poor.

RAY A. KROC (1902–84), American fast food entrepreneur

The difference between a moral man and a man of honor is that the latter regrets a discreditable act, even when it has worked and he has not been caught.

HENRY LOUIS MENCKEN (1880–1956), American philologist, editor and satirist: *Prejudices: Fourth Series*

Character is much easier kept than recovered.

THOMAS PAINE (1737–1809), English philosopher and writer: *The American Crisis*

Polonius:
This above all – to thine own self be true.
And it must follow, as the night the day,
Thou canst not then be false to any man.

WILLIAM SHAKESPEARE (1564–1616), English dramatist and poet: *Hamlet, Act I*

The person that loses their conscience has nothing left worth keeping.

IZAAK WALTON (1593–1683), English writer

A little sincerity is a dangerous thing, and a great deal of it is absolutely fatal.

OSCAR WILDE (1856–1900), Irish poet, dramatist and wit: *The Critic as Artist*

In matters of grave importance, style, not sincerity, is the vital thing.

OSCAR WILDE: *The Importance of Being Earnest*

Knowledge

The intelligent are to the intelligentsia what a man is to a gent.

STANLEY BALDWIN, 1st Earl Baldwin of Bewdley (1867–1947), British statesman (Attributed)

I've learned one thing – people who know the least anyways seem to know it the loudest.

ANDY CAPP (Reginald Smythe, 1917–98), comic strip character

To know a little of anything gives neither satisfaction nor credit, but often brings disgrace or ridicule.

LORD CHESTERFIELD, Philip Dormer Stanhope, 4th Earl of (1694–1773), English statesman and writer: *Letter to his son, 4 October 1746*

Knowledge is the only instrument of production that is not subject to diminishing returns.

JOHN MAURICE CLARK (1884–1971), American economist and professor

Learn as though you would never be able to master it; hold it as though you would be in fear of losing it.

CONFUCIUS (Kong Zi) (551–479 BC), Chinese philosopher: *Analects*

We might all be happier if we knew less about what was going on in the world.

BILL DEEDES (1913–), British journalist and politician

The more extensive a man's knowledge of what has been done, the greater will be his power of knowing what to do.

BENJAMIN DISRAELI, 1st Earl of Beaconsfield (1804–81), English statesman, prime minister and novelist

The world's great men have not commonly been great scholars, nor its great scholars great men.

OLIVER WENDELL HOLMES, SR (1809–94), American physician, professor and author: *The Autocrat of the Breakfast Table*

No one can know everything.

HORACE (Quintus Horatius Flaccus) (65–8 BC), Roman poet and satirist: *Carmina*

Knowledge is proportionate to being … You know in virtue of what you are.

ALDOUS (LEONARD) HUXLEY (1894–1963), English novelist and essayist: *Time Must Have a Stop, chapter 26*

Knowledge is of two kinds: we know a subject ourselves, or we know where we can find information upon it.

SAMUEL JOHNSON (1709–84), English lexicographer, essayist and poet: quoted in James Boswell, *The Life of Samuel Johnson*

The height of cleverness is to conceal one's cleverness.

FRANÇOIS LA ROCHEFOUCAULD, Duc de La Rochefoucauld (1613–80), French writer: *Maxims*

'Know thyself' is a good saying, but not in all situations. In many, it is better to say 'Know others'.

MENANDER (?342–?292 BC), Greek comic dramatist: *Thrasyleon*

A good listener is not only popular everywhere, but after a while he gets to know something.

WILSON MIZNER (1876–1933), American playwright

Since we cannot be universal and know all that is to be known of everything, we ought to know a little about everything.

BLAISE PASCAL (1623–62), French philosopher, mathematician and physicist: *Pensées*

A little learning is a dangerous thing.

ALEXANDER POPE (1688–1744), English poet and satirist: *An Essay on Criticism*

Knowledge is power.

PROVERB

Knowledge is, in most of those who cultivate it, a species of money, which is valued greatly, but only adds to our well-being in proportion as it is communicated, and is only good in commerce. Take from the wise the pleasure of being listened to, and knowledge would be nothing to them.

JEAN-JACQUES ROUSSEAU (1712–78), Swiss-born French philosopher and writer: *La nouvelle Heloise*

I know perfectly well that I don't want to do anything; to do something is to create existence – and there's quite enough existence as it is.

JEAN-PAUL SARTRE (1905–80), French philosopher, dramatist and novelist: *Nausea*

There is only one good, knowledge, and one evil, ignorance.

SOCRATES (?470–399 BC), Athenian philosopher: *Diogenes Laertius*

Science is organised knowledge.

HERBERT SPENCER (1820–1903), English philosopher: *Education, chapter 2*

The desire of knowledge, like the thirst of riches, increases ever with the acquisition of it.

LAURENCE STERNE (1713–68), Irish-born English novelist: *Tristram Shandy*

We are creating and using up ideas and images at a faster and faster pace. Knowledge, like people, places, things, and organisational forms, is becoming dispensable.

ALVIN TOFFLER (1928–), American writer: *Future Shock*

The things we know best are the things we haven't been taught.

VAUVENARGUES, Marquis de Luc de Clapiers (1715–47), French moralist: *Reflections and Maxims*

Laziness

I could slack for Britain.

IAIN BANKS (1944–), Scottish author

Go to the ant, thou sluggard: consider her ways, and be wise.

The Bible, Authorised (King James) Version, Proverbs 6:6

Idleness is only the refuge of weak minds.

LORD CHESTERFIELD, Philip Dormer Stanhope, 4th Earl of (1694–1773), English statesman and writer: *Letter to his son, 20 July 1749*

We have a system that increasingly taxes work and subsidizes nonwork.

MILTON FRIEDMAN (1912–2006), American economist

He is idle that might be better employed.

THOMAS FULLER (1654–1734), English physician, writer and compiler: *Gnomologia*

The greatest obstacle to progress is not man's inherited pugnacity, but his incorrigible tendency to parasitism.

WILLIAM RALPH INGE (1860–1954), English theologian: *Outspoken Essays: First Series, 'Patriotism'*

Well, we can't stand around here doing nothing, people will think we're workmen.

SPIKE MILLIGAN (1918–2002), Irish comedian: *The Goon Show*

The devil finds work for idle hands to do.

PROVERB

The hardest work is to go idle.

PROVERB

Laziness is often mistaken for patience.

PROVERB

One of these days is none of these days.

PROVERB

Laziness is nothing more than the habit of resting before you get tired.

JULES RENARD (1864–1910), French author

I am happiest when I am idle. I could live for months without performing any kind of labour, and at the expiration of that time I should feel fresh and vigorous enough to go right on in the same way for numerous more months.

ARTEMUS WARD (Charles Farrar Browne) (1834–67), American humorist, editor and lecturer: *Pyrotechny*

To do nothing at all is the most difficult thing in the world, the most difficult and the most intellectual.

OSCAR WILDE (1856–1900), Irish poet, dramatist and wit: *Intentions, 'The Critic as Artist'*

Loyalty

An ounce of loyalty is worth a pound of cleverness.

ELBERT (GREEN) HUBBARD (1856–1915), American businessman, writer and printer: *The Note Book*

You want loyalty, hire a cocker spaniel.

MICHAEL LEWIS (1960–), American non-fiction writer: *Liar's Poker*

The greater the loyalty of a group toward the group, the greater is the motivation among the members to achieve the goals of the group, and the greater the probability that the group will achieve its goals.

RENSIS LIKKERT (1903–81), American educator and organisational psychologist

The successful conduct of an industrial enterprise requires two quite distinct qualifications: fidelity and zeal.

JOHN STUART MILL (1806–73), English philosopher and economist: *Principles of Political Economy, book I*

If you live to be 100, I hope I live to be 100 minus 1 day, so I never have to live without you.

A(LAN) A(LEXANDER) MILNE (1882–1956), English writer and dramatist: *Winnie the Pooh*

It is easier for a man to be loyal to his club than to his planet; the by-laws are shorter, and he is personally acquainted with the other members.

E(LWYN) B(ROOKS) WHITE (1899–1985), American humorist and essayist

If you are not too long, I will wait here for you all my life.

OSCAR WILDE (1856–1900), Irish poet, dramatist and wit

Luck

I don't know anything about luck. I've never banked on it, and I'm afraid of people who do. Luck to me is something else: hard work and realizing what is opportunity and what isn't.

LUCILLE BALL (1911–89), American actress

We must believe in luck. For how else can we explain the success of those we don't like.

JEAN COCTEAU (1889–1963), French writer and film director

Shallow men believe in luck. Strong men believe in cause and effect.

RALPH WALDO EMERSON (1803–82), American poet, essayist and philosopher

The man who glories in his luck
May be overthrown by destiny.

EURIPIDES (?480–406 BC), Greek tragic dramatist: *The Suppliant Women*

He who is not lucky, let him not go a-fishing.

THOMAS FULLER (1654–1734), English physician, writer and compiler: *Gnomologia*

It is a great piece of skill to know how to guide your luck even while waiting for it.

BALTASAR GRACIÁN (1601–58), Spanish prose writer and Jesuit priest: *The Art of Worldly Wisdom*

Some folk want their luck buttered.

THOMAS HARDY (1840–1928), English novelist and poet: *The Mayor of Casterbridge*

True luck consists not in holding the best of the cards at the table: Luckiest he who knows just when to rise and go home.

JOHN (MILTON) HAY (1838–1905), American statesman and man of letters: *Distichs*

I am a great believer in luck, and I find the harder I work the more I have of it.

STEPHEN BUTLER LEACOCK (1869–1944), Canadian economist and humorist: *Literary Lapses*

It is better to be born lucky than rich.

PROVERB

Luck never gives; it only lends.

SWEDISH PROVERB

Life is not a spectacle or a feast; it is a predicament.

GEORGE SANTAYANA (1863–1952), American philosopher and poet

Luck is the residue of diligence.

SAYING

Depend on the rabbit's foot if you will, but remember it didn't work for the rabbit.

R. E. SHAY

Luck is not something you can mention in the presence of self-made men.

E(LWYN) B(ROOKS) WHITE (1899–1985), American humorist and essayist

Motives

You will find in politics that you are much exposed to the attribution of false motives. Never complain and never explain.

STANLEY BALDWIN, 1st Earl Baldwin of Bewdley (1867–1947), British statesman: quoted in Harold Nicolson, *Diaries and Letters*

We are all selfish and I no more trust myself than others with a good motive.

LORD BYRON, George Gordon Byron, 6th Baron Byron of Rochdale (1788–1824), English poet

We must judge a man's motives from his overt acts.

LORD KENYON (1917–93): *Judgment in Rex v. Waddington*

It's motive alone which gives character to the actions of men.

JEAN DE LA BRUYÈRE (1645–96), French satiric moralist

We should often feel ashamed of our best actions if the world could see all of the motives which produced them.

FRANÇOIS LA ROCHEFOUCAULD, Duc de La Rochefoucauld (1613–80), French writer: *Maxims*

When you buy a vase cheap, look for the flaw; when a man offers favours, look for the motive.

JAPANESE PROVERB

Take away the motive, and the sin is taken away.

SPANISH PROVERB

When a stupid man is doing something he is ashamed of, he always declares that it is his duty.

GEORGE BERNARD SHAW (1856–1950), Irish dramatist and critic: *Caesar and Cleopatra, Act 3*

The light of lights looks always on the motive, not the deed, the shadow of shadows on the deed alone.

W(ILLIAM) B(UTLER) YEATS (1865–1939), Irish poet and dramatist

Power

When you doubt your power, you give power to your doubt.

ANON

Knowledge is power.

FRANCIS BACON, 1st Baron Verulam, Viscount St Albans (1561–1626), English writer, philosopher and statesman: *Meditationes sacrae*, 'De haeresibus'

Money is economical power.

WALTER BAGEHOT (1826–77), English economist and journalist: *Lombard Street*

Power without principle is barren, but principle without power is futile.

TONY (ANTHONY CHARLES LYNTON) BLAIR (1953–), British politician and prime minister

Power tends to corrupt and absolute power corrupts absolutely. Great men are almost always bad men … There is no worse heresy than that the office sanctifies the holder of it.

JOHN EMERICH EDWARD DALBERG, 1st Baron Acton (1834–1902), English historian: *Letter to Bishop Mandell Creighton, 5 April 1887*

The attempt to combine wisdom and power has only rarely been successful and then only for a short while.

ALBERT EINSTEIN (1879–1955), German-Swiss-American physicist

Men, such as they are, very naturally seek money or power; and power because it is as good as money.

RALPH WALDO EMERSON (1803–82), American poet, essayist, and philosopher: *The American Scholar*

There is always room for a man of force, and he makes room for many.

RALPH WALDO EMERSON, *The Conduct of Life*, 'Power'

You shall have joy or you shall have power, said God; you shall not have both.

RALPH WALDO EMERSON, *Journals*

Influence those who influence others.

JOHN FAIRCHILD (1927–), American publisher: *Motto*

Men of power have no time to read; yet the men who do not read are unfit for power.

MICHAEL FOOT (1913–), English politician: *Debts of Honour*

There is nothing fortuitous about the tendency for power to beget countervailing power; it is organic. However it does not work evenly. The buttressing of weak bargaining positions has become, as a result, one of the most important of the functions of government.

JOHN KENNETH GALBRAITH (1908–2006), Canadian-born American economist, diplomat and writer: *The American Economy, Its Substance and Myth*

Under all forms of government the ultimate power lies with the masses. It is not kings nor aristocracies, nor landowners nor capitalists, that anywhere really enslave the people. It is their own ignorance.

HENRY GEORGE (1839–97), American economist: *Protection or Free Trade, chapter 1*

We look forward to the time when the power of love will replace the love of power. Then will our world know the blessings of peace.
WILLIAM EWART GLADSTONE (1809–98), British statesman and prime minister

Power is not happiness. Security and peace are more to be desired than a name at which nations tremble.
WILLIAM GODWIN (1756–1836), English political philosopher and novelist: *An Enquiry Concerning Political Justice*

The sole advantage of power is that you can do more good.
BALTASAR GRACIÁN (1601–58), Spanish prose writer and Jesuit priest: *The Art of Worldly Wisdom*

Only he deserves power who every day justifies it.
DAG HAMMARSKJÖLD (1905–61), Swedish statesman and secretary-general of the United Nations: *Markings*

Idealism is the noble toga that political gentlemen drape over their will to power.
ALDOUS (LEONARD) HUXLEY (1894–1963), English novelist and essayist: *New York Herald Tribune, 25 November 1962*

Great power, which incites great envy, hurls some men to destruction; they are drowned in a long, splendid stream of honours.
JUVENAL (Decimus Junius Juvenalis) (?AD 60–?140), Roman satirist: *Satires*

Power is the ultimate aphrodisiac.
HENRY KISSINGER (1923–), German-born American academic and diplomat: quoted in *Guardian, 28 November 1976*

All life is a game of power. The object of the game is simple enough: to know what you want and get it.
MICHAEL KORDA (1933–), British writer: *Power in the Office*

Nearly all men can stand adversity, but if you want to test a man's character, give him power.

ABRAHAM LINCOLN (1809–65), American statesman and president

Affluence means influence.

JACK LONDON (John Griffith London) (1876–1916), American novelist and adventurer (Attributed)

Power? It's like a dead sea fruit; when you achieve it, there's nothing there.

SIR (MAURICE) HAROLD MACMILLAN, Earl of Stockton (1894–1986), British statesman and prime minister: quoted in Anthony Sampson, *The New Anatomy of Britain*

Economic power is headstrong and vehement, and if it is to prove beneficial to mankind it must be securely curbed and regulated with prudence.

POPE PIUS XI (Achille Ratti) (1857–1939), Italian ecclesiastic and pope: *Quadragesimo anno, 15 May 1931*

Next to enjoying ourselves, the next greatest pleasure consists in preventing others from enjoying themselves, or, more generally, in the acquisition of power.

BERTRAND (ARTHUR WILLIAM) RUSSELL, 3rd Earl Russell (1872–1970), English philosopher and mathematician: *Sceptical Essays, 'The Recrudescence of Puritanism'*

You can have power over people as long as you don't take everything away from them. But when you've robbed a man of everything, he's no longer in your power.

ALEXANDER ISAYEVICH SOLZHENITSYN (1918–), Russian novelist

Power corrupts, but lack of power corrupts absolutely.

ADLAI (EWING) STEVENSON (1900–68), American statesman

Of Lord Northcliffe:~

He aspired to power instead of influence, and as a result forfeited both.

A(LAN) J(OHN) P(ERCIVALE) TAYLOR (1906–90), English historian: *English History 1914–1945*

Men are not corrupted by the exercise of power, or debased by the habit of obedience; but by the exercise of a power which they believe to be illegitimate, and by obedience to a rule which they consider to be usurped and oppressive.

ALEXIS (CHARLES HENRI MAURICE CLÉREL) DE TOCQUEVILLE (1805–59), French politician and political writer: *Democracy in America*

The balance of power.

SIR ROBERT WALPOLE, 1st Earl of Orford (1676–1745), English statesman and prime minister: *Speech, House of Commons, 13 February 1741*

Purpose

Ready, fire, aim!

ANON

Here is a test to find out whether your mission in life is complete. If you're alive, it isn't.

RICHARD BACH (1936–), American author: *Jonathon Livingstone Seagull*

One should always think of what one is about; when one is learning, one should not think of play; and when one is at play, one should not think of one's learning.

LORD CHESTERFIELD, Philip Dormer Stanhope, 4th Earl of (1694–1773), English statesman and writer: *Letter to his son, 24 July 1739*

First things first, second things never.

SHIRLEY CONRAN (1932–), British writer: *Superwoman*

The secret of success is constancy to purpose.
BENJAMIN DISRAELI, 1st Earl of Beaconsfield (1804–81), English statesman, prime minister and novelist: *Speech, House of Commons, 24 June 1870*

Never forget that the purpose for which a man lives is the improvement of the man himself, so that he may go out of this world having, in his great sphere or his small one, done some little good for his fellow creatures and laboured a little to diminish the sin and sorrow that are in the world.
WILLIAM EWART GLADSTONE (1809–98), British statesman and prime minister

Work for something because it is good, not just because it stands a chance to succeed.
VACLAV HAVEL (1936–), Czechoslovakian writer and politician

Life, to be worthy of a rational being, must be always in progression; we must always purpose to do more or better than in time past. The mind is enlarged and elevated by mere purposes, though they end as they begin by airy contemplation.
SAMUEL JOHNSON (1709–84), English lexicographer, essayist and poet: *To Hester Thrale, 29 November 1783*

Year by year we are becoming better equipped to accomplish the things we are striving for. But what are we actually striving for?
BERTRAND DE JOUVENEL (1903–87), French writer

If people want a sense of purpose they should get it from their archbishop. They should certainly not get it from their politicians.
SIR (MAURICE) HAROLD MACMILLAN, Earl of Stockton (1894–1986), British statesman and prime minister: quoted in Henry Fairlie, *The Life of Politics*

We set sail within a vast sphere, ever drifting in uncertainty, driven from end to end.

BLAISE PASCAL (1623–62), French philosopher, mathematician and physicist: *Pensées*

If you don't know where you are going, you will probably end up somewhere else.

DR LAURENCE J. PETER (1919–90), Canadian educator and RAYMOND HULL (1919–): *The Peter Principle*

My mother said to me, 'If you become a soldier, you'll be a general; if you become a monk, you'll end up as the Pope.' Instead, I became a painter and wound up as Picasso.

PABLO PICASSO (1881–1973), Spanish artist

A radical is a man with both feet firmly planted in the air.

FRANKLIN DELANO ROOSEVELT (1882–1945), American statesman and president: *Broadcast, 26 October 1939*

Liberty means responsibility. That is why most men dread it.

GEORGE BERNARD SHAW (1856–1950), Irish dramatist and critic: *Man and Superman, Maxims for Revolutionists*

There are two things to aim at in life: first, to get what you want; and, after that, to enjoy it. Only the wisest of mankind achieve the second.

LOGAN PEARSALL SMITH (1865–1946), American-born Englishman of letters: *Afterthoughts*

Reputation

Have regard for your name, since it will remain for you longer than a great store of gold.

The Apocrypha, Ecclesiasticus 41:12

It pays to be obvious, especially if you have a reputation for subtlety.
ISAAC ASIMOV (?1920–92), Russian-born American science-fiction writer

I have built my reputation on honesty; I have sometimes been too honest.
DAVID BLUNKETT (1947–), British politician

I'm dealing with my drinking problem and I have a reputation for getting things done.
BRIAN CLOUGH (1935–2004), English footballer and manager

A single lie destroys a whole reputation for integrity.
BALTASAR GRACIÁN (1601–58), Spanish prose writer and Jesuit priest: *The Art of Worldly Wisdom*

Work is the price which is paid for reputation.
BALTASAR GRACIÁN, as above

Reputation is fine but you have to keep justifying it. In a sense, it makes it harder because people's expectations of you are higher. So, you have to fulfil those expectations. Or, try to exceed those expectations. But, it becomes more difficult as time goes on.
SIR DEREK JACOBI (1938–), English actor and director

Worldly wisdom teaches that it is better for the reputation to fail conventionally than to succeed unconventionally.
JOHN MAYNARD KEYNES (1883–1946), English economist: *The General Theory of Employment, Interest and Money*

The world more often rewards the appearances of merit than merit itself.
FRANÇOIS LA ROCHEFOUCAULD, Duc de La Rochefoucauld (1613–80), French writer: *Maxims*

Our reputation is more important than the last hundred million dollars.

RUPERT MURDOCH (1931–), Australian-born media executive

It is generally much more shameful to lose a good reputation than never to have acquired it.

PLINY THE YOUNGER (Gaius Plinius Caecilius Secundus) (?AD 62–?113), Roman writer and administrator: *Letters*

Reputation is often got without merit, and lost without crime.

PROVERB

A man's good deeds are known only at home; his bad deeds far away.

CHINESE PROVERB

Cassio:

Reputation, reputation, reputation! O, I have lost my reputation! I have lost the immortal part of myself, and what remains is bestial.

WILLIAM SHAKESPEARE (1564–1616), English dramatist and poet: *Othello, Act 2*

One's reputation is like a shadow, it is gigantic when it precedes you, and a pigmy in proportion when it follows.

CHARLES MAURICE DE TALLEYRAND (1754–1838), French diplomat

One man lies in his work, and gets a bad reputation; another in his manners, and enjoys a good one.

HENRY DAVID THOREAU (1817–62), American essayist and poet: *Journal, 25 June 1852*

Associate yourself with men of good quality if you esteem your own reputation; for 'tis better to be alone than in bad company.

GEORGE WASHINGTON (1732–99), American statesman and president: *Rules of Civility*

One can survive everything nowadays, except death, and live down anything except a good reputation.

OSCAR WILDE (1856–1900), Irish poet, dramatist and wit: *A Woman of No Importance*

Risk

Don't refuse to go on an occasional wild goose chase – that's what wild geese are for.

ANON

I don't believe the story for a minute. But there's a 50 per cent chance I'm wrong.

ANON

Never be afraid to try something new. Remember, amateurs built the ark; professionals built the Titanic.

ANON

Take risks: if you win, you will be happy; if you lose, you will be wise.

ANON

Living at risk is jumping off the cliff and building your wings on the way down.

RAY BRADBURY (1920–), American writer

Uncertainty kills business.

SIR MICHAEL EDWARDES (1930–), British industrialist: quoted in Cary L. Cooper and Peter Hingley, *The Change Makers*

Yes, risk taking is inherently failure-prone. Otherwise, it would be called sure-thing-taking.

TIM MCMAHON, American businessman

For fools rush in where angels fear to tread.

ALEXANDER POPE (1688–1744), English poet and satirist: *An Essay on Criticism*

Unless you enter the tiger's den you cannot take the cubs.

JAPANESE PROVERB

Why not go out on a limb? Isn't that where the fruit is?

FRANK SCULLY (?–1964), American author

Behold, the fool saith, 'Put not all thine eggs in the one basket' – which is but a manner of saying, 'Scatter your money and your attention', but the wise man saith, 'Put all your eggs in the one basket and – watch that basket.'

MARK TWAIN (Samuel Langhorne Clemens) (1835–1910), American novelist and humorist: *Pudd'nhead Wilson, chapter 15*

Self-Interest

My parents acted immediately when I was kidnapped: they rented out my room.

WOODY ALLEN (1935–), American film director and actor

'If everybody minded their own business,' the Duchess said in a hoarse growl, 'the world would go round a great deal faster than it does.'

LEWIS CARROLL (Charles Lutwidge Dodgson) (1832–98), English writer and mathematician: *Alice's Adventures in Wonderland, chapter 6*

Even wisdom has to yield to self-interest.

PINDAR (?518–?438 BC), Greek lyric poet: *Pythian Odes*

Every man for himself, and the devil take the hindmost.

PROVERB

I know on which side my bread is buttered.
PROVERB

Look after number one.
PROVERB

We have always known that heedless self-interest was bad morals;
we now know that it is bad economics.
FRANKLIN DELANO ROOSEVELT (1882–1945), American statesman and
president: *Speech, 1937*

The world is governed by self-interest only.
(JOHANN CHRISTOPH) FRIEDRICH VON SCHILLER (1759–1805), German
playwright, poet and historian: *Wallenstein's Death*

Everyone's interest if checked by everybody else's would in reality
represent the common interest. But when everyone is seeking his
own interest at the expense of others as well as developing his
own means, it does not always happen that he is opposed by
equally powerful forces. The strong thus find it in their interest
to seize and the weak to acquiesce, for the least evil as well as the
greatest good is a part of the aim of human policy.
JEAN CHARLES LEONARD SIMONDE DE SISMONDI (1773–1842), Swiss
historian and economist: *Nouveaux principes d'économique politique, volume 1*

Every individual ... generally, indeed, neither intends to promote
the public interest, nor knows how much he is promoting it. By
preferring the support of domestic to that of foreign industry he
intends only his own security; and by directing that industry in
such a manner as its produce may be of the greatest value, he
intends only his own gain, and he is in this, as in many other
cases, led by an invisible hand to promote an end which was no
part of his intention.
ADAM SMITH (1723–90), Scottish economist and philosopher: *The Wealth of
Nations, book 4*

It is not from the benevolence of the butcher, the brewer or the baker that we expect our dinner, but from their regard to their own interest.

ADAM SMITH (1723–90), Scottish economist and philosopher

Self-interest is the enemy of all true affection.

PUBLIUS CORNELIUS TACITUS (?AD 55–?120), Roman historian and orator: *History*

Vision

Cherish your visions. Cherish your ideals. Cherish the music that stirs in your heart, the beauty that forms in your mind, the loveliness that drapes your purest thoughts, for out of them will grow all delightful conditions, all heavenly environment; of these, if you but remain true to them, your world will at last be built.

JAMES ALLEN (1864–1912), English inspirational writer

Where there is no vision, the people perish.

The Bible, Authorised (King James) Version, Proverbs 29:18

'Men of action', whose minds are too busy with the day's work to see beyond it. They are essential men, we cannot do without them, and yet we must not allow all our vision to be bound by the limitations of 'men of action'.

PEARL S(YDENSTRIKER) BUCK (1892–1973), American novelist and humanitarian: *What America Means to Me*

Why be an average person? All the great achievements of history have been made by strong individuals who refused to consult statistics or to listen to those who could prove convincingly that what they wanted to do, and in fact ultimately did do, was completely impossible.

ERIC BUTTERWORTH (1916–2003), American spiritual teacher

Prospect is often better than possession.

THOMAS FULLER (1654–1734), English physician, writer and compiler:
Gnomologia

Never look down to test the ground before taking your next step:
only he who keeps his eye fixed on the far horizon will find his
right road.

DAG HAMMARSKJÖLD (1905–61), Swedish statesman and secretary-general
of the United Nations: *Markings*

Your vision will become clear only when you look into your
heart. Who looks outside, dreams. Who looks inside, awakens.

CARL JUNG (1875–1961), Swiss psychiatrist and psychologist

A leader has the vision and conviction that a dream can be
achieved. He inspires the power and energy to get it done.

RALPH LAUREN (1939–), American fashion designer

Visionary people are visionary partly because of the very great
many things they don't see.

BERKELEY RICE (1937–), American writer: *The New York Times Magazine, 17
March 1968*

Vision is the art of seeing things invisible.

JONATHAN SWIFT (1667–1745), Anglo-Irish satirist and churchman:
Thoughts on Various Subjects

As long as you are going to think anyway – you might as well
think BIG!

DONALD TRUMP (1946–), American entrepreneur

Index

Also published by Lawpack

YOU CAN'T MARRY YOUR MOTHER-IN-LAW
AND OTHER COMMON LEGAL MISCONCEPTIONS

'I just loved this little pocket-sized book.
A most entertaining collection of witty
vignettes on how the law *really* works.'

The Woman Writer

£6.99
ISBN 978 1 905261 28 4
176 pages

www.lawpack.co.uk